THE
REFERENCE
SHELF

POLITICAL CHANGE
IN SOUTHEAST ASIA

edited by DONALD ALTSCHILLER

THE REFERENCE SHELF

Volume 61 Number 5

THE H. W. WILSON COMPANY

New York   1989

THE REFERENCE SHELF

The books in this series contain reprints of articles, excerpts from books, and addresses on current issues and social trends in the United States and other countries. There are six separately bound numbers in each volume, all of which are generally published in the same calendar year. One number is a collection of recent speeches; each of the others is devoted to a single subject and gives background information and discussion from various points of view, concluding with a comprehensive bibliography that contains books and pamphlets and abstracts of additional articles on the subject. Books in the series may be purchased individually or on subscription.

Library of Congress Cataloging-in-Publication Data

Main entry under title:

Political change in southeast Asia / edited by Donald Altschiller.
    p.   cm. — (The Reference shelf ; v. 61, no. 5)
    Includes bibliographical references.
    Summary: A collection of essays discussing political tension and change in South Korea, the Philippines, Cambodia, Malaysia, and Sri Lanka.
    ISBN 0-8242-0784-X
    1. Asia, Southeastern—Politics and government.   2. Korea (South)--Politics and government—1960- [1. Asia, Southeastern—Politics and government.   2. Korea (South)—Politics and government.]
I. Altschiller, Donald.   II. Series.
DS526.7.P64   1989
320.959—dc20   89-28448
                                              CIP
                                              AC

Cover: A teeming throng of anticommunist protesters confront riot police in front of National Assembly in Seoul, South Korea.
Photo: AP/Wide World Photos

Printed in the United States of America

CONTENTS

PREFACE

The vast and populous continent of Asia, together with its neighboring Pacific islands, comprises twenty-seven countries, some ancient, some founded very recently, some democracies, some dictatorships. Throughout the region, the winds of political change are blowing strongly, affecting the stability of governments and societies. This book examines these developments and considers some of the consequences of these changes for American interests.

An introductory section provides an overview of political trends in the continent, with a close look at changing superpower relations in the region. To facilitate its own internal reforms, the Soviet Union must reach new accommodations with old East Asian rivals—Red China and Japan—radically different societies with little in common but their lingering mistrust of Soviet aims. Whereas Japan's economic primacy is incontestable and growth of its political influence continues unabated, the situation in China is murky indeed in light of the events of spring 1989 in Tiananmen Square. The Chinese economy expanded rapidly after economic reforms and an open-door policy were launched in 1979. However, Deng Xiaoping and old bureaucratic elites with a stranglehold on the levers of social power refused to carry out needed political reform. The brutality the communists exercised in crushing the pro-democracy student movement threatens to return China to the devastation that accompanied the rule of the pre-Deng "Gang of Four." The overview is followed by five sections, each of which focuses on a country whose distinct political and ethnic character is of special interest.

The first country thus treated is South Korea, which has emerged prosperous from its war-torn past but has experienced continuing tensions because of the American military presence, the calls for reunification with North Korea, and the rising expectations of its people. The following section deals with the Philippines, where democratic aspirations led to a relatively bloodless "People Power" revolution in which the corrupt and tyrannical Ferdinand Marcos regime was dealt a stunning defeat, leading to the ascension to the presidency of Corazon Aquino. Filipinos now face the daunting task of putting their society to rights. The continued stranglehold of elites, massive poverty, huge foreign debts, and the at-times resented presence of American military installations threaten to tear the country apart if the democratic system cannot respond to popular aspirations, thus forcing those who seek democratic self-rule and economic reform to turn to vigilantes and communist insurgents to accomplish their aims.

The next section focuses attention on Cambodia (or the People's Republic of Kampuchea, as it is now called), a particularly thorny special case. Hun Sen's Vietnamese-controlled "occupation" government has begun to stabilize, but, as Vietnamese troops begin to withdraw, the combined opposition forces united by the figure of Sihanouk will doubtless seek to topple the government. Many fear a takeover by the Khmer Rouge, the dreaded Red Chinese–supported murderers who waged a war of annihilation against opponents under Pol Pot's leadership when they ruled Cambodia in the 1970s and who, for the time being, stand in uneasy alliance with Sihanouk. Their current subdued image is quite possibly a ploy to lessen opposition to their participation in a Cambodian coalition government or even to gain them eventual victory through votes, along democratic lines.

The last two sections deal with Malaysia and with Sri Lanka, where in both countries democratic institutions and prosperity are imperiled by ethnic conflict. These two cases provide a study in contrasts: In Malaysia, despite economic difficulties due to falling commodity prices and scandal-ridden government dealings, ethnic tensions have by and large not erupted in bloodshed. However, the internal balance of power is steadied only by government intervention, which keeps the majority Malays, despite their relative lack of business skills, artificially in equilibrium with the Chinese and Indian minorities and which uses press censorship to ease racial tensions. Sri Lanka, on the other hand, is torn by fighting between the minority Hindu Tamils, a comparatively well-educated group which is demanding autonomy in the northeastern province and at least equal treatment under the law, and the majority Buddhist Sinhalese. The involvement of India in the fighting, occasioned in part because Tamil Nadu is the ancestral homeland of many of the Sri Lankan Tamils, is a further complication in this conflict.

The editor wishes to thank the publishers who have granted permission to reprint their material in this compilation.

DONALD ALTSCHILLER

November 1989

I. OVERVIEW OF POLITICAL TRENDS IN ASIA

EDITOR'S INTRODUCTION

With superpower relationships in Asis in flux, and with economic change, sometimes bringing explosive growth, having come to the area, vast political shifts characterize Southeast Asia today. One major factor in the equation is Soviet involvement in the region, as Donald S. Zagoria, professor of government at Hunter College and the Graduate Center of the City University of New York, points out in the first article in this section, "Soviet Policy in East Asia: A New Beginning?," reprinted from *Foreign Affairs*. Past alliances and interventionist policies have left a lingering mistrust of the Soviets; recent economic and political developments have also resulted in a lack of control of allies. The net result is that the Soviets are increasingly finding that they must pay heed to the demands of their longtime regional allies while remaining cognizant of U.S. interests. The second article, "When Ideology Bows to Economics" by Douglas Stanglin with Dusko Doder and Mike Tharp, from *U.S. News & World Report*, elaborates on the themes of the first and attributes some of the abovementioned effects to Moscow's peace offensive in the region and the economic primacy of Japan. It also posits the thesis that the U.S. presence in Korea and elsewhere is still instrumental in preventing regional arms races. Finally, an editorial reprinted from the *New Republic* addresses the question "Is democracy beginning to flower in Asia?" and provides the answer "Yes," at least in some countries, citing encouraging developments in South Korea, Taiwan, and the Philippines in particular. The editorial goes on to warn, however, that the U.S. must maintain strong diplomatic, military, and economic support to "kindle a genuine and gradual Asian democratic thaw," even if it means opposing our "allies."

SOVIET POLICY IN EAST ASIA:
A NEW BEGINNING?[1]

Under Mikhail Gorbachev the Soviet Union has greatly increased its efforts to improve relations with the countries of East Asia, particularly China, but also Japan and South Korea, and with Southeast Asia, Australia and New Zealand. There has been a new diplomatic flexibility, frequent visits, a drive for better trade links, an effort to join regional economic organizations such as the Asian Development Bank and the Pacific Economic Cooperation Council (PECC), a variety of arms control proposals and a determined effort to change the poor image of the Soviet Union in the region.

In a number of speeches, especially those in Vladivostok in July 1986 and Krasnoyarsk in September 1988, Gorbachev has said he wants to lower the level of military activity in the Pacific, to help resolve regional tensions, to improve Moscow's bilateral relations with all the countries in the region, to advance multilateral cooperation, particularly economic cooperation, and generally to create a "healthier" situation.

There is no euphoria about Gorbachev in Asia, as there may be elsewhere, but his initiatives have had an impact, particularly on China and South Korea. A summit meeting between Gorbachev and Deng Xiaoping will take place early in 1989, the first such meeting between two top Soviet and Chinese leaders in 30 years. An informal dialogue between Moscow and Seoul has begun and both sides are anxious to expand economic and even political relations. Moreover, it seems likely that Moscow and Tokyo will also reach some sort of modus vivendi in the near future, despite their territorial dispute. And if Vietnamese troops withdraw from Cambodia, as Moscow is now pressing Hanoi to do, a major constraint on Soviet relations with the member countries of the Association of Southeast Asian Nations (ASEAN) will be removed.

[1]Reprint of an article by Donald S. Zagoria, professor of government at Hunter College and the Graduate Center of the City University of New York and the Whitnew H. Shepardson Fellow at the Council on Foreign Relations for 1988–1989. Reprinted by permission of *Foreign Affairs*, vol. 68, no. 1, 1989. Copyright © 1989 by the Council on Foreign Relations Inc.

In sum, the Soviet Union may well succeed in normalizing relations with East Asia during the next few years. The Soviet Union, however, has not become a status quo power. Moscow now seeks to revive atrophied diplomatic instruments unused by former and longtime Foreign Minister Andrei Gromyko in order to increase, not to reduce, Soviet influence abroad. Thus, this new Soviet moderation offers both challenge and opportunity for the United States. The challenge arises from the fact that the moderation may actually result in a less aggressive stategy but a more active and effective Soviet diplomacy. The opportunity is to take advantage of the new Soviet moderation in an effort to reduce the U.S. security burden and to ease global and regional tensions.

II

Even if Moscow improves its relations with the Asia-Pacific countries, it will remain at a considerable disadvantage in the region. The United States, despite all the talk about decline, continues to be the predominant power in the Pacific. It has presided in recent decades over a vigorous expansion of trade, investment and growth among the East Asian countries. The United States has a highly effective ally in Japan, which seeks to support, and not to challenge, U.S. leadership. The two countries have a compelling stake in maintaining and strengthening the web of security and economic ties that sustain an open world economy and the defense of Western interests. The United States also has a number of other allies and friends in the Pacific, several of them bound by treaty commitments, and all of them sharing an interest in maintaining a robust American presence in Asia in order to balance other "close-in" powers which they fear most. By contrast, the Soviet Union has only military power in East Asia; its economic relations are minimal, and its few allies in the region are poor, politically isolated and without much influence.

The Soviet Union is also at a disadvantage because it is still regarded with suspicion virtually everywhere in the region. Despite the latest Soviet force reductions, China remains encircled by Soviet military power. Japan insists on a settlement of its territorial dispute with the Soviet Union before substantial progress toward easing tensions can be achieved. Most Southeast Asian countries are reluctant to allow a large Soviet presence because of fears that the Soviets may aid local insurgents. Moreover, the failure of Stalinist economics, which has become increasingly evident all over the communist world, has made the Soviet Union virtually irrelevant as an ideological model in a region consisting of the fastest-growing market economies in the world. The extreme underdevelopment of Siberia and the Soviet Far East, a vast region with a tiny population and a weak infrastructure, will handicap any Soviet effort to develop more active economic relations with East Asia's market economies.

There is also a basic dilemma in Moscow's new effort to woo East Asia through flexible diplomacy. In the past, the Soviet Union's principal method of expanding its influence was through military power and aggressive behavior. If Moscow now seeks influence through diplomacy and trade, its leverage will be limited because it has little to offer. If, on the other hand, it resorts once again to employing its military power—as it did in the 1970s when it deployed SS-20 missiles, invaded Afghanistan and supported Vietnam's invasion of Cambodia—it will again mobilize a coalition of powers against it.

Despite these difficulties, Gorbachev's diplomacy has already scored some successes. The Soviet leader has laid the groundwork for a summit meeting with Deng Xiaoping by showing more flexibility than any of his predecessors. He accepted the Chinese position in the dispute over the Amur River border and he has systematically addressed all three of China's declared "obstacles" to normalization of Sino-Soviet relations: Soviet troops on the Chinese border, the Soviet occupation of Afghanistan and the Soviet support of Vietnam's occupation of Cambodia. Some Soviet troops have already been withdrawn from Mongolia and, in his recent U.N. speech, Gorbachev promised to pull out a "considerable" number of those remaining; Soviet military exercises and forces elsewhere on the Chinese border have been reduced; the Soviet army has begun a withdrawal from Afghanistan; and Moscow is now negotiating directly with China on Cambodia, while urging the Vietnamese to withdraw. The only substantial obstacle remaining is Vietnam's continuing occupation of Cambodia. But even this could be overcome in the near future. The shape of a political settlement in Cambodia is likely to be one of the chief topics for discussion at the upcoming Deng-Gorbachev summit.

There has also been an acceleration of Sino-Soviet trade. The Soviet Union is now China's fifth-largest trading partner, and border trade is expanding with particular rapidity. Total trade grew from $363 million in 1982 to $2.6 billion in 1986, a sevenfold increase. According to one Soviet specialist on China, there are plans for five or six hydroelectric plants along the Amur River. The Soviets are also suggesting Sino-Soviet cooperation in joint ventures in the Soviet Far East, and the Chinese are interested. And the Soviets are helping to refurbish 17 plants that they originally built in China in the 1950s, and are building seven new ones.

Moscow and Beijing are again referring to each other as "comrades," and offering positive assessments of each other's reforms. Indeed, they are rediscovering a common identity as socialist states, now that both are determined to develop a new, non-Stalinist and more pragmatic version of socialism. Party-to-party relations may even be resumed. The Chinese have already reestablished relations with most of the East European communist parties.

In short, the deep freeze in Sino-Soviet relations has ended, and a new stage is beginning.

Both sides have poweful motives to continue this process of normalization. Each believes that its most urgent priority for the next decade or more is to modernize its economy; this requires a peaceful international climate, reduced defense spending and calm along the 4,500-mile Sino-Soviet border. They both hope to increase their flexibility and maneuverability in the great power triangle that includes the United States. By improving relations with Moscow, Beijing also hopes to pressure Moscow's client state, Vietnam, to withdraw from Cambodia quickly and to accept China's (and the West's) preferred solution to the Cambodian problem—a dissolution of the existing pro-Hanoi government of the People's Republic of Kampuchea (P.R.K.) and its replacement by a genuinely neutralist four-party coalition led by Prince Norodom Sihanouk. Most important, now that Gorbachev is withdrawing from Afghanistan and concentrating on improving Russia's stagnant economy, the Chinese see a much reduced Soviet threat for some time to come. Within the next few years it is therefore likely that there will be a border settlement and a substantial mutual withdrawal of Soviet and Chinese forces from the border.

There are also economic considerations. For both Moscow and Beijing, barter trade preserves scarce foreign exchange. And, for China, Soviet technology is more appropriate than Western technology for those enterprises built by the Soviets in the 1950s.

A return to a 1950s-type alliance, however, seems out of the question. Even the development of an intimate and trusting relationship seems highly unlikely. For years to come, China's two major concerns will be security and development, and in each category China has much more to gain from the West than the Soviet Union. In the strategic realm, so long as the Soviet Union has the most powerful army on the Eurasian continent, keeps one-third of its nuclear weapons in the Far East, maintains a huge Pacific fleet off China's coast, and supplies arms to two of China's adversaries, India and Vietnam, the Chinese will want to maintain stable relations with the West in order to balance Soviet power. China's view of the United States as a crucial counterweight to the Soviet Union in Asia is implicit in a variety of Chinese writings and explicit in informal conversation with Americans.

Moreover, there is a continuing wariness in China, as there is in the West, about Gorbachev's motives. In a 1986 book, *The Soviet Far East Military Buildup*, Chinese analyst Yao Wen-bin warned that the new Soviet "peace offensive" in Asia was designed to divide the "anti-hegemonic" forces and to sow discord in U.S. relations with China, Japan and other Asian countries. Even more recently, the Chinese noted that Gorbachev's announced reduction of 500,000 troops worldwide was in part designed to weaken European defense efforts, dampen defense cooperation between the United States and Europe, and strengthen calls for a U.S. troop withdrawal from Europe.

A basic constraint on any Sino-Soviet rapprochement will be the geopolitical rivalry between the two great continental land powers, which is bound to continue. China and Vietnam will also continue to eye each other warily, even after Hanoi withdraws from Cambodia. Hanoi keeps a large portion of its 1.2-million-man army on the Chinese border and there is a continuing territorial dispute over the Spratly Islands in the South China Sea. China will therefore continue to be wary of Vietnam's alliance with Moscow. To balance that combination, China and Thailand are developing a much closer military relationship. The two countries have recently agreed to set up a war reserve stockpile on Thai territory. In Korea, which borders on China's strategic province of Manchuria, the Chinese are concerned—although they do not say so publicly—about growing military ties between Moscow and Pyongyang. In South Asia the Chinese are still worried about the Soviet-Indian connection and continuing Soviet pressure on Pakistan.

In the economic sphere, China's relations with the Pacific market economies are almost certainly going to continue to be much more important than its economic relations with the Soviets. China conducts less than five percent of its trade with the Russians whereas its trade with Japan, the United States and other Pacific countries constitutes more than two-thirds of its booming trade.

In sum, the Chinese, for their own reasons, will not move so close to Moscow as to jeopardize their relations with the West. The power balance in East Asia will not be changed. The probable normalization of Sino-Soviet relations will occur without trust or intimacy, and the West should not fear it. Indeed, such a détente between the two great Asian land powers—if it leads to a Soviet withdrawal from Afghanistan, a Vietnamese withdrawal from Cambodia and a general reduction of tension in Asia—is in the West's interest, particularly as long as both Moscow and Beijing are preoccupied with domestic reform and seek stable relations with all the Western powers.

The main impact of the Sino-Soviet détente will be on Moscow's Asian allies. North Korea and Vietnam will find it more difficult to play China off against Russia. As a result, pressures will grow for North Korea to come to terms with South Korea and for Vietnam to accommodate itself to China and ASEAN. The principal effect on India will be to move it in the direction of better relations with China and the United States. Thus, the Soviet Union's allies in Asia may be forced to reconsider some of their past policies, which could in turn open new opportunities for an astute American policy.

III

For Gorbachev, reaching a modus vivendi with Japan will probably be his greatest single challenge in East Asia. He wants technological assistance from Japan in order to develop Siberia, and he needs Japan's support if the Soviet Union intends to join the dynamic Pacific economy.

Gorbachev has taken a number of small steps to improve relations with Japan. Soviet Foreign Minister Eduard Shevardnadze has resumed regular exchanges with his Japanese counterpart after a lapse of a decade, and Gorbachev has expressed a desire to visit Japan. This would be the first such visit by a Soviet leader in the postwar period. In contrast to earlier Soviet comments that dismissed Japan as a stooge of the United States, Gorbachev has made positive statements about Japan's growing role and importance in global diplomacy. And in contrast to their former rigid and unyielding manner, Soviet diplomats have adopted a new style which the Japanese press refers to as "smile diplomacy." Moscow has appointed a new Japanese-speaking career diplomat, Nikolai Soloviev, as the Soviet ambassador to Japan.

Even on the territorial issue of returning the northern islands, Moscow is displaying new flexibility. While Soviet officials used to say that the issue was closed and there was nothing to discuss, they now concede it is a problem that needs to be resolved. when Shevardnadze visited Japan in December, he signed a communiqué implicitly recognizing the existence of a territorial dispute. As a result, preparations are now under way for a summit between Gorbachev and Prime Minister Noboru Takeshita sometime later this year.

Both Moscow and Tokyo have strong incentives to compromise. For the Soviets, easing relations with Japan is essential to gaining entrance to the Asian Development Bank and the PECC and to achieving access to Japanese technology, objectives which now rank very high on Gorbachev's agenda. For its part, Tokyo will not want to be left out of what may be a worldwide rapprochement with the Soviet Union. Moreover, if European and American businessmen and bankers encourage trade with Moscow, the Japanese private sector will want to do the same.

But even if Gorbachev is able to reach an understanding of sorts with Tokyo, the Soviet Union and Japan will continue to be adversaries. First, the territorial dispute will not be fully resolved. The Soviets are unlikely to return all the disputed islands because they are of considerable strategic importance. The islands straddle the passage between the Sea of Okhotsk and the Pacific Ocean and are extremely valuable for the Soviet navy, which hides many of its missile-firing submarines in the Sea of Okhotsk. Control of the disputed islands allows the Soviets to monitor the entrances and exits to that strategically vital body of water. Without such control, Soviet submarines would have to operate in the open waters of the Pacific, where the American navy would pose a much greater threat. Moreover, the Soviets fear that returning the islands to Japan would set a precedent for other countries from which the Russians took territory during World War II to make their own territorial demands on the U.S.S.R., thus opening a Pandora's box of irredentist aspirations at a time when ethnic tensions are already on the rise inside the Soviet Union. In any case, the Soviets have little incentive to give back any of the islands without obtaining a major concession in return.

A second constraint on Soviet-Japanese relations is Japan's firm alliance with the United States. Despite serious trade problems, both Tokyo and Washington have very powerful economic and strategic incentives to strengthen an alliance that has been the cornerstone of Pacific prosperity and security. Indeed, military cooperation between the two Pacific allies has been growing steadily during the past decade because of their common view of the Soviet Union as a hegemonic threat. Japan has been gradually but perceptibly increasing its contribution to Pacific security. Tokyo has already deployed more modern destroyers than the United Kingdom has in its entire navy; the Japanese also have four times more P-3 aircraft for antisubmarine warfare than the American Seventh Fleet and as many modern aircraft defending their homeland and sea-lanes as the United States uses for its entire continental defense. Japan has also become the largest donor of economic development assistance to such key Asian countries as China, the Philippines and India.

Meanwhile, the Soviets have built up forces in the Sea of Okhotsk and the northern part of the Sea of Japan, and the United States and Japan are making efforts to counter this buildup. Thus, the region around the Japanese archipelago is becoming one of the major theaters of the U.S.-Soviet military rivalry in Asia.

Third, the limitations of the Soviet economy combined with recent structural changes in the Japanese economy make it unlikely that economic relations between the two countries will improve rapidly. In the 1970s Japan was one of the top three capitalist countries in trade with the Soviet Union. But by 1981 Japan had fallen to fifth among the capitalist nations trading with Moscow. Japanese enthusiasm for getting involved in large Siberian development projects has largely evaporated because, since the 1970s, Japan has established a more fuel-efficient production method for its industries and greatly diversified its sources of oil supply. At a time of plentiful oil and relatively low energy prices, the Japanese have lost much of the appetite they once had for exploring Siberian coal and gas reserves. Of some 100 joint ventures the Soviets have signed recently, Japan's share is only a meager five projects—a good indication that Siberia is no longer as alluring for Japanese business.

In any case, there is a legacy of mistrust that is bound to inhibit any substantial warming of relations. The two countries have been at odds for most of this century and have yet to sign a peace treaty ending World War II. They fought four times, the last time in 1945 when the Red Army entered Manchuria in the final weeks of World War II. The Japanese still regard this as a "stab in the back" that violated the Soviet-Japanese treaty of neutrality in 1941. Moreover, the Soviets kept over half a million Japanese prisoners in the Soviet gulag and many of them never returned home. As a result of this history, Japanese public opinion polls regularly show that the Soviet Union is the least liked and most distrusted of all foreign countries.

Within the Japanese elite, and particularly among the professional diplomats who are Soviet specialists, dislike of the Soviet Union is deeply rooted. This stems in part from the crude and condescending behavior that the Russians displayed toward Japan during the Gromyko era. As a result, perhaps more than any other country in the Western alliance, the Japanese are extremely cautious and skeptical about the changes in the Soviet Union under Gorbachev.

IV

In Korea the Soviet are playing a new game designed to have the best of both Koreas. They are increasing their strategic relations with North Korea while demonstrating new flexibility toward South Korea. Since Kim Il Sung's visit to Moscow in 1984, the Soviets have supplied Pyongyang with new military hardware, including SU-25 ground attack aircraft, the most effective of the Soviet Union's attack planes; MiG-29 Fulcrum aircraft, one of the most sophisticated planes in the Soviet arsenal; and SA-5 Gammon surface-to-air missiles along with the advanced Tin Shield early warning radar network, the first time this system has been deployed outside the Soviet Union. All of this contrasts with Moscow's reluctance in the 1970s to supply the volatile North Korean dictator with advanced weapons. For its generosity, Moscow has been able to gain overflight rights over North Korean territory and its Pacific fleet has made calls at North Korean ports. North Korea has also toned down its independent foreign policy and fallen in with Gorbachev's general line.

Meanwhile, Moscow is holding out olive branches to the Republic of Korea. Despite Pyongyang's boycott, the Soviets attended the Olympic Games in Seoul, and in his speech at Krasnoyarsk in September 1988 Gorbachev signaled his intention to expand economic relations with South Korea. Both sides have now agreed to set up trade offices in each other's capital. Recently two influential Soviet orientalists, Georgii Kim and Mikhail Titarenko, visited Seoul and indicated that the Soviet Union was now ready to have regular informal exchanges with the R.O.K. In sum, the Soviets, like the Chinese, are pursuing a de facto "two Koreas" policy.

Seoul has responded favorably to Soviet overtures. For domestic reasons, President Roh Tae Woo wants to adopt a policy more in line with growing South Korean nationalism—a policy of avoiding excessive dependence on the United States. There are also economic motives: President Roh has authorized some of his top business leaders to visit Moscow to scout the possibilities for trade, investment and joint ventures. South Korea also hopes to prod North Korea into negotiation; Roh is adopting a more flexible policy toward the North than any previous South Korean leader has ever dared. He is wisely encouraging the United States and other Western countries to be more flexible toward Pyongyang in an effort to end North Korea's long isolation. And Roh has formally proposed a six-power conference including the Soviet Union to help resolve the Korean issue.

Over the longer run, however, Seoul's enthusiasm for its new Moscow connection may wane once South Korean businessmen discover the realities of doing business in the Soviet Union. South Korea's leading firms are already seeking Japanese co-participation in Siberian joint ventures, but receiving only a lukewarm response. This is bound to cool Korean enthusiasm. Moreover, Seoul may soon discover that Moscow's influence in North Korea is limited. Finally, since South Korea is still highly dependent on the American market and surrounded by communist states, including a volatile North Korea, these economic and geopolitical realities will dictate a continuing interest in a strong alliance with the United States. The best that Seoul can hope for—and it is not negligible—is to overcome its past diplomatic isolation by the major communist powers (it is already engaging in substantial trade with China) and to diversify its export markets.

In Southeast Asia, as in Korea, the Soviets are trying to have it both ways. While increasing military and economic assistance to Vietnam, which has now reached a level of $3 billion a year, Moscow is pressuring Vietnam to withdraw from Cambodia in order to improve relations with China and ASEAN. The Vietnamese have promised to withdraw all their troops from Cambodia by 1990 after withdrawing some 50,000 of them in 1988.

The Soviets are courting ASEAN instead of condemning it as an "imperialistic" bloc, as they once did. Mr. Shevardnadze toured Indonesia and Thailand in 1987, the first such visit by a Soviet foreign minister in 20 years. The prime ministers of Malaysia, Australia and Thailand have all visited Moscow with their foreign ministers, and the presidents of the Philippines and Indonesia are expected to follow suit. Moscow is also seeking to become a "dialogue partner" of ASEAN, along with the United States, Japan and the European Economic Community.

There is at least one basic problem with Moscow's new strategy in Korea and Indochina: the Soviets do not control either North Korea or Vietnam. The North Koreans have maintained a militant and uncompromising posture toward South Korea for the last three decades, while insisting on their own solution to the unification issue. On several occasions they have resorted to terror, most recently when two North Korean agents planted a bomb on a South Korean passenger airliner. The North Koreans have adamantly refused any serious discussions with South Korea about defusing their conflict unless the Americans agree to withdraw from Korea. Moreover, while Moscow and Beijing are reforming their economies and opening up to the outside world, North Korea remains a bastion of Stalinism, xenophobia and ideological fanaticism. Whether all this will change after Kim Il Sung passes from the scene remains to be seen.

Similarly, in the case of the Cambodian conflict, the Vietnamese are free agents. Hanoi sees itself threatened in Cambodia by China and its Khmer Rouge allies. It is unlikely that Vietnam, after withdrawing from Cambodia, will allow its P.R.K. protégé to be replaced by a genuinely neutralist government. That is the most plausible reason for Hanoi's continuing refusal to agree to an international peacekeeping force in Cambodia after it withdraws its troops.

Moscow is therefore limited in the amount of pressure it can put on either Pyongyang or Hanoi. Kim Il Sung, the North Korean dictator, does not trust the Russians, and in Vietnam Moscow does not want to risk eviction from strategically important bases in Cam Ranh Bay. Thus despite Moscow's efforts to gain greater flexibility in Korea and Southeast Asia, the scope for expanding its influence may be limited by the recalcitrance of its allies.

V

Improving its bilateral relations with all the countries of the region is one general Soviet objective in East Asia. Another is to increase Soviet trade with, and involvement in, the dynamic Pacific economy. While most of the Asia-Pacific countries, including China, have become increasingly integrated into the Pacific economy, the Soviet Far East has been isolated from it. An important part of the explanation for this is that previous Soviet leaders, especially Leonid Brezhnev, pursued a "guns over growth" development strategy in Siberia. They invested in military assets instead of exploiting the vast economic resources in the eastern regions of the Soviet Union. And because of their obsession with military secrecy, the Soviet leaders closed off the Soviet Far East to outsiders. Now the Soviets say they intend to open up the area and turn parts of it into special economic zones designed to attract foreign investors, joint ventures and tourists. At a recent weekend conference in Vladivostok, the capital of the Maritime Province which had previously been closed to foreigners, the Soviets said they want to triple their Pacific trade in the next 12 years.

Soviet trade with the Pacific in 1986 amounted to only about six percent of total Soviet trade and of this portion, almost 65 percent was with other socialist countries—China, Vietnam, Mongolia and North Korea. (By contrast, U.S. trade with the region exceeds its trade with Europe and constitutes more than one-third of its total trade.) For most of the market economies in the region, trade with the Soviet Union is both minimal and unbalanced. The Soviets import far more than they export because Soviet exports are simply not competitive either in terms of price or quality. In the past six years Soviet trade with the ASEAN countries has declined by half to less than $500 million, and only about 20 percent of that are Soviet exports. And while China's trade with South Korea was more than $2.5 billion last year, Soviet trade with South Korea reached only $200 million.

The basic obstacle to expanded Soviet trade with East Asia is structural. Due to the very nature of the command economy, Soviet enterprises do not have much incentive to export. They are not in competition with each other or with foreign companies. They have little interaction with foreign customers or foreign competitors. They have an assured domestic market for their goods. And they do not have the "survival motive" so important in the Western market economies, because the state has traditionally made sure that Soviet enterprises do not go under. Even if all of these problems were resolved by a dramatic move toward market reforms, the Soviet enterprises would have to start producing high-quality, reasonably priced manufactured goods that could compete on world markets. This is unlikely to occur any time soon.

Moreover, despite a good deal of rhetoric about a new economic policy in the Soviet Far East, economic realities dictate that Siberian development will be put on the back burner because of its enormously high cost and difficulty. Any large increments of new investment will almost certainly go into the European regions of the U.S.S.R., where the cost of labor and capital is much lower and the infrastructure is more highly developed.

There will also be severe obstacles to attracting substantial numbers of foreign investors to participate in joint ventures in the Soviet Far East. The Soviets will have to make the conditions for doing business and repatriating profits more attractive than they are now. They will need to develop the Far East by investing substantially in roads, railways and ports. They will need to open Vladivostok for more than a weekend conference and change it from a port oriented largely to military purposes to one adapted to commerce. And even if they do all of these things, foreign companies will still have to do business in a Soviet economy that remains notorious for its bureaucratic rigidities, shortages of raw materials and general inefficiency.

Finally, in addition to structural problems, the Soviets lack a business culture. Except for some remnants of entrepreneurship in Armenia and the Baltic states, the Soviet system has produced a nation of bureaucrats who fear taking risks and have little desire to market products aggressively. It could take a generation for the Soviets to change this.

In sum, even if all goes exceptionally well with Gorbachev's economic reform efforts, the Soviets will probably remain a marginal player in the Pacific economy for years and probably decades to come.

VI

Yet another professed Soviet objective in East Asia is regional arms control and force reductions. In his speech at Krasnoyarsk, Gorbachev made a seven-point proposal: to freeze the level of nuclear weapons in the region; to invite all naval powers in the region for consultations on freezing naval forces; to have a multilateral discussion on reducing military confrontation in Northeast Asia; to eliminate U.S. military bases in the Philippines in exchange for Soviet withdrawal from Cam Ranh Bay; to discuss ways to prevent incidents in the open sea and in the airspace above it; to have an international conference for turning the Indian Ocean into a peace zone; and to develop a negotiating mechanism to examine these other proposals.

So far the dominant reaction in the West to Gorbachev's arms control initiatives has been one of skepticism. Two American officials recently observed that the Soviet proposals were one-sided. Capping naval force levels, they said, would inhibit Japan from making greater contributions to its own defense. Freezing naval and air deployments in the region, they argued, makes more sense for the Soviet Union, a land-based power, than it does for the United States, a naval power which relies on a strategy of forward deployment. As they pointed out, "sea lanes are to America what railroad lines are to the Soviet Union. We cannot imagine the Soviets agreeing to constrict their own vital arteries." If the Soviets really want to eliminate tensions in Asia, American officials argue, they must reverse the recent growth in Soviet land, naval and nuclear forces which threaten Asia. One-third of all Soviet forces are stationed in the Pacific region, with particular concentration along the Sino-Soviet border, the Kamchatka Peninsula and the Sea of Okhotsk.

Some Chinese newspapers were also skeptical about Gorbachev's proposals. They suggested that these ideas were designed to weaken American naval superiority in the region and to preempt a Japanese naval buildup.

The Japanese are even less enthusiastic. They insist that the Soviet Union must adopt a more defensive posture in the Soviet Far East, recognize Japan's legitimate security interest in its alliance with the United States and move toward some settlement of the territorial dispute to show that it is really interested in defusing regional tensions. Japanese officials point out that arms control is not an end in itself but merely a means for achieving stability. In Europe a German settlement preceded the Helsinki conference on European security. In Asia, they argue, the first task is not arms control but an effort to resolve the political disputes.

There is a good deal of merit in all of these objections to Gorbachev's proposals. The basic fact is that the Soviet Union seeks to overcome American naval superiority in the Pacific through naval arms control, just as NATO is now seeking to overcome Soviet superiority in Europe through conventional arms control. But the United States has little incentive to rectify the imbalance in the Pacific, any more than the Soviet Union has a great incentive to rectify it in Europe. Moreover, the United States has a vital interest in maintaining a robust naval presence in the Pacific in order to reassure its allies of its credibility and to help maintain regional stability. So long as the Soviet Union, North Korea and Vietnam retain huge land armies in Asia, the latter two with Soviet support, the United States will be under pressure from its allies in the region to continue to maintain visible naval and air superiority.

Nor will the Japanese or Chinese have any interest in freezing naval deployments, since they both perceive themselves to be at a great disadvantage to the Soviet Union.

An appropriate Western response to Gorbachev's Krasnoyarsk proposals would be to point out precisely why his proposals are one-sided and then go on to suggest some ways of reducing tension in the Pacific that are in everyone's interest. It is to this that I now turn.

VII

Because of several new factors, especially economic development, international relations in East Asia are undergoing a substantial change. First, the region's extraordinary economic growth, which has now been sustained over several decades, is leading to the rise of many new sources of power, including Japan, China and such middle powers as the Republic of Korea. As a result, the old bipolar world is eroding and a new multipolar system is emerging. By the end of he century Japan could have a GNP of $4 trillion, comparable to that of the United States today; China could have a GNP close to $1 trillion; and the R.O.K. could have a GNP of some $400-$500 billion. East Asia already produces close to 20 percent of world GNP, not far behind North America, which now produces 27 percent. By the end of this decade East Asia will probably contribute as much as North America to world GNP. This change in relative economic power does not mean an end to the postwar structure in which the United States has occupied the central role. But it does mean that the United States will have to treat its allies in East Asia as partners rather than clients.

Second, the vigorous expansion of trade, investment and other economic ties within the Pacific region is contributing to a new type of "positive sum" international relations in which all the players benefit from a growing pie, develop a stake in maintaining an open trading system and, in the process, create a set of peaceful and friendly relations among themselves.

The more moderate post-Mao China, which has given up support of revolutionary violence in favor of concentrating on economic development at home, is already being integrated into the Pacific economy and developing an interest in peaceful relations with all the countries of the region. Provided Gorbachev's market reforms go far enough, and the Soviet Union begins to reallocate resources away from the military and toward the civilian sector—as the Chinese have done—the Soviet Far East may also be integrated eventually into the Pacific economy. Looking further into the future, North Korea and Vietnam could also be absorbed.

A third prominent feature of East Asian international relations is that, for the first time in postwar history, a major reduction of tensions among all four major powers in the region is now taking place. There is no "odd man out." The United States and the Soviet Union, after four summits, an accord on intermediate-range missiles and the beginning of a Soviet withdrawal from Afghanistan, are at the foothills of a new détente. Sino-Soviet relations are improving rapidly and Soviet-Japanese relations will probably also improve in the near future.

This positive change in the pattern of relations among the four powers is not occurring at the expense of other relationships. The U.S.-Japanese alliance, despite many problems, remains firm. Both American and Chinese leaders describe their relationship as stable and mutually beneficial. Chinese-Japanese relations are developing a strong economic momentum, particularly now that Japanese Prime Minister Noboru Takeshita has promised Beijing some $6 billion in soft loans and an increase in Japanese investment in China.

To be sure, there are many uncertainties in the rapidly changing strategic situation in East Asia and there will be many barriers on the road toward a more peaceful and stable environment. After 40 years of cold war between the two superpowers, several decades of Sino-Soviet hostility and a century of mistrust between Russia and Japan, suspicions among all the major powers are still strong.

Nevertheless, the prospects for a breakthrough in easing tensions have not been better since the end of World War II. And the opportunities now unfolding—particularly the new Soviet diplomacy in the region—need to be explored.

If the Gorbachev leadership is serious about cooperating with the United States in reducing tensions in the Pacific and in joining the Pacific economy, it must stop pursuing policies that threaten American vital interests. In particular, it needs to engage in some "new thinking" about the role of American alliances. A Japan freed from the American embrace might become more, not less, dangerous to Moscow.

Furthermore, the Soviet Union must also be told to stop making arms control proposals so one-sided that they increase suspicions of its intentions. For example, Gorbachev promotes nuclear-free zones in Korea and Southeast Asia. Such proposals, if implemented, would constrict only U.S. forces.

If the Soviet Union wants to join international economic organizations in Asia, it should first be required to furnish much more data about its own economy than is presently available. It should also indicate what specific contributions it is prepared to make to such organizations. Will it, for example, become a contributor to Asian Development Bank projects? And, once it joins, will it use such organizations to exploit economic frictions between the United States and its allies, or will it seek to play a constructive role in the region?

The Western governments also need to discourage untied bank loans to the East bloc and to decide under what conditions they will grant government-backed loans to the Soviet Union and lift various restrictions on trade. There should be some effort to link these loans to Western political objectives—progress in arms control, ameliorating regional conflicts, improving the human rights situation in the Soviet Union and cutting back Soviet arms sales abroad.

On the security front, there should be few if any reductions in the American conventional or nuclear presence in Asia and no change in the strategy of forward deployment that the United States has successfully pursued for more than 40 years. There should, however, be a five-part agenda for creating a more peaceful situation: reducing regional tensions; engaging in reciprocal unilateral restraint; holding a dialogue on naval doctrine at the highest levels; exchanging data on defense budgets and force projections; and establishing an effective crisis-management regime.

First, reducing regional tensions should be given the highest priority because it is the one issue on which the major powers have a strong common interest. In Korea, all four of the major powers want to avoid a new Korean war, to help bring about a détente between North and South Korea, to open up Pyongyang to the global community and to improve their own relations with the two Koreas. Now that Moscow and Beijing are both improving their relations with South Korea, the United States and Japan, with Seoul's approval, can try to improve their relations with Pyongyang. The immediate objective of all four powers should be to get the two Koreas into a new dialogue which eventually leads to a substantial drawdown of forces along the 38th parallel, family reunification, the beginning of trade, and a variety of contacts between Seoul and Pyongyang. Ultimately, both Koreas should sign a peace treaty and enter the United Nations.

In Cambodia, all four powers should press the Vietnamese to withdraw soon and to allow the formation of a four-party coalition under Prince Sihanouk. The transition to the new government should take place under international supervision. Steps must also be taken to prevent the Khmer Rouge from returning to power alone after the Vietnamese leave.

Second, the two superpowers could begin to take unilateral steps to reduce their military confrontation in the Pacific. Gorbachev told the U.N. that the Soviet Union would begin to make substantial unilateral reductions of troops stationed along the Sino-Soviet border. Naval and air power directed against Japan and the United States should also be reduced. Washington, in turn, might cut back on military exercises.

Third, high-ranking Soviet and American naval officials should enter into regular exchanges to discuss their respective naval doctrines and future force projections in the Pacific. Such a dialogue in itself would be a major confidence-building measure. The American navy ought to be prepared to discuss its "maritime strategy," and the Soviet admirals should discuss their own "ocean bastion" strategy while making available data about their own forces and force projections in the Pacific. At present, all data on Soviet forces come from Western sources.

Fourth, the superpowers ought to exchange data on their respective defense budgets and plans. Soviet officials say they themselves do not know how much the Soviet Union is spending on defense and that they will be able to make such information available only after they have made price reforms scheduled for the early 1990s. But many knowledgeable Americans are skeptical of such contentions. At the very least, the Soviet military could furnish data on conscripts, military manpower, numbers of divisions and their readiness, numbers of airplanes and combat ships planned in coming years, and so forth.

Fifth, the incidents-at-sea talks, which have been going on for more than a decade—and which have been among the most successful of the various Soviet-American dialogues—could be expanded in an effort to institute a better system for crisis management in the Northwest Pacific.

The new American administration, while remaining cautious about Soviet intentions, needs to respond constructively and not defensively to Gorbachev's offers to lower tension. A measured response, as sketched above, would be appropriate.

There are two basic advantages to be derived from such an approach. First, in terms of public diplomacy, we should not allow Gorbachev to pose as the peacemaker in Asia and the United

States to appear rigid and unimaginative. It should be made clear how and why the Pacific became such a source of tension in the first place. From Stalin's occupation of Japan's northern territories in 1945 and the unleashing of North Korea against South Korea in 1950 to Brezhnev's aggressive policies in the 1970s, culminating in the Soviet invasion of Afghanistan, it has been the Soviet Union that has been largely responsible for the existing cold war in Asia. Moreover, we should also make clear that the Soviet Union and its Asian allies are presiding over failed, over-militarized and isolated economies due to policies of their own choosing while the liberal trading system we brought into being has led to an unparalled burst of economic growth among our allies in East Asia.

Second, we need to test Gorbachev to find out whether his peace proposals are simply one-sided and self-serving or whether he is ready to address the legitimate security interests of the United States and its allies in the region. In Europe, the West has correctly made conventional and asymmetrical force reductions the key test of Soviet intentions. We need a similar test in Asia, one that focuses on ending the regional conflicts on terms that are satisfactory to the Western coalition.

WHEN IDEOLOGY BOWS TO ECONOMICS[2]

Suddenly, Asian nations are finding merit in old enemies. India's Prime Minister Rajiv Gandhi, who counts Moscow as his principal patron, now talks reconciliation in China. Cambodian Prime Minister Hun Sen, who is fighting the Khmer Rouge guerrillas, pops up in Thailand, which bankrolls them. Sino-Soviet rapprochement seems merely a matter of time. With lucrative trade as the reward, Tokyo and Moscow discuss a formal end, finally, to World War II—the return of the disputed Kurile Islands to Japan. Everywhere in Asia, it seems, relationships spawned by the cold war are eroding as new U.S.-Soviet ties render them

[2]Reprint of an article by Douglas Stanglin with Dusko Doder and Mike Tharp. Reprinted by permission from *U.S. News & World Report*, F. 6, 1989, pp. 30-31. Copyright © February 6, 1989, *U.S. News & World Report*.

meaningless. In their place is emerging a new order built on economic pragmatism but bringing with it the danger of new instability.

The diplomatic shuffle comes at an awkward time for America, once the superpower arbiter of the Pacific. The U.S. military presence in the region is under increasing strain from nationalist movements, particularly in the Philippines and South Korea. Economic pressures, principally the outsize budget deficit at home, are forcing Washington to rethink defense commitments. The prospect leaves many Asians ambivalent. Few are eager for U.S. retrenchment as Japanese economic and diplomatic power expands, yet they hardly hesitate to compete with the U.S. for markets in the region. The combination fuels in America both protectionism and reluctance to spend more for allied defense. But President Bush clearly understands the need to reaffirm U.S. interests. He has added Beijing to his schedule after he attends the funeral of Emperor Hirohito later this month.

Moscow's Visible Hand

The pending Sino-Soviet rapprochement is the latest dramatic evidence of the political transition rattling Asia. Mikhail Gorbachev is extending his charm offensive into the Pacific by promising new economic links and pledging cutbacks in missiles and troops. He is meeting China's tough preconditions for improved relations: Ending his Afghan War, easing tensions on the Sino-Soviet border, pressing Vietnam to withdraw from Cambodia. Foreign Minister Eduard Shevardnadze is expected in Beijing this week to plan a spring visit by Gorbachev, the first Sino-Soviet summit since the 1950s.

The wrenching realignment now shapes policies in even the smallest Asian countries. It was actually set in motion almost 17 years ago by an abrupt thaw in Sino-American relations. China and the U.S. found in each other welcome leverage against a mutual rival, the Soviet Union, even though Moscow and Washington were on the lip of Détente I at the time. The convenient bond created, in effect, a strategic Sino-Soviet-American triangle upon which all three have come to play in the pursuit of interests around the Pacific Rim.

Until recently, Moscow's leg had been the weakest. The Soviet Union was bogged down in the old ideological debate with Bei-

jing and was suspect to other nations because of its invasion of
Afghanistan and support for Vietnam in Cambodia. But Gorbachev began to change all that with a seminal 1986 speech in Vladivostok, dealing Moscow into the Asian game and proclaiming
new "bonds of interdependence." Exploiting steadily improving
U.S.-Soviet ties, Gorbachev soon had his own leverage within the
triangle, leading finally to the warming of relations with Beijing.
Among China's preconditions, only withdrawal of the remaining
90,000 Vietnamese troops in Cambodia, now in prospect, awaits
fulfillment.

The consequences are evident throughout the region: Gandhi has called amicably on not one but two old enemies, Pakistan
and China; China has opened direct talks with Vietnam about the
future of Cambodia; Thailand's Foreign Minister went to Hanoi
for the first high-level visit in 13 years to prospect for trade and
investment; Cambodia's Hun Sen was in Bangkok last week, the
first such contact in a decade, to discuss trade and tourism.

The transition is producing even stranger bedfellows, prov-
ing Marco Polo's dictum that trade precedes politics. South Korea and Taiwan, traditional anti-Communist bastions, enjoy
multibillion-dollar trade ties with China, the Soviet Union and
Eastern Europe. South Korea's two-way trade with the socialist
bloc exceeded $3 billion last year, and Seoul has even begun di-
rect trade with North Korea. The Taiwanese are quietly investing in Chinese plant projects.

Luring Foreign Capital

In the new Asia, economics is in, ideology is out. "Countries
are being driven to improve frozen or strained or hostile political
relationships to maximize trade and investment," says Harry Har-
ding, a China specialist at the Brookings Institution. Like the Soviet Union, Beijing needs peace along its borders to focus on
domestic economic reforms—hence the warming of ties with
Moscow, New Delhi and Hanoi. Also, like the Soviet Union, it
needs a stable international environment to lure foreign capital
and technology. Smaller countries welcome the example: Vietnam begins to court Washington now that Moscow can ill afford
to foot the bill for its allies.

The new economic flexibility has provided a fallow field for
Japan. It is now the single largest foreign investor in nearly every

Asian economy, including China's. Within 10 years, the combined GNP of 10 East Asian countries will be three fourths the
GNP of all of North America. Of that, Japan's share will account
for nearly 80 percent. Asian neighbors already export more manufactured goods to Japan than the U.S. does. Japan's total trade
with Asian countries, even excluding China, now exceeds that
with America.

The strategic implications are staggering. Prime Minister Lee
Kuan Yew of Singapore said recently that Japan will replace the
U.S. as Asia's dominant power in the next decade. Money will do
it, according to Seah Chiang Nee, a Singapore columnist. Today,
he writes, "a country, or a corporation, with $2 billion to invest
may wield greater influence among countries hungry for jobs,
capital, technology and export markets than a country with a
costly military arsenal."

Diplomacy, Tokyo Style

Japan's political profile is rising rapidly as well. In Afghani-
stan, its diplomats are part of the international group overseeing
Soviet troop withdrawal and stand ready to take the same role in
Cambodia. Japan has abruptly suspended economic assistance to
Burma pending reforms by the new and oppressive military re-
gime. It was the first time Tokyo has tied aid to political perfor-
mance. Japanese companies are now poised to invest heavily in
Vietnam once Hanoi pulls out of Cambodia.

But for all its economic strength, Japan must tread carefully
in translating it into advantage. Neighbors resent Japan's influence and fear its eventual return to militarism. Although Tokyo
is trying to broker relations between the two Koreas, neither
Seoul nor Pyongyang seems interested in its help. Even Japanese
officials most eager for reunification and stability on the Korean
Peninsula acknowledge that Japan's former colonial role there
puts it in a "delicate situation."

Economic competition may become a critical counterweight
to Japan's domination of the Asian market. Some experts predict
a proliferation of subregional groupings that will compete with
each other. China is careful to broaden its trade relations to avoid
overdependence on one nation or trading group. It is Australia's
third-largest trading partner and does a thriving exchange with
the four "economic dragons"—Singapore, Taiwan, Hong Kong

and South Korea. In Indochina, proximity alone should make
Thailand and Vietnam natural economic allies. Bangkok businessmen, eager to tap the Vietnamese labor pool, were prominent in the official Thai delegation that recently visited Hanoi.

Pressure in Korea

As economic relationships grow in importance, Washington
may find it harder to rationalize its military presence. Two of its
primary security concerns of the 1960s, Indochina and the For-
mosa Strait, have been overtaken in the less ideological environment. A third, the Korean Peninsula, where the U.S. has 42,000
troops, will also fade in importance if the two Koreas actually reduce their confrontation.

The Soviet threat, Washington's bedrock rationale for military presence in the Pacific, is less persuasive to some Asians. The
Filipinos and Soviets recently held the highest-level military contacts in more than a decade, and Manila and Washington now
squabble over renewing U.S. base rights in the Philippines.
Gorbachev has encouraged that argument by offering to pull his
forces from Vietnam's Cam Ranh Bay if the U.S. will shut down
its Philippine bases. The offer, the U.S. replies, hardly corre-
sponds to strategic reality.

But strategic reality is in flux. The Soviet Union, China and
Japan are groping for position—Japan being the economic superpower without nuclear weapons. America's relative influence has
declined accordingly as others compete for markets. "The presence of American forces in the region obviates the need for other
countries to build their own," the Brookings Institution's Har-
ding says. "It dampens that and therefore prevents regional arms
races." That is a valid objective for Washington. It is not enough
to sustain the primacy of the past. The U.S. has no wish, nor can
if afford, to become primarily an arbiter or buffer between newly
competitive Asian countries.

Novel constellations are forming in Asia, causing a realignment in which the decisions of smaller nations, to an extent un-
imaginable as recently as a decade ago, will determine status. If
the next century is to be the century of the Pacific, as many strate-
gists now predict, and not merely of Japan, the other main players
are only now emerging.

THE VOTING FIELDS[3]

It's been a democratic spring in Southeast Asia. The momentum of the Philippines' revolution 18 months ago has continued
with Korea's back-flip into democracy and the end of 40 years of
martial law in Taiwan. But there have been democratic twinges
in the rest of the region as well. Thailand held a quiet election
in May 1986 with a turnout of 61 percent (higher than for elections in the United States). Amid growing calls for a liberalized
press, it chalked up its tenth year without a military coup, a
record in its postwar existence. In Malaysia's 1986 election the
anti-Western Islamic Fundamentalist Party was decisively repudiated. Las April Indonesia's 164 million people enjoyed one of the
most incident-free "elections" in their history. Even in this
"directed democracy," dominated by President Suharto and his
Golkar party, embarrassingly major gains, especially among the
young, were won by an opposition party (the PDI) that argued for
greater democratization. In Hong Kong polls suggest overwhelming public support for the first direct elections in the colony's history, scheduled for 1988. Whether this precedent will
survive the 1997 takeover by Beijing is, of course, another matter.

There is even some surprising news from Vietnam and its client states, Laos and Cambodia. The latest reports point to an ever
so grudging *glasnost*, Vietnamese-style, led by the new Party chair-
man Nguyen Van Linh, nicknamed "little Gorbachev." The
"elections" of April 20 were hardly more than a routine backing
for the Marxist government, but the methods were new. The
number of candidates increased from 600 to 829, contesting 496
seats. For the first time public meetings were held in which ordinary Vietnamese could openly voice any—except fundamental—
complaints. In Lang Son province, according to Radio
Hanoi, candidates even withdrew from the race after popular
"objections," whatever that means.

The persecution of Buddhism and ethnic minorities is unabated, and the forced march to the Marxist-Leninist nirvana

[3]Reprint of an editorial in *The New Republic*, 197:7–9, August 10–17, 1987. Reprinted by permission.

continues. But there is still a new pragmatism in the air. Some of this is "follow the Russian leader." But more important is the growing economic success of the Western-style "democracies" in the region, leading to increased demands for real democracy within them. This is prodding their Communist neighbors to liberalize at least their economies in order to compete.

The signs are everywhere. In Cambodia last year the Vietnamese-controlled Heng Samrin regime followed the time-honored democratic tradition of collecting taxes, rents, and utility fees from private businesses. It makes a pleasant change from confiscating them. Premier Hun Sen openly defended reliance on the private sector. "The fact that we're giving our population the opportunity to exercise freedom in the economy and small industry is not as dangerous as the fact that poverty continues to exist," was his touchingly bizarre apology for capitalism last year.

Even in Laos there has been a relaxation of central controls to rescue the country from a great leap forward that resulted in a per capita income lower than Bangladesh, and a drop in industrial production of some 40 percent over the last five years. Alongside all this postmodern Communist realism, the old Leninist leaders are gradually dying off, leaving space for a new generation to take over. It means a pivotal few years for Asian democracy.

Two potential developments threaten this rosy picture. The first is the chance of an outbreak of U.S. protectionism, or a serious downturn in the world economy, either of which could clobber economies already hit by the decline in commodity prices in the last few years. The second is a rise in conservatism in the region, either from Communist hard-liners in Vietnam or disgruntled generals in the democracies still to be born.

To counteract the first, Congress needs to avoid self-defeating and democracy-defeating protectionism, including the hidden protectionism of vast agricultural subsidies, especially of American rice. The promise of liberalized trade with the world's largest market can be an important Western lever for democracy. In the last three years ASEAN's trade with the United States increased by $2 billion, to $16 billion. Its trade with the rest of the world declined by $3 billion.

To deal with the second threat, a clear policy for promoting democracy among our allies needs to be developed as a companion to the Reagan administration's clear ideas about promoting democracy among our enemies. The Philippines, South Korea, and Taiwan have all been hailed as achievements of the Reagan approach. Unfortunately, it stretches the imagination to believe this. In none of these cases were there insurgencies consistently supported by the administration. NOr was there any direct—or indirect—military intervention. In all three, an organic and genuine democratic force put intolerable pressure on a regime that the United States then abandoned at a critical juncture. The achievements were primarily those of the Filipino, Korean, and Taiwanese peoples, and securer for it. The successful U.S. policy (part accidental, part deliberate) was: diplomatic distance, an intimate but not partisan relationship with the regime, loud support for nonviolence, and a consistent and vocal commitment to greater democratization. Gently did it.

This administration—and the next—should build on these achievements with a twofold policy. With the Communist states, the choice is between a hostile stalemate and a risky diplomatic opening that exploits the recent liberalization. We think the time is ripe for the latter. The MIA issue, though important, is not the only common interest we have with the Vietnamese, and should be treated as a separate humanitarian issue, as George Shultz reaffirmed last week. For the rest, the United States should use the carrot of tentative economic contact with the Vietnamese, to be expanded if their withdrawal from Cambodia, said to be planned for 1990, really looks like it's happening.

The administration, to its credit, has begun the process. It ended the ban on economic aid to Vietnam-controlled Laos last year, and initiated joint excavations with Vietnamese of MIA sites. Last December it held the first diplomatic discussions at the assistant-secretary level with Vietnam in Hanoi. But along with encouraging the end of Vietnamese control in Cambodia, steps must taken to ensure that a Cambodian tyranny does not succeed the current one. This means counteracting the influence of the Khmer Rouge by backing the democratic forces within the Cambodian resistance, namely the followers of Prince Sihanouk. A meager $3.35 million was given last year. As an almost textbook case of genuine freedom fighters, Sihanouk's forces could use a lot more. The aim should be to give them a dominant voice in a transitional regime, before elections can be supervised. The rest will be up to the Cambodian people.

In the non-Communist states, pro-democratic forces should be given firm backing, on the Korea-Philippines model. If the administration wants to argue that its "successes" in those two countries weren't just luck and hindsight, here's a chance to prove it. In Korea itself, where the generals are already grumbling, the battle is far from over. Pressuring Chun to include opposition members in his interim Cabinet and sending observers to the elections when they take place would be two useful measures. In Taiwan the ending of martial law should be seen as the beginning—not the end—of democratization. Gradual repeal of repressive legislation still in force curtailing freedom of speech and habeas corpus should be made conditional for continue U.S. support.

In Thailand the United States should continue to support the government militarily (Reagan gave them 12 F-16 fighter bombers in 1985, and over 9,000 U.S. troops took part in joint exercises with the Thais last year). But it should use the aid to push the government toward an elective premiership, and a weakening of the dominance of the military in the unelected upper chamber. With the Communist resistance now crushed, there's no excuse for inaction. It should also firmly support the freer press laws now being considered in the country. Further south, Malaysia's imminent renegotiation of its delicate ethnic truce, enshrined in the New Economic Plan, is stirring up trouble in the country and a government crackdown is under way. Wide powers of summary arrest and non-jury trials for crimes punished with the death penalty are signs of a growing authoritarianism. But the genuine popular support for a tolerant and democratic regime (as the last elections showed) and the need for greater U.S. investment provide an opening for the administration. Strong diplomatic pressure could tip the balance for democracy, or at least hold it steady.

In Indonesia a successor to Suharto will be needed in the next few years. It's a good time for us to back vociferously growing elements in the country who want to see a limited presidential term and greater press freedom. In Hong Kong the United States should persuade the British to support direct elections soon, if necessary before the Chinese revise their own Basic Law—a mini-constitution for a Chinese-run Hong Kong that is now being drafted by Beijing and will probably be approved by China's National People's Congress in 1990. With democracy already in place, it will be harder to budge by the time the Chinese take over.

Singapore's "democracy," where "opposition" means one contrary deputy in the national chamber and where repressive legislation openly outlaws any hints of dissent, is no place for the United States to keep silent. The administration should press for repeal of the Internal Security Act, which allows for detention without trial and which was used in May to imprison ten Catholic social workers and a progressive theater company for a "Marxist conspiracy." Given Singapore's complete reliance on Western investment, the leverage is there.

"Constructive Engagement" are now two dirty words. In Southeast Asia, they needn't be. Using a mix of diplomatic, military, and economic pressure to kindle a genuine and gradual Asian democratic thaw is one of the most fruitful policy initiatives now available to any administration. Korea and the Philippines were largely surprises. They shouldn't have been. If future Pol Pots and Marcoses are to be avoided in Southeast Asia, now's the time to do a little for democracy, and to do it well.

II. SOUTH KOREA

EDITOR'S INTRODUCTION

Modern Korean history has been shaped by China, Russia, and, especially, Japan. Korea's most recent history stems from the stalemated Korean War, which left a divided country—Communist-ruled North Korea and pro-Western South Korea. In the first article, "The End of the Hermit Kingdom," reprinted from *Ethics & International Affairs*, Robert J. Myers, an authority on Korean affairs, analyzes the complex political history of modern South Korea. The following article, "The Republic of Korea: Great Transition and Coming Crisis," by Ramon H. Myers, seminar fellow at The Hoover Institution, describes the dangers inherent in South Korea's internal fragmentation along economic and political lines. Next, in "South Korea's Rise to Prominence," reprinted from *Current History*, Young Whan Kihl, professor of political science at Iowa State University, expresses his hope that South Korea's increasing economic and political success, while leading to rising expectations that in many cases cannot be immediately satisfied, will result in the tolerance necessary for rational solutions, thanks to better education of the populace. Finally, Doug Bandow, a senior fellow at the Cato Institute and formerly an aide to President Reagan, advocates in "It's Time to Reassess the U.S.-Korea Defense Treaty," reprinted from *USA Today Magazine*, the withdrawal of U.S. troops to encourage South Korea to assume responsibility for its own national defense.

THE END OF THE HERMIT KINGDOM[1]

I

Korea did not enter the American consciousness until June 1950, when the North Koreans attacked the South Koreans in an effort to unify the country, which was split in two at the conclusion of World War II by a hasty agreement between Stalin and Truman. While the future of Korea, then a Japanese colony, was occasionally raised at Big Four meetings during World War II, no decision had been reached. The history of Korea was known only to a handful of scholars and missionaries. Under threats in the nineteenth century from its neighbors—China, Russia, and Japan—Korea had withdrawn into itself, earning the sobriquet of "The Hermit Kingdom," as well as the more lyrical "Land of the Morning Calm." Japan finally prevailed in the struggle, annexing all of Korea in 1910. The colonial period remains a bitter memory in Korea. "The forced enslavement of Korea by Japan for almost half a century left Korea poverty-stricken and a target for exploitation by the colonizer. This was a most tragic period in Korean history because Koreans lost their self-respect, both as Koreans and as human beings. The exhilaration of Koreans on the day of liberation from Japan in 1945 was therefore beyond description." (Han Sung-joo and Robert J. Myers, eds., *Korea: The Year 2000*, Carnegie Council on Ethics and International Affairs [Maryland: University Press of America, 1987] p. 119) The U.N.-supervised elections in South Korea led to the election of Syngman Rhee, the American-backed candidate. Rhee, playing the role of super-patriot, was more interested in the reunification of the divided country than anything else. Economic development was not high on his priority list. Nor was it high on the list of his communist counterpart, Kim Il Sung, who struck across the demarcation line at the 38th parallel in June 1950. American and U.N. forces supported the South, while the Chinese supported the North.

[1]Reprint of an article by Robert J. Myers, editor-in-chief, *Ethics & International Affairs* 2: 99-114, 1988. Reprinted by permission.

The Korean War (1950–1953) ended in a stalemate at the 1945 demarcation line. This is where the whole tragedy began, leaving a devastated and still divided country, whose social and economic conditions could best be described as egalitarian—no one had much. Yet in that rubble, many ideas of the hierarchical past were being reevaluated and the possibility of a new society with democratic elements arose, a possibility that did not become explicit until several years later. In the meantime, the Rhee brand of nationalist authoritarianism was insufficient to begin the road to recovery and economic development. By 1960 popular discontent sparked student demonstrations, supported by the population at large, ending the Rhee regime. Rhee's nationalism aimed at restoring lost pride and creating a feeling of importance. The stalemated war was hard for Rhee to accept; reunification was farther away than ever. While the obsession for reunification continued with Rhee, he did not have the ability or sense of purpose to create the first two pre-conditions for the nation's future—stability and economic development. With no democratic institutions in place, no middle class in sight, the successor regime of Prime Minister Chang Myon failed to provide leadership or direction. Its salient characteristics were instability and drift.

Into this vacuum on May 16, 1961 stepped Major General Park Chung Hee, the Korean military being the only powerful institution in the nation. This marked the end of the "nationalism" era and ushered in the beginning of the economic development "garrison state." Growth and anti-communism were the watchwords. Nationalism remains an important element in Korean society, but not its total inspiration.

It was clear to Park Chung Hee and his close associates, such as Kim Jon Pil (later prime minister and an opposition candidate, albeit conservative, in the December 1987 elections) that the future was linked to an export-led economy. The first five-year plan was launched in 1962, followed by the five-year plans of 1967, 1972, and 1977. The key to breaking the poverty of a traditional, agrarian society was industrialization. South Korea's future prosperity grew from an abysmal economic base. In the early 1960s, South Korea's per-capita income was less than $100 (U.S. dollars). Government funds were loaned to favorite large industries (the *chaebol*); South Korea's international debt rose to over $45 billion by 1985 (in contrast to the U.S. debt, these funds were spent for infrastructure and factories, which produced revenues;

the external debt is now down to the mid-$30 billions and falling). The economy was further spurred by the Vietnam War. Progress was rapid. While government intervention was important in creating targets and key industries, essentially South Korea had a market economy. Government intervention was discreet, based on the Japanese model. This approach, as the world knows, protects the domestic manufacturing market as well as agriculture. (The question of Korea opening its domestic markets remains unanswered to this day.)

While all of this was going on, the military dictatorship performed its obvious legitimizing functions, providing security along the demilitarized zone (DMZ), against the possibility of a renewed assault by North Korea with the aid of its Chinese and Soviet allies. As a corollary, in South Korea itself, a strong anti-communist ideology and tight press censorship kept internal unrest and dissent below the surface. Any opposition to the government during this time of the "garrison state" was considered subversive. The external situation to the North and the internal situation domestically were nonetheless attuned to the reality of the times. The stationing of American troops, mainly at the DMZ, was part of the U.S. strategy of communist containment, and the strict anti-communist internal policies of South Korea found a resonance in the United States. As time went on, however, internal pressures were mounting in the 1970s for the Park Chung Hee regime. Cracks were developing in the twin pillars of stability and economic growth. One development theory insists that once economic development is under way and takes hold, the likelihood increases for the parallel path to democratic government. This is not necessarily a value judgment, that is, economically advanced countries prefer democratic government. It is simply that as the society becomes more complex and more educated, trained citizens are required. The "middle class" develops new centers of power, which temper the power of the state.

The assassination of Park Chung Hee in 1979 produced a brief interregnum before another military coup, led by General Chun Doo Hwan. As President, Chun Doo Hwan initiated the Fifth Republic but continued Park's policies, unmindful until perhaps 1985 of the profound changes that were occurring in the society at large. One leading reason for the acceptance of the "garrison state" rationale long after it had reached its apogee was the failure on the part of Korean and American leaders to recognize the changing strategic reality in North Asia. The change in these strategies corresponded with President Richard Nixon's opening to the People's Republic of China in 1972.

II

There were three elements in the strategic situation that have altered politics in South Korea and in the whole Korean peninsula. First is the emergence of a new China, which has regained its strength, self-confidence, and self-assurance. This China is unlikely to support North Korea in a new war on South Korea. In November 1950 the Chinese entered the Korean War to ensure a friendly state on its Manchurian border. The intervention was massive. Chinese troops took over the war-fighting responsibility from the decimated North Koreans. In 1988, given China's modernization goals, and after a substantial reduction in the size of its armed forces, there would appear to be no national interest served by reopening the Korean War. On the contrary, while nourishing its relations with North Korea, China is rapidly expanding its economic and cultural ties with South Korea. The latter is urging formal diplomatic relations, a point raised publicly by President Roh Tae Woo in the December election campaign. This goal is strongly supported by the Japanese Prime Minister Noboru Takeshita.

The second change in the strategic equation is the Soviet Union. There again, given Moscow's priorities—to restructure its own economy and concentrate on its problems with the U.S., Europe, and the Eastern bloc—promoting a war on the Korean peninsula would not be practical. This would also enormously complicate relations with China, which the Soviet Union is seeking to improve. Changes in Sino-Soviet relations cannot be considered evidence that the basic principles of interstate relations have been suspended or repealed, that threats of war and actual conflict are now out of the question. Rather, in trying to consider the likely interests to be pursued by both major communist powers, launching a war in Northeast Asia, independently or in conjunction with North Korea, is not in the cards. A variation of this thinking as applied to Western Europe was reportedly behind the judgment of the U.S. Joint Chiefs of Staff to proceed with the INF treaty with the Soviet Union. (*The New York Times*, January 3, 1988) Nonetheless, these ideas die slowly. The Pentagon report of the Commission on Integrated Long-Term Strategy stated that Soviet military power in East Asia, combined with North Korean forces, poses a threat to the South. Therefore, the report concludes, U.S. forces will remain in South Korea until no threat is visible. From the official U.S. military view, nothing has changed over the past 30 years. (*Korean Herald*, January 13, 1988) This is not an argument to withdraw U.S. troops from Korea, but rather to find a large strategic rationale, assuming a gradual improvement in South-North relations. Professor Paul Kennedy, author of *The Rise and Fall of the Great Powers*, writes in terms of U.S. commitments and resources. For example, "in East Asia the balance of power is shifting toward the local biggies, China and Japan. And in many ways it could be argued that they could take over the role of provider of stability and influence in the area. A fast fix might be to say, 'O.K., we'll get American troops and the air force out of Korea just as soon as we possibly can.'" This might set the stage for some kind of second Korean War. "The commitments to Korea need to be thought through, not only in terms of discussions with the South Koreans, but multilateral confidential discussion with the Japanese and China. In other words, the role of diplomacy becomes very important in the strategy of reducing commitments." (*The New York Times*, January 24, 1988)

The third factor is the increasing strength of the South Korean armed forces and the economy vis-à-vis North Korea. There is a rough military parity (not necessarily in each weapons category) that makes a North Korean attack a very high-risk enterprise indeed. Assuming that its communist neighbors would not significantly support an attack, the North would be faced by the South, plus 40,000 American troops and air and naval support, committed by the security treaty. The only rationale left to support the possibility of an attack is the irrationality of the aging North Korean tyrant, Kim Il Sung, or of his son Kim Jong Il, a variation of Richard Nixon's "mad dog argument" during the Vietnam War. The North Korean full-scale military attack idea is no longer credible. Beyond regrettable terrorist attacks and non-participation in the 1988 Olympics in Seoul, there is little that North Korea and its 18 million inhabitants can do to the modern world.

All of these points demonstrate a completely different balance of power and a new era of reconciliation of great power interests that was not the case in June 1950. The rhetoric in South

Korea of the imminent danger of a North Korean attack still continues (despite the experience of the December 1987 election), but this is because of the trauma of the Korean War generation, now moving from the scene. A "new war on the peninsula" as a constructive way of uniting the two Koreas seems most unlikely. Basing one's international and domestic policies on the most unlikely scenario carries with it high costs. South Korea has paid for this, perhaps more than its leaders have realized. The rhetoric of imminent hostilities with North Korea has increasingly worked against the current interests of the South Korean ruling elite. Why would international financial institutions and private foreign banks lend money to South Korea by the billion if they believed an imminent North Korean attack was to be taken seriously? Why would the South Korean authorities seek to hold the Olympics . . . [in 1988] and expect the sports fans of the world to attend? Why has this myth persisted so long in the face of the new reality, encompassed by the strategic shift already evident and contrary to the realities in both North and South Korea? The short answer is that the military elite of South Korea became addicted to this psychology as a way of continuing its monopoly of political power. As the events of 1987 have shown, it was Korea's good fortune that the regime of President Chun Doo Hwan finally changed its course, nudged vigorously, to be sure, by students, labor, and the general population. The government finally recognized the face of the society that it in fact had created. The attack by North Korean agents on a Korean airliner in November 1987, just before the elections, reminded everyone of the capacity of the North Koreans to commit terrorist acts. The Rangoon outrage in 1983 was the worst; yet inexcusable as these attacks are, they are marginal to the power competition between the two Koreas, which clearly the South has won.

III

If it is true that the objective situation outside Korea has radically changed since the 1950s and that the ruling military elite held power by the perpetuation of a myth, what finally changed the perception and then the reality? A triggering event, one can argue, was the decision of the Olympic Organizing Committee in 1981 to hold the 1988 summer Olympics in Seoul. Both the Chun government and its many opponents were highly in favor of this unexpected turn of events for quite different reasons. The Chun government saw the Olympics as international recognition of its economic achievements and as evidence of the government's heretofore questioned legitimacy. The oppositionists, particularly in the scholarly and technocratic communities, saw it as a means toward faster modernization, Korea's movement into the international economic order. Internationalization meant the imposition of not only world standard economic norms but inevitably world standard political norms as well. This would provide a sturdy shield against government oppression, and a powerful force for pluralism and democratic change. After all, the world's publicity light would be upon Korea. The real winner was the democratic impulse in Korean society, not a justification for the perpetuation of an absolute government. (President Chun, to his credit and as a testimony to his own political insight, told an American observer in the summer of 1987: "I am an anachronism.")

The second and decisive event was the decision of President Chun Doo Hwan on April 13, 1987 to cut off the arguments in the National Assembly over the question of the direct election of the president. Chun, having agreed already to give up power in February 1988, felt that this was a sufficient concession and the new constitution and direct election questions could be decided after the power transfer. He had already made an unprecedented concession. The trade-off was to select his heir apparent, former fellow general Roh Tae Woo at the Democratic Justice Party (DJP) convention. This did not wash (to the surprise of many, including myself). The nascent democratic process, the new correlation of business, labor, and academic power, was bubbling up too quickly. The U.S. Department of State had already spoken out for the need for change, in an address by Gaston J. Sigur on February 6, 1987. The street demonstrations and labor strikes, beginning in earnest in June, compelled the DJP candidate Roh Tae Woo to propose, on June 29, 1987, a series of concessions to meet the demand for direct elections and to diffuse the demonstrations. President Chun promptly accepted Roh's initiative. Clearly the principle of economic growth could no longer guarantee stability. Hyun Hong Choo, a leading member of the DJP in the National Assembly and a key supporter of President Roh explained it this way: "What sets the leadership of the Fifth Republic apart from the earlier ones is its realization that economic

progress is no longer a sufficient condition for political legitimacy. Surely, it is a necessary condition, the absence of which will
rock the very foundation of the country. The result of high economic development was the decoupling of politics from economics. Political legitimacy has to be established on its own merit."
(*Progress in Democracy: The Pacific Basin Experience* [Seoul: The Ilhae Institute, 1987] p. 69) The inadequacy of just the two pillars,
stability and economic development, was clearly evident in the
streets of Seoul in June 1987. The days of the "garrison state"
were numbered.

IV

The military rulers of South Korea (albeit in civilian clothes)
were blinded in their perception of politics and social change by
their very success. Their economic accomplishments were known
as "the Korean miracle," a miracle discovered in Korea. The ideological explanation was that political stability plus hard work
equals economic success, or in short, the triump of the Confucian
society.

The rediscovery of "Confucianism" in the West in the 1960s
in the context of modern economic development is one of the
wonders of our day. A largely discredited system of feudal hierarchical society was suddenly thrust upon the world's public at the
popular level as the wave of the future. Confucianism is essentially an ethical code, created by its founder two centuries B.C. It was
woefully short of economics; in fact wealth and commerce were
explicitly eschewed by its founder. For example, in James Legge's
translation of *The Chinese Classics*, "The Master said: 'With coarse
rice to eat, with water to drink, and my bended arm for a pil-
low;—I have still joy in the midst of these things.'" (James Legge,
The Chinese Classics [Hong Kong: The London Missionary
Society] Book VII, ch. XV, p. 64) This paradox between then and
now deserves a brief comment to place the virtues and defects of
Confucianism in a more utilitarian light.

The early Korean dynasties quickly and even avidly came under the sway of Chinese cultural, political, and military influence,
at the same time preserving their own language, arts, and culture.
Buddhism to this day (along with shamanism or folk religion) is
highly influential among about 70 percent of the population;
Confucianism reached its peak among the Koreans in the last

dynasty, the Yi. More Confucian than the Chinese Ch'ing dynasty, the Yi was easily overthrown by the Japanese in 1910 and the country was converted into a colony. The lopping off of the Emperor, the key figure in the Confucian hierarchical system, both weakened the Confucian tradition in Korea and spurred the growth of Christianity, for Jesus Christ to replace the god that failed. In China itself, Confucianism, with its static system, was generally considered one of the principal reasons that modern capitalism did not develop in China. Such a closed hierarchical social and political structure did not, therefore, encourage large-scale entrepreneurship. The idea of progress was unknown; the Chinese world moved in an unending series of cycles, hoping to emulate the virtues of some past utopia. The Mandate of Heaven could be withdrawn, not so much by the accumulation of virtue in the opponents of the Emperor, but on the sturdy arms of disaffected armed peasants. There are many fine things to be said about Confucius and Chinese philosophy in general, but as a lever for economic development in a modern sense, there is a strong case to go elsewhere.

While some scholars saw in this dynastic cycle proof of its democratic nature, to many this was a charitable conclusion. Lo Bang, the current Chinese literary gadfly, anathema to both the Mainland and the Taiwan governments, has written a highly critical book on the dark side of Chinese culture, *The Ugly Chinaman*. While Allan Bloom in *The Closing of the American Mind* excoriates Americans for being too relativistic, too quick to concede on whatever grounds the superiority of someone else's value system, Mr. Lo is one of the few to attack the Middle Kingdom's philosophy. "Our culture has been shaped largely by Confucianism, which does not contain a single element of equality, a key concept in building the modern democratic system," Mr. [Lo] Bang wrote. The Confucian tradition "nurtures bullies," ranging from "tyrannical emperors to despotic officials and ruthless mobs." As for the famed Confucian scholars, "The minds of the literati were stuck on the bottom of an intellectually stagnant pond, the soy sauce vat of Chinese culture." (*The Washington Post*, January 5, 1988) The Confucian economy consisted of agriculture and merchant trading. The uniqueness of the "Confucian work ethic" is also highly suspect. Plenty of other—non-Sinitic—nationalities also work hard. Confucian deference to authority may account for part of the Asian economic success inspired by authoritarian long hours and coercive labor practices—comparative labor advantage—but that has built-in limitations, as the case of South Korea has demonstrated. While it may be true that the ideal Confucian society can be used to exploit labor, that was probably not the expectation of the founder. In any case, the actuality is that a society run by an authoritarian government, based on a monopoly of military and political power, can for a time be economically successful. One needs to inquire if that means economic efficiency is the only goal, and whether values, such as the "good life," calling for consideration of distribution and the purposes of a society, do not come into question.

In the case of South Korea, the insufficiency of the Confucian-rationalized authoritarian government was gradually recognized. An economy with no overall inflation was the result of low wages, which in turn made possible the competitive export-led economy. President Park promoted the welfare of the backward agricultural sector at the expense of the industrial labor force for political support. The astounding gain each year in GNP was not reflective of similar increases in per-capita income. (Between 1983 and 1987, for example, Korea's GNP grew at an average rate of 10.1 percent, the highest rate in the world, according to the Bank of Korea.) In 1987 when a Korean scholar friend who was opposed to the government was reminded by a government official how much better off he was economically than in the immediate past, his response was, "But remember, we are not animals." Clearly, something was missing. With 98 percent of the population literate (compared to 90 percent in the U.S.), there were longings for popular participation in decision making and a vision of social justice. These additional two pillars were what was missing in the Korean system of government. Why was there this degree of discontent in South Korea in 1985 to mid-1987? Why was there a sudden congealing of democratic sentiment as the way out of the dilemma of authoritarian rule? The democratic moment had come for the reasons we have already suggested and the street demonstrations proved the point. Koreans were uncomfortable having decisions made in the streets, but for a time, this seemed to be the only avenue open to them.

V

Beyond democratic longings, there was also the all-pervasive perception that the former more or less egalitarian society was tilting toward the rich. Under President Park, for example, the spread was 1 to 3 between the bottom and the top, while under President Chun it was 1 to 6 or 7 (not of course in either case counting the handful of very rich). This phenomenon is the well-known Kuznet's effect, that high growth rates are associated with increasing inequality until a leveling process begins at a later stage. Most Korean laborers did not feel that they were receiving a fair share of the fruits of their labor. In brief, the questions of social justice and popular participation in government had somehow eluded the vast majority of citizens. Tales of government favoritism to the giant companies with low-interest loans, financial scandals and corruption involving favor and influence arose from time to time in the South Korean press, despite the censorship system. The Korean stock market provided the evidence that the companies were riding high on the backs of the workers. The strikes in the summer of 1987 in both the large and small production and service groups seriously disrupted the economy, and the justness of the workers' complaints was generally accepted. The timing was superb. With the election coming up, the government had little choice but to support the workers, even though the strikes were illegal. Raises of 15 to 20 percent or more were commonplace. The government sided with the workers, encouraging the management to meet the workers' demands and get on with business. The long-term adjustment between the demands of labor and the requirements for profit maximization have yet to be resolved. The significance of the strikes and how the government handled them shows that there is a growing consensus in South Korea that a degree of untidiness will be accepted in the economic arena in the name of social justice.

In addition, the problem of political participation was on the minds of the student rioters and labor strikers in the summer of 1987. The 1981 Chun constitution provided for the indirect system of presidential elections, wherein electors were selected from each district after the National Assembly pattern. This allowed the government in effect to gerrymander the results. This aspect, applied to the presidential elections—as well as for election to the National Assembly—was the unfair aspect of the Korean system, and not fraud at the polls. The direct election idea was highly

risky for the ruling party, but it accepted this idea to end the demonstrations and strikes in order to establish confidence among
the populace in the legitimacy and fairness of the political process. The issue in the election was which candidate could most
successfully blend the four factors of stability, economic development, popular participation, and social justice in his program.
Other important factors were regionalism and personality. The
winner received only a plurality of 36.6 percent, while the two
principal opponents, Kim Young Sam and Kim Dae Jung, each
had about 26 percent. Most analysts consider that about 80 percent of the total vote was for conservatives, showing the essentially cautious nature of the society and its likely level of tolerance
for future disorder.

VI

One can say with considerable confidence that democratic
roots are being put down in Korea in a very receptive and nourishing soil. South Korean democracy is not a Western, or more
specifically, American invention. The South Koreans are sophisticated thinkers, and their difficulty in being democratic in their
actions stems from their cultural heritage (insofar as it is Confucian) and their inability to compromise easily. Politics still carries
a high level of principle, a Korean political moralism that is finally
being overcome. (Susan Chira, "South Koreans Obsessed by
Dreams of Democracy," *The New York Times*, December 15, 1987)
Politics as the art of the possible is now being practiced. This is
not to downgrade the need for morality in political action, in the
Niebuhrian sense, but is rather the recognition that moralism, a
crusading spirit on any issue, does not lead to sound results. One
sees from the politics of the past year that Koreans now have their
collective eye on both process and results.

The odds are that they will enthusiastically embrace democracy. In a conference on Asian democracy in Seoul on July 1–2,
1987, Arthur Schlesinger, Jr. said, "Democracy will be, I believe,
more than a passing episode in human history. In the end, it
seems a natural aspiration because it responds in a deep sense not
only to the needs of society but to the needs of human nature itself—because democracy expresses that complex amalgam in every breast of human courage with human frailty, of the desire to
create with the impulse to destroy, or the capacity to do good with

the compulsion to do evil. Democracy rests not only on the mixed economy but even more profoundly on the mixed nature of man." (Schlesinger in *Progress in Democracy*, *op. cit.*, p. 18)

South Korean democracy gets its start on a relatively egalitarian basis, in the sense that there is universal education. This is not to suggest that a highly literate population cannot make serious political mistakes; it does mean, however, that reasons for nonparticipation or disembarment from the franchise—such as gender or race or property ownership, which were the impediments to the flowering of democracy in the U.S., do not exist in South Korea. There is no mechanism to prevent a citizen from voting, as was demonstrated in the 90 percent voter turnout; no barriers, and no apathy. Korean voters evidently think that their voice matters. The importance of participation might be catching in other Asian societies, where there seems no obvious opportunity to compete successfully. If today's minority cannot be tomorrow's majority (for whatever reason), the well-spring of that country's chances for real democracy will dry up, "political competition, far from being a source of instability, serves as the safety valve on the boiler and prevents pent up steam from exploding the system." (*Ibid.*)

Democratic outcomes are obtained at a certain cost, particularly for a country whose political tradition of the past 40 years was heavily influenced by the threat to the North, justifying (to many) the "garrison state," discussed previously. The claim of democracy's supporters that this system is the best way to resolve division and dissent was generally accepted in South Korea. The new democratic process will work its own way. The four-part formula—stability, economic development, popular participation, and social justice—is flexible. The arguments in Korean politics in the future will be on how these four parts are put together in opposition to organize itself as a real political party instead of a mass movement. The new formula does not guarantee the success of any particular political groupings, but it does speak well to the prospects for a democratic, dynamic, and internationally significant South Korean nation.

The South Koreans will need all the optimism they can muster in the next few years after they successfully conclude the Olympics and some of their euphoria vanishes. One general internal problem that requires attention is the surprising strength of regionalism in political matters. One would think that this would lessen under the impact of modern communications and transportation in the succeeding generations. Regionalism is not necessarily a bad thing unless it is carried to the point of national divisiveness.

Two other matters loom large, trade and defense. The trade problem comes from two directions, China and the United States, for quite different reasons. With the appreciation of the won, a survey by the Korean Foreign Trade Association (KFTA) shows that 57.2 percent of foreign buyers are considering shifting import sources from South Korea—42 percent to China. (*The Korean Herald*, January 12, 1988) Beyond the won, China will soon be a tenacious competitor against all kinds of Korean manufactured products and will probably soon be entering the General Agreement on Tariffs and Trade (GATT). For one thing it will have considerably lower labor costs (a familiar story!). While the U.S. has been taking almost 60 percent of Korea's exports, this percentage will fall, not so much because of protectionism but because of weak finances. America will have to pick and choose its trading partners to reduce the trade deficit. Also, it will in time have to reduce its military spending, not because it wants to or because of a new view of security in Northeast Asia, but because it can't afford not to. So the Korean economy may contract and its defense bill may rise.

This brings us, however, to the question of cooperation between the two Koreas. While a number of South Koreans write about "reunification," this would appear to be in the distant future. If our analysis is correct about the decline of the North's fortunes, sometime within the next few years the often aborted discussions between the North and the South will begin again. Minimum results will be communication by mail, some travel, and trade. There is considerable domestic pressure in the South for negotiations, since 15 percent of the population originally come from the North. The pace will depend upon the level of desire on the part of the North to enter the modern world.

Finally, there is the likelihood, based on the points raised in this discussion, that Korea will develop its own new style of politics that will be less threatening to the society in general, again evidence of a turn from the sterotype of Confucius. In the past, to reinforce his Mandate of Heaven, the Korean president showed a stern and dour visage to his own people and to the world. President Roh Tae Woo has dared to smile. While such symbolism cannot be quantified, nonetheless the old story of Korea as the "Hermit Kingdom" will remain a historical fact but not the image of the future.

THE REPUBLIC OF KOREA: GREAT TRANSITION AND COMING CRISIS[2]

What I can say today is to offer some insights into the great crisis now engulfing Korean society, based upon different developmental patterns in other East Asian countries. Part of my argument is that South Korea has entered a great transition in which there seems to be no turning back, but this transition is now beset with enormous problems.

Let us view the rapidity of change over the past 25 years. In 1965 nearly 30 percent of the people resided in cities of over 2,000 persons. By 1990 roughly 70 percent will be living in cities. The economy is now predominantly manufacturing and services, with agriculture employing only 23 percent of the workforce. Agriculture contributed only about 12 percent of the gross domestic product in 1987, whereas it was around 40 percent in the early sixties. The speed with which resources, particularly human, have moved from villages and agricultural activity to the cities and engaged in services and manufacturing has been breathtaking.

Associated with this great transformation has been the growth of population, with an increasing share of the population becoming younger. With a population of 42 million in 1987, there were around 5 million elementary students, around 6 million secondary students (middle and high school) and around 1.5 million college students, to make for a total student body of around 12.5 million, or 30 percent of the Korean population. In other words, around one out of every three persons is being supported to learn and spend time in school, compared to only one out of seven persons in the early sixties.

[2]Reprint of a speech by Ramon H. Myers, Seminar Fellow at The Hoover Institution. *Vital Speeches of the Day*, vol. LV, no. 14, May 1, 1989. Reprinted with permission.

Finally, the Korean economy has become integrated into the world economy. A high proportion of GDP (gross domestic product) originates in foreign trade, and foreign direct investment in Korea is substantial. Moreover, the country's foreign debt stands at $42 billion. Any major changes in foreign trade quickly produce ripple effects in the domestic economy and society alike.

The Emergence of Tensions

The extraordinary changes just cited have produced a differentiated society of skilled and professional groups in new urban networks, along with the typical urban anomie and social deviation that accompany all rapid changes of this kind. Meanwhile, Korea's political system had hardened during the 1960s and 1970s into a new form. A large, autocratic political center, located in the country's capital, had formed patron-client networks extending out to the provinces and down to the cities and towns, and were based upon personal-particularistic ties. Although this political center pushed policies of rapid economic growth, kept a tight rein on the money supply, kept the national budget deficit under control, and resorted to international borrowing only because credit was so easy at that time, the center failed to build political institutions to resolve grievances and tensions. Communities could not elect their own leaders and enjoy self-government.

New tensions began to build up in the late seventies and eighties, created in large measure by the expansion of this huge, complex political center and by the dramatic growth of a new, urban society and economy increasingly interacting with the international market. Hardworking, frugal, law-abiding and belt-tightening as the Koreans were—and they demonstrated those native qualities for nearly twenty years—more and more city people by the 1980s began to demand more freedom of expression and participation in political affairs. Unfortunate events of violence and repression and arrests of dissidents also intensified fear and anger toward the political center, which was ruled by the Democratic Justice Party (DJP) and its strong man. Events came to a head in 1987 when the DJP's Roh Tae Woo took the party's helm, made a dramatic promise of elections, and pledged that if he was elected, a referendum would be held within a year's time.

These tensions came from the new demands made on the political center by farmers' associations, trade unions, church organizations, student groups and other activist opponents. All of these groups held grievances toward the political center. They demanded political reform and democratic, legal procedures to ensure government accountability. Where these new ideas of democracy, justice, equality, human rights, etc. came from is hard to say. But the circulation of such ideas in Korean society became more obvious by the early 1980s, perhaps speeded up by a new sense of widespread grievances and deprivation. They produced severe tensions not supportive of consensus-building in Korean society. Although political pluralism in which new parties could compete in political elections to select the nation's new leaders came in December 1987, there had been no ideological and social consensus-building.

As you all know, the 1987 elections produced a narrow victory for Roh and his party to control the executive branch of government, but not the National Assembly. Kim Young Sam, Kim Dae Jung and Kim Jung Pil had formed their own parties to run separately, and final votes merely divided the National Assembly. Since the elections, important government business in the National Assembly these past months had been stalled. Opposition members have only demanded official investigations and trials for individuals affiliated with the previous government, beginning with Chun Doo Hwan. Roh has blocked some of these investigations, but attempts to bring Chun to trial still go on. Meanwhile, no serious legislation can be approved, and no real consensus-building between the parties has taken place.

Further political fragmentation came on January 22 of this year, when a dissident organization, said to be the largest in the nation's political history, was formed, pledging a grass-roots democratic movement and a continued struggle against home-vintage dictatorship and foreign influence. The so-called "Coalition for a National Democratic Movement" was formalized, adopting a collective leadership system that included such prominent dissident figures as Lee Pu-yong and Lee Chang-bok. The Rev. Moon Ik-hwan, Paek Ki-wan and Kye Hoon-je serve as advisers, with Chang Ki-pyo as secretary-general and Kim Kun-tae as chief policy maker. Although the three opposition parties (the Party for Peace and Democracy, the Reunification Democratic Party and the New Democratic Republican Party) all issued statements wel-

coming this new political party, the Democratic Justice Party was
extremely nervous about its formation.

Political fragmentation is now severe, and social disinte-
gration also has become serious. Several thousand labor-
management strikes and disputes have erupted over the past two
years. Student rioting on campuses and in congested street areas
also continues. Associated with this rioting and violence has been
the shrill rhetoric of anti-American jingoism, especially among
student and radical dissident groups. Various reasons account
for this. First, many radical students believe in ideas like
"dependency theory," a mix of neo-Marxist views to explain how
and why developing countries become excessively dependent
upon rich countries like the United States. U.S. demands that Korea open some of its agricultural and telecommunication markets,
etc. have produced a backlash, causing farmers and even workers
to organize. When U.S. tabacco interests lobbied and persuaded
the U.S. government to bash Korea and insist that larger imports
of U.S. tobacco be allowed, Korean tobacco growers were required to cut back their cultivation of tobacco. In the last few
years, most of these farmers switched to growing red peppers on
their land, and the large increase in the pepper supply on the
market drove prices down, producing large losses for these same
farmers. Examples of this sort explain the driving force behind
anti-Americanism in certain quarters.

Still another source of grievance has been those Koreans who
had suffered some kind of perceived or actual injustice from the
former military-led government. Many people in Kwangju,
where the worst riot in that city's history occurred in 1980, are
still bitterly opposed to the Roh government. Such anger was revealed at the trial of Kim Hyon Hui, the North Korean spy who
confessed to the bombing of a South Korean airliner over Burma
in November 1987. Many women who lost loved ones in that incident came to the trial to express their rage. Many of these people
even believed that the government had caused the bombing in order to perpetuate its rule. This incredible interpretation shows
how rumor has stimulated anti-government passions.

Have widespread grievances become so severe that many
groups will unite to topple the present government? I do not
know, but there appears to be little consensus in Korean society
today. Few speak out to insist on tolerance and a cooling of passions. Few defend the government, whose power has been enor-

mously curbed since last year's elections. Few stand up to speak out against the daily violence that rocks Korean society. If political fragmentation paralyzes government action, and if every group keeps on battering the political center, can Korean society remain integrated to support a political democracy? This is my deep worry as the Korean people prepare to vote in the mid-April 1989 referendum.

Korea's political system does not seem capable of resolving grievances so that tensions can be reduced. There is now so much acrimony, hatred and suspicion among political leaders. The opposition leaders Kim Young Sam and Kim Dae Jung deeply resent each other and cannot join forces to establish a constructive opposition party. Businessmen are afraid to support the Democratic Justice Party and give it money as in the past. Many groups now demand more from the government than it can guarantee: higher wages from business to satisfy labor; unreasonable reforms to satisfy radical students; higher farm prices to satisfy farmers.

Yet a recent development in the press provides some hope. Since January 1989, the *Chosen Il-bo* has become more critical of Kim Dae Jung's Party for Peace and Democracy. That has angered the PPD, which publicly exhorted the people to boycott the newspaper. (That call reflects an odd standard for democracy.) The PPD also has brought a civil suit against the paper. Senior press editors are reportedly demanding that their younger journalists tone down their critical editorials and report the facts. The popular press could become an important new power broker in Korean society if it became more evenhanded and reported facts impartially instead of consistently bashing the government.

Yet I worry about whether Korea's political center can hold out and meet the increasing demands being imposed on it. Adding to the center's great difficulties is a trade-bashing stance adopted by the United States, whose officials now seem ready to meddle in currency manipulation and to pressure the Korean government to open markets in ways that would destroy social integration in the country. When Bush visited Korea a few weeks ago, he neither strongly praised the leadership for its democratic progress nor urged calm and patience in Korean society. Instead, he lectured the Korean legislative and political leaders on free trade. This sent the wrong signal, very likely making anti-Americanism worse, not better.

The Threat from Pyongyang

Over the past 25 years, Kim Il-song's government has always broken off negotiations with South Korea by the demand that American troops be withdrawn from the Korean Peninsula. North Korea has never sincerely negotiated to reduce tensions and establish a long-lasting dialogue with South Korea. Her aim instead seems to have been to split America from South Korea in order to initiate military aggression and unify Korea under Pyongyang hegemony. In the past few years, Kim Il-song's negotiating tactic has remained the same: elevate expectations in South Korea and then destroy them by imposing the impossible demand of American troop withdrawal. That diabolical tactic could intensify cleavages in South Korean society by enabling dissident-radical groups to use the anti-American issue as a means to blame the government for producing a breakdown in North-South negotiations. Therefore, Pyongyang's leaders appear to understand only too well the fragmentation in South Korea, and are trying to manipulate the crisis in the South to topple the Roh government.

Let me conclude by making the following simple points. Korea has already embarked on a great economic and social transformation. In order to increase productivity, keep exports competitive, and meet obligations to repay interest and principal on its U.S. $42 billion foreign debt, the economy must be continuously restructured. But restructuring the economy also means painful social change. If social change cannot occur without severe politicization—and more politicization imposes demands on a weak political center—then the government cannot carry out its functions of maintaining national security, domestic order, and social tranquility.

Korea now confronts a major crisis, which few Americans realize is extremely serious for the stability of that country. My purpose today is to share with you my great worry about the future of that country over the next six to twelve months. If the present democratic government can survive the referendum in mid-April and can deal the pressing domestic issues so that calm and normalcy can return, then we can breathe a sigh of relief and have some optimism about Korea's future. But if the present government falls and violence worsens in the country, Korea will be in grave difficulties. Even her good friend the United States will be unable to help.

SOUTH KOREA'S RISE TO PROMINENCE[3]

In the late 1980's, South Korea is a success story in terms of its impressive gains in the political economy of development. The "economic miracle" of South Korea, sustained by remarkable achievements in recent decades, has made the country one of East Asia's newly industrializing economies. The unfolding drama of the "political miracle" under way since 1987 has also forced South Korea to progress along the path of political development. Only two years ago, in 1987, the country was engulfed in political turmoil and violent street demonstrations. Nevertheless, an orderly and peaceful transition of power took place on February 25, 1988, after the general election to choose a new President in December, 1987.

Under President Roh Tae Woo, South Korea's sixth republic is not politically stable, because the ruling Democratic Justice party failed to win the majority of seats in the April 26, 1988, National Assembly election. Nevertheless, the interparty dialogue and accommodation within the Parliament has kept alive the hope for rekindling democracy in South Korea. Moreover, if the current experiment in democratic politics succeeds, South Korea will emerge as an advanced third world nation in the 1990's. The hosting of the 1988 Seoul Olympics enhanced the prestige and status of South Korea as a progressive nation. Already a medium-sized industrial power, South Korea's participation in regional development projects has been much sought after by other nations.

What makes the Korean situation still fluid, however, is the geopolitics of Korea as a divided nation. In the 44 years since the country was partitioned in 1945, the socialist North and the capitalist South have pursued different paths of political development and socioeconomic modernization. Although they have remained isolated from one another, the two Korean states have suc-

[3]Reprint of an article by Young Whan Kihl, professor of political science, Iowa State University. Reprinted with permission from *Current History*, April 1989. Copyright © *Current History* 1989.

ceeded—largely through internal efforts—in developing their
respective societies. By the late 1980's, two fully developed and
entrenched Korean states had emerged: unfortunately, they confront one another across a narrow band of the demilitarized zone
(DMZ) that bisects the peninsula.

Because of different rates of economic growth and sociopolit-
ical development and varying capabilities to adjust to the changing environment, the balance between the two Koreas has come
to favor the South over the North. In the last 25 years, South Korea has begun to outperform the North economically because of
its dynamic economic growth. South Korea's rise to regional
prominence in the late 1980's is a reality, and this has implications for the future of inter-Korean relations and the regional
balance of power.

As the Korean peninsula glacier is exposed to the thaw in the
external environment, peaceful competition between the two Koreas rather than military confrontation will become the agenda.
In this endeavor, South Korea's expanded regional role is acquiring greater significance; its participation in regional trade is
sought after not only by its traditional allies—the United States
and Japan—but also by the neighboring Communist countries of
China and the Soviet Union, which see Seoul as a trading and investment partner.

South Korea's Options

The strategic environment surrounding the Korean peninsula has begun to change in the late 1980's. The balance of power
is shifting not only between the two Korean states but also between the Koreas and the four major powers with an active interest in the Korean peninsula: China, the Soviet Union, Japan and
the United States. As each of the four major powers seeks to rede-
fine its policy vis-à-vis the two Koreas, the ability of each Korean
state to maneuver among the major powers will be a decisive factor in determining Korea's destiny.

The talks on normalizing Sino-Soviet relations, for instance,
will undermine North Korea's "much-vaunted deftness in playing
China and the Soviet Union off against each other." The failure
to improve Japanese-Soviet relations already has given South Korea a window of opportunity to evolve trade ties with the Soviet
Union, especially in connection with the ambitious Soviet plan to

develop the Soviet Far East and the Siberian region. China's pragmatic open door policy under its "Four Modernizations" policy has led South Korea to increase its informal trade ties with China, in spite of the North Korean objection to Beijing's cultivating trade links with Seoul. Indirect Chinese–South Korean trade in 1987 approached US$3 billion.

The successful hosting of the 1988 Seoul Olympiad yielded tangible benefits to South Korea in establishing external links with the Soviet Union and North Korea's allies in East Europe. Hungary and South Korea, having already exchanged permanent missions in late 1988, are negotiating to upgrade their relations and to establish diplomatic ties. Such a move is likely to be followed by similar acts by other East European countries as their mutual trade relations expand.

The summit meetings held by United States President Ronald Reagan and Soviet President Mikhail Gorbachev, in the wake of the signing of the Intermediate Nuclear Forces (INF) treaty in 1987, lessened tensions and increased the prospect for greater peace and security in the region. As long as South Korea perceives a North Korean threat, however, the Korean peninsula will continue to suffer tension. Still, the resumption of an inter-Korean dialogue in the summer of 1988, after a hiatus of 30 months, slightly improved the atmosphere.

The bold initiative aimed at improving relations with North Korea that was announced by South Korea's President Roh Tae Woo on July 7, 1988, may enhance the prospects for a peaceful resolution of the Korean dispute.

Political Development

Since Roh Tae Woo was elected President by a plurality of 36.6 percent of the popular vote, his government is not strong or stable enough to rule decisively. Moreover, during his presidential campaigns, Roh pledged publicly that if elected he would stand for a vote of confidence after the Seoul Olympiad, although the venue of this referendum was left undefined.

A major political event in South Korea's sixth republic was the holding of the thirteenth National Assembly election on April 26, 1988. This general election chose 224 of the 299 members of the National Assembly (the remaining 75 are to be chosen at large). The election was a defeat for the ruling Democratic Justice party because it deprived the Roh Tae Woo government of a majority in the legislature. The party captured 125 seats in the Assembly. The remaining 174 seats were won by three main opposition parties: the Party for Peace and Democracy, led by Kim Dae Jung, with 70 seats; the Reunification and Democracy party, under Kim Young Sam, with 59 seats; the New Democratic Republican party, under Kim Jong Pil, with 35 seats; the remaining 10 seats were captured by independents.

For the first time in the history of the Republic, the ruling party lost its majority in the National Assembly. The defeat of the ruling party deprived President Roh of the luxury of a compliant National Assembly. Although this has increased instances of a legislative-executive branch confrontation, undermining political stability, it may be a "blessing in disguise." The ruling party and the opposition will be forced to play the game of political compromise. If successful, this will improve the chances for democracy and may accelerate political development in South Korea.

In spite of the sporadic student-led antigovernment demonstrations in the street, a political lull prevailed in South Korea in the late summer and early fall of 1988. The party leaders had agreed to a temporary political truce during the Seoul Olympiad, from September 17 to October 4, 1988. Once the Olympic games were over, the National Assembly resumed its investigatory probing of the charges of corruption and irregularities during the administration of President Chun Doo Hwan (1980–1988).

When the National Assembly investigation uncovered the extensive irregularities, the public outcry for the arrest and trial of Chun's lieutenants as well as Chun himself intensified. The irregularities of the Chun era ranged from a financial scandal (in connection with the fund-raising for the Ilhae Institute to assist the families of those killed during the October, 1983, Rangoon bombing) to the cover-up of repressive measures and human rights violations in connection with the mistreatment of political prisoners and the 1980 Kwangju uprising. Many members of Chun's family have already been arrested, tried and convicted. Other criminal indictments and civil suits will follow when the National Assembly probes are completed.

The public pressure on Chun himself, coupled with violent university student demonstrations demanding Chun's arrest, forced the former President to take a stand on the charges against him and his associates. On November 23, 1988, in a televised speech from his residence in Seoul, Chun publicly apologized to the nation for the mistakes he had made. Asking for forgiveness, he left Seoul for an internal rural exile.

Since Roh was Chun's political associate and former classmate in the military academy, his reputation and legitimacy were challenged as a result of Chun's confession. As Chun's political successor, Roh and his sixth republic must win the support of the majority of the South Koreans.

In an attempt to soothe the public, President Roh appealed to the nation to forgive his now-disgraced predecessor. In a televised address, he presented a six-point formula, promising to "liquidate past wrongdoing and carry out bold reforms" in the new era. These included the settlement of the 1980 Kwangju massacre and other human rights violations, the revision of several "evil laws" and the appointment of a special task force to probe corruption in the fifth republic.

As part of his pledge to do away with Chun's legacy of authoritarianism, President Roh reshuffled his Cabinet in December, 1988, replacing all but four portfolios. On December 21, 1988, he released 281 political prisoners and granted a sweeping amnesty involving 2,015 "politically motivated offenders."

The initial reaction to Roh's appeal, especially the reaction of the opposition parties, has not been encouraging. The question of Roh's legitimacy is at stake, as is the survival of his government, because Roh was a participant in the regime that he now condemns. The future of the sixth republic is therefore precarious.

Economic Development

While political turmoil and street demonstrations were under way, South Korea's economy continued to grow in 1986–1988. The major economic indicators show that the real growth of South Korea's gross national product (GNP) was one of the fastest in the world in 1986–1988, with an annual growth rate of 12.5 percent in 1986, 12.2 percent in 1987 and an estimated 12.1 percent in 1988.

The engine of South Korea's economic powerhouse is the export-led strategy of industrialization. The foreign trade sector of the economy has grown rapidly, and the country's export of manufactured products doubled and tripled within a few years. In

1988, South Korea's trade volume surpassed the $100-billion level, enabling South Korea to become one of the world's 10 largest trading nations. South Korea's $112-billion trade volume in 1988 was surpassed only by such developed industrial democracies as the United States, Japan, the countries of the European Community (EC) and Canada. In 1988, the South Korean export volume grew at a faster rate despite an unfavorable climate for the Korean won's rise against the dollar, wage increases and increased trade disputes.

In this export-driven strategy, access to the overseas market, especially the huge United States market, has been crucial for success. The United States and Japan have seen South Korea's largest and second largest trading partners, absorbing approximately 38 percent and 16 percent of the total export volume, respectively, in 1987.

As the protectionist pressures in world trade have escalated, however, South Korea's trade expansion trategy may not work as well as it worked in the past. For the time being, South Korea is trying to diversify its export markets by establishing trade links with European countries and the ASEAN (Association of South East Asian Nations) countries.

Coinciding with the 1988 Seoul Olympics, Hungary and South Korea established trade missions in each other's capital. Both countries subsequently agreed to upgrade their missions early in 1989, headed by diplomats with ambassadorial rank, a step that amounts to de facto diplomatic normalization. Hungary was the first Communist nation to open diplomatic ties with South Korea; other East European countries, including Yugoslavia, Poland, Czechoslovakia and Bulgaria, are expected to follow suit in spite of North Korea's strenuous objections. Seoul has agreed to lend $125 million to Hungary to initiate joint venture projects.

The Soviet Union also dispatched consular officials to Seoul before the Seoul Olympics. This act was preceded by Soviet cultural diplomacy, involving the tour of the Bolshoi Ballet and symphony orchestra in the major cities in South Korea. Seoul and Moscow have agreed to establish trade offices in 1989.

Social Progress

In the summer of 1987, violent street demonstrations led to escalating labor and industrial disturbances. The worker strikes and stoppages spread like wildfire, causing temporary plant shutdowns and disruption of the economy. Since one of the secrets of South Korea's "economic miracle" is its disciplined labor force and the low cost of its labor, the workers' belated demands for higher wages and the right to collective bargaining will increase the cost of industrial production. South Korea's competitiveness in the world marketplace will also be affected adversely.

Rapid urbanization and population migration continue to deepen the process of industrialization of Korean society. So far the rural exodus has supplied the work force for industrial projects. Many of the migrants from the countryside are young people with a basic seconday education and they can easily become a skilled labor force.

As the standard of living continues to improve, middle class Koreans are playing a new role in maintaining political and social stability. The reaction of middle class citizens to the student demonstrations, for instance, was the key to former President Chun's decision to back down from his hard-line position in the summer of 1987 and his subsequent decision to apologize publicly.

Rapid industrialization and urbanization in South Korea have also unleashed the process of pluralistic democracy. Social groups and organizations, for instance, are better able to articulate their demands. The workers and farmers are beginning to express their attitudes toward policy issues. The farmers have also become more vocal in their protests against foreign pressure to open South Korea's agricultural market. The press and the intellectuals are beginning to express their opinions. The equitable sharing of the economic pie and the growing gap between the rich and the poor will also become agenda and policy issues as the economy continues to expand.

Foreign Policy

South Korea has become more active in diplomacy and more skillful in its diplomatic moves. President Roh, for instance, began a 12-day state visit to four Asian-Pacific nations (Malaysia, Australia, Indonesia and Brunei) on November 3, 1988, to promote closer diplomatic ties and increase trade.

On October 18, 1988, President Roh Tae Woo addressed the
United Nations General Assembly, proposing a six-nation consultative conference on Northeast Asia. This proposal was intended,
the Seoul authorities claimed, as a response to Soviet President
Mikhail Gorbachev's initial proposal in his Krasnoyarsk speech
about two months earlier.

The proposed consultative conference, according to Roh,
would discuss a "broad range of issues concerning peace, stability,
progress and prosperity" in Northeast Asia, including a permanent peace arrangement between North Korea and South Korea.
Unlike the Gorbachev proposal, Roh's plan would include the
United States as a key member of the six-nation consultative
body, in addition to the Soviet Union, China, Japan and the two
Koreas.

On his return trip, President Roh also conferred in Washington, D.C., with United States President Ronald Reagan. The
United States–South Korean alliance was reaffirmed; President
Reagan praised Roh for the successful hosting of the Seoul Olympics and for the gains he had made in democratizing Korean politics.

United States– Korean Relations

United States–South Korean relations have been friendly
since the mutual security treaty was signed and ratified in 1953,
after the conclusion of the Korean War. Recently, however, several bilateral issues between Seoul and Washington have become
tense. These include trade, security, burden sharing, and the issue of United States troop withdrawal.

Nonetheless, the United States and South Korea have maintained mutually beneficial economic relations. With growing
United States trade deficits, however, bilateral trade disputes
have escalated. In 1987, the United States importation of South
Korean products reached $18.3 billion, while United States ex-
ports to South Korea were $8.7 billion. Since 1982, the unfavor-
able balance of United States trade with South Korea reached a
record $9.5 billion in 1987. This led to United States pressure on
South Korea to liberalize its protected domestic market. Such
pressure, especially on agricultural products, is resisted by South
Korea's "nationalist" voices. Anti-American sentiment has also
emerged for the first time to undermine the structure of security
between the two nations.

South Korea is negotiating with the United States on the relocation of the United States military command in South Korea, away from its present location in central Seoul to a rural area. Relocating United States military facilities, including the return of a golf course under American control, will dampen growing anti-American sentiment in South Korea. The other outstanding issue involves the renegotiation of the terms by which South Korea's armed forces are kept under the operational control of the United States military commander.

The United States troop withdrawal from South Korea, the demand that North Korea has consistently stressed, is now openly debated by some radicals in South Korea. The middle class, however, seems more concerned about the disruption of political stability that might follow a speedy withdrawal of United States troops.

The Unification Issue

On July 7, 1988, the Roh government announced a new six-point initiative toward North Korea. The policy has been hailed as bold and positive. In his October 18, 1988, address to the United Nations General Assembly, President Roh Tae Woo reiterated his desire to improve relations with North Korea and proposed to turn the DMZ into a peace zone.

What has thus far impeded progress in inter-Korean negotiation is the North Korean demand for the withdrawal of United States troops from South Korea. North Korea has also demanded an immediate halt to the United States–South Korean annual joint military exercises called "Team Spirit." Several levels of inter-Korean dialogue and negotiation, however, have been carried out simultaneously, including the interparliamentarian talks to arrange for an eventual meeting between the National Assembly in the South and the Supreme People's Assembly in the North, and the Red Cross talks to arrange for the reunion of 10 million dispersed families scattered through the country since the Korean War years.

In late December, 1988, South Korea announced that it would agree to a North Korean proposal to hold high-level political and military talks to ease tension on the Korean peninsula. In a letter from South Korean Prime Minister Kang Young Hoon to Yon Hyong Muk, his counterpart in the North, the Seoul gov-

ernment suggested that Prime Ministers from the two sides meet
to discuss ways to cooperate, build mutual trust in military matters, and pledge noninterference in each other's affairs. Such a
meeting will lay the foundation for a subsequent summit meeting
between President Roh Tae Woo and North Korea's President
Kim Il Sung. One political issue to be settled at such a meeting
will be whether or not to adopt a joint declaration on mutual non-
aggression and noninterference in each other's affairs, including
a formula for promoting reunification.

Prospects

In the late 1980's, South Korea has seen rapid political
change, continuous economic growth and steady social progress.
South Korea has become one of the world's most dynamic countries in terms of political, economic and social changes that have
been positive in their impact on society. As the country prepares
to enter the decade of the 1990's, South Korea will emerge as an
important regional power in Northeast Asia.

Politically, South Korea has gained momentum toward democracy. The launching of the sixth republic in 1988 was the first
peaceful transfer of power in the 40-year-old history of the Republic of Korea. Since 1948, the country has undergone a series
of important political changes.

Economically, in the late 1980's South Korea has become one
of East Asia's most successful newly industrialized countries
(NIC's). Averaging an annual growth rate of 10 percent in the decade of the 1980's, South Korea has made rapid progress in
economic development. In 1987, the economy registered an impressive GNP of $118.6 billion and a per capita GNP of
$2,826. This is a remarkable achievement; in about 25 years
South Korea's per capita income multiplied 35 times, from a low
of $82 in 1961 to $2,826 in 1987.

Even if the projected growth rate is slower in the year after
1988, the total GNP is expected to almost double in four to five
years, from $118.6 billion in 1987 to an estimated $226 billion
in 1991. The GNP per capita likewise is projected to increase
from $2,826 in 1987 to about $5,100 in 1991.

As South Korea continues to progress economically, the
country will also develop politically. Koreans will also become
more enlightened and more tolerant of diversity, as standards of

living continue to improve. It can be hoped that a culture of pluralism and democracy will take root in the soil of South Korea in the 1990's.

IT'S TIME TO REASSESS
THE U.S.-KOREA DEFENSE TREATY[4]

Thirty-eight years ago, North Korean troops crossed the 38th parallel. U.S. forces soon intervened, along with small foreign contingents under the auspices of the United Nations, later followed by hundreds of thousands of "Chinese People's Volunteers." The front eventually stabilized near the original boundary, and the combatants signed an armistice in July, 1953. The war cost America 54,000 dead and at least $75,000,000,000—5.6% of its aggregate Gross National Product (GNP) between 1950 and 1953.

When discussions over a permanent peace proved fruitless, the U.S. initiated a mutual defense treaty with the Republic of Korea (ROK). The agreement itself does not guarantee military assistance, but the presence of 40,000 American soldiers acts as a "tripwire," making U.S. intervention automatic. While Pres. Carter proposed withdrawing American forces from the peninsula, Pres. Reagan has strengthened official ties to Seoul. U.S. troops will remain in the ROK "as long as the people of Korea want and need that presence," pledged then-Defense Secretary Caspar Weinberger in 1983.

Is such a permanent military guarantee really in America's interest? The security commitment is expensive—the U.S. not only maintains an infantry division in the ROK, but also earmarks forces located elsewhere in the Pacific for Korea's naval and air defense. All told, the U.S. spends nearly $25,000,000,000 annually to defend South Korea.

Moreover, the defense guarantee threatens to suck the U.S. into another bloody conflict far from home. The Korean border,

[4]Reprint of a magazine article by Doug Bandow, a senior fellow at the Cato Institute. Reprinted from *USA Today Magazine*, 117:63–65, July 1988. Copyright © 1988 by the Society for the Advancement of Education.

marked by a heavily fortified "demilitarized zone," remains one of the most hostile in the world; indeed, the two Koreas are still technically at war, and small, but deadly, military clashes are common. Since 1953, 90 Americans have died in border skirmishes.

Finally, there is a political cost to stationing U.S. troops in Korea. The ROK appears to be moving successfully toward democracy, but recently inaugurated Pres. Roh Tae Woo faces several potentially daunting challenges, including the growing scandal involving the brother of former Pres. Chun Doo Hwan, severe labor unrest, and Roh's repudiation by nearly two-thirds of the electorate. Should the liberalization process stall, the U.S. will be blamed, fairly or not, for America's record in that country has not been a good one. "It's not that we don't like Americans," said one demonstrator in the summer of 1987, "but for 37 years you've been supporting the wrong guy here."

U.S. involvement in Korea grew naturally out of World War II, which left that nation, like Germany and Austria, divided between East and West. Efforts to unify the peninsula collapsed, leading to the creation of the ROK and the Soviet-backed Democratic People's Republic of Korea (DPRK). In 1949, the Truman Administration withdrew its troops and—partially in reaction to southern strongman Syngman Rhee's repressive rule and threat to liberate the northern "lost territories"—refused to sell the ROK tanks, anti-tank weapons, or other heavy equipment. In January, 1950, Secretary of State Dean Acheson explicitly excluded Korea from America's defense perimeter; five months later, the DPRK invaded the South.

The Korean War, a "police action" in Truman's words, was not a popular conflict, coming so soon after the end of World War II. Today, the public appears ready to reconsider America's commitment to Korea. A 1986 Chicago Council on Foreign Relations poll found that, while 64% of opinion leaders would send troops to defend the ROK, and 24% of the public backed military intervention. Their skepticism is fully warranted. Even if U.S. involvement made sense when South Korea's military was little more than a domestic constabulary and Japan had been disarmed, the world has changed.

The most important contrast between then and now—which makes the likely consequences of withdrawing U.S. troops so very different today—is the development of the ROK. After the war, much of that country lay in ruins; per capita income was barely $134 a year.

However, the ROK's current per capita income of $2,300—more than a 15-fold increase—places it near the top of the developing world and is three times that of the DPRK. South Korea's economy grew an astounding 12.5% in 1986 and 12.2% in 1987, while the DPRK's economy has been essentially stagnant since 1970. The ROK dramatically has broken into the auto and computer markets and competes around the world for construction projects. In fact, South Korea is one of the leading trading nations, running an annual surplus with the U.S. of some $10,000,000,000. North Korea, in contrast, has defaulted on $800,000,000 in foreign loans and suffers from severe economic bottlenecks and shortages. Moreover, the ROK's population (43,300,000) is more than twice that of the DPRK (20,500,000).

Military Strength

North Korea is stronger militarily. Like most communist nations, it has invested a disproportionate share of its resources in defense and maintains a substantial numerical edge in manpower, aircraft, combat naval vessels, tanks, and other equipment.

However, warns Congressional staffer Stephen Goose, these statistical differences "are usually overstated, almost always misleading, and often meaningless." South Korea is now without its own advantages, including the mountainous terrain, which, according to a 1980 Congressional Budget Office (CBO) study, "is such a dominant factor in assessing the military balance between the two Koreas that conventional measures of military strength do not fully apply." Geography greatly would constrain the DPRK's use of armor, for instance. The CBO estimates that North Korea could bring only about half of its tanks immediately to bear in an invasion, and the ROK, given its extensive fortifications, could achieve as much as a three-to-one kill ratio.

Moreover, South Korea's weapons are generally newer, more sophisticated, and more reliable than those of the DPRK. This factor, says Goose, is "the single most important aspect" of the military equation. The ROK's soldiers also are better-trained.

In any case, the South's quantitative military deficiencies are an understandable result of the American defense commitment. After all, the ROK has let U.S. forces carry much of its defense burden—the 40,000 American personnel on the peninsula and additional Pacific-based contingents would enter any conflict al-

most immediately, followed by large numbers of ground troops
from the continental U.S. and possibly Europe. Moreover, some
South Korean analysts, like Prof. Sang Woo Rhee, director of the
East Asian studies center at Sogang University, contend that the
U.S. has blocked South Korean attempts to acquire more ad-
vanced weapons for political reasons.

Indeed, recent events clearly show that the ROK is not locked
into a position of inferiority. South Korean military spending
grew sharply following the limited troop withdrawals from the
peninsula initiated by Pres. Nixon. The South has outspent the
North since the mid-1970's, with outlays climbing from
$558,000,000 in 1974 to $3,500,000,000 in 1984. Moreover,
during the last decade, Seoul has devoted twice as much resources
as Pyongyang to procurement; the ROK, which could not even
produce rifles little more than a decade ago, is now manufacturing F-5 aircraft, howitzers, AIM-9 missiles, and rocket-launchers.

In 1987, Seoul's Defense Minister, Lee Ki Baek, told a forum
at the Center for Strategic and International Studies in Washington that this country expects to achieve a military balance with
the North within two of three years. Equally optimistic is Eulk-
won Kim of the Ilhae Institute: "There's a maxim in military
strategy that if you have only 70% of the enemy's objective capability, you can defend against him, and within the next one to two
years, South Korea will have reached that level." (In fact, standard Soviet offensive doctrine calls for an advantage of six-to-one
in artillery, five-to-one in tanks, and three-to-one in manpower,
which the DPRK does not have.)

Moreover, it will be almost impossible for North Korea to
maintain its military edge in the years ahead. A 1985 Rand Corporation study estimates that the North would have to devote
36–42% of its GNP—more than twice the current share—to the
military simply to match an expenditure of six–seven percent of
GNP by Seoul. Moreover, the ROK's advantages will increase as
its economy expands at an annual rate several times that of the
DPRK. Concluded Rand: "South Korea's economic, technological, and military capabilities can be expected to grow substantially relative to those of North Korea during the next decade. The resulting balance should increasingly and predominantly favor the
South."

In short, there is no reason the ROK could not defend itself,
given time to remedy its current military weaknesses and assum-

ing no direct intervention by either the U.S.S.R. or the People's Republic of China (PRC), and their involvement in any conflict is highly unlikely. Although the Soviets armed the DPRK before the last war and China, while not involved in the initial attack, essentially took over the North Korean war effort when the allied army neared the Yalu River, the attitudes of both the PRC and the U.S.S.R. have changed dramatically since then.

For instance, China now places a high priority on the peninsula's stability—in keeping with the PRC's extensive reform program. Beijing has indicated that it would not support a North Korean invasion; in 1983, China began pressing Pyongyang to take a more flexible position in reunification talks. Moreover, China and South Korea have initiated a variety of cultural exchanges. Trade between the two nations runs some $1,500,000,000 annually—more than between Beijing and the DPRK—and the governments successfully have defused several potentially serious confrontations involving PRC defectors. In 1987, South Korea's assistant foreign minister, Park Soo Gil, said that "it isn't a matter of if we're going to have closer relations with China, but when."

In contrast to the PRC, the Soviet Union has done little to improve its ties to South Korea, which were frozen after the 1983 shooting down of the Korean Air flight (KAL 700). While the U.S.S.R. has been strengthening its relationship with North Korea and supplying Pyongyang with advanced weaponry, American aid to Seoul still has been three times the combined Soviet and Chinese assistance to the DPRK. More important, there is no evidence that the Soviets would like Pyongyang to start a war over which they would have no control. Indeed, the U.S.S.R., though it publicly supports the North's claim to be the peninsula's sole legitimate government, privately has encouraged the DPRK to follow the two-Germany model.

Even if the Soviets wanted to support a North Korean invasion directly, it would be difficult for them to do so. According to the Congressional Budget Office, "the territory is so constraining" near the 10-mile Soviet/DPRK border, "that the operation would have to be considered very risky." Given the short border, the irregular terrain, and the presence of only two potential supply routes, "a Soviet invasion would require the acquiescence of China for both the initial troop movement and subsequent supply convoys—an unlikely prospect." Such geographic

and political realities undoubtedly have contributed to a climate
in which, according to one U.S. diplomat in Seoul, "none of us
[China, America, and the Soviet Union] wants war on the Korean
Peninsula."

Japanese National Interests

Moreover, a militarily revitalized Japan could provide a major
counterweight to Chinese and Soviet influence on Korean affairs.
It has an interest in preserving Korea's stability since part of the
Korean Peninsula is only 35 miles from the Japanese islands. In
fact, over the years, Japan has provided Seoul with substantial
amounts of economic aid, including $4,000,000,000 in loans in
1983 alone.

In the future, Japan could help redress any military imbalance
created by an American pull-out. Japan's 1987 military outlays,
roughly $32,000,000,000, placed it third in the world, according
to Katsuro Sakoh, president of the Institute for Pacific Studies.
While Japan's armed forces—470 combat aircraft; 52 destroyers
and frigates; and 3,700 tanks, armored vehicles, and artillery
pieces—may lag behind those of the leading military antagonists,
they are not insignificant. Japan clearly would have an incentive
to do far more if America brought its troops home.

Even with the changed circumstances between 1950 and
1988, does America dare risk reducing its military role in East
Asia? Since the integrity of South Korea is simply not critical to
this nation's security, it can. While a friendly government in
Seoul is obviously helpful to the U.S., this country's defense posture would not be worsened materially without that Asian out-
post. Indeed, American intervention in 1950 resulted more from
outrage over what was seen as a communist attempt to swallow
a helpless friend than concern about U.S. security. Not only had
the Joint Chiefs of Staff declared the Korean peninsula to be strategically unimportant, but, before the DPRK invasion, even Gen.
Douglas MacArthur said that it was not necessary for the U.S. to
defend Seoul.

The peninsula is, of course, the center of great power rivalries, but the U.S. never will be able to match the pressure that
China and the Soviet Union could place on this nearby territory.
The sea lanes adjoining South Korea are vital for the U.S.S.R.
and China, not this nation. Communist control of the South

might extend the reach of the Soviet Far Eastern Fleet—though North Korea jealously has guarded its independence, permitting no foreign bases—but China would be more threatened by that development than the U.S.

Japan certainly would feel less secure if the DPRK controlled the entire peninsula, but even in the late 1940s, neither the Joint Chiefs nor Gen. MacArthur believed that preservation of the ROK was necessary for Japan's defense. That country is already within range of Soviet, Chinese, and North Korean forces and could meet any increased danger after an American withdrawal through greater defense expenditures of its own. After all, no one in Asia doubts the military prowess of the Japanese.

We do have other interests in Korea—economic and cultural, as well as the simple desire to help prevent a semi-free country from being swept into a Stalinist dark age—but they hardly warrant an American promise to go to war. This nation should reserve military intervention for instances where its own survival genuinely is threatened.

In any case, there is no reason to believe a U.S. pull-out would lead to a communist conquest of the South. The disaster of 1950 occurred because the ROK was not prepared for war. Today, South Korea has twice the population and five times the GNP of North Korea; the ROK's military is strong and eventually will outstrip that of the DPRK. South Korea also could seek to build military ties with Japan.

Therefore, the U.S. should announce its intention to cancel the mutual defense treaty at the end of a set period of time, during which it would withdraw its military units. The U.S. should offer to sell the ROK any non-nuclear military equipment that is desired, avoiding a repetition of America's original blunder of refusing to help equip the South Korean military before withdrawing U.S. troops in 1949. The U.S. also should encourage the ROK and Japan to enter into a bilateral security arrangement. In any case, at the end of the transition period, South Korea would have "graduated" from the American military safety net; that nation's defense then would be its own responsibility.

For 35 years, the U.S. has sought to deter a repeat North Korean invasion. It's now time to turn that responsibility over to the ROK. A withdrawal from Korea still would allow the U.S. to maintain a significant presence in the Pacific. However, dropping this commitment, and thus the potential for unnecessary military involvement in a Korean conflict, would increase our own security. Moreover, doing so would improve our political relations with Seoul, since America's reputation no longer would be held hostage to the vagaries of the ROK's volatile domestic politics. In the short run, a pull-out might leave the U.S. less able to influence any given Korean policy; in the long run, however, American-Korean relations likely would be more stable and productive.

Disengagement would not be risk-free, but no foreign policy is without costs. Americans now pay a very high price to ensure the safety of a nation that is capable of defending itself. Chancing an unlikely foreign "loss" would be a small price to pay for the very real benefits of strengthening the U.S. economy and reducing the likelihood of war.

III. THE PHILIPPINES

EDITOR'S INTRODUCTION

The virtually bloodless overthrow of Philippine dictator Ferdinand Marcos in 1986 surely ranks as one of the great victories for democracy in the 1980s. "Indeed, Corazon Aquino has become the best advertisement for the democratic alternative in years," writes Sandra Burton, a correspondent for *Time* magazine, in "Aquino's Philippines: The Center Holds," a *Foreign Affairs* article that traces Aquino's rise to power. The following article, "Democracy in the Philippines" by Belinda A. Aquino, associate professor of political science at the University of Hawaii at Manoa, chronicles the issues, such as human rights, the debt problem, the American bases, vigilantes, and the faltering economy, with which Corazon Aquino must grapple, revealing the necessity for the Philippine president to lead and truly reform to fulfill her mandate. In the final article in this section, "'Total War' in the Philippines," reprinted from the *Nation*, Ninotchka Rosca expresses her dissatisfaction with the situation in Aquino's Philippines, where the elite has retained its hold and suppression has continued, even intensified, causing human rights organizations to feel suspicious, even increasingly coming to the conclusion "that within the system, there can be no salvation."

AQUINO'S PHILIPPINES: THE CENTER HOLDS[1]

I

In a year of setbacks for U.S. foreign policy, the peaceful transition of power in the Philippines was a major success story. The ascension of Corazon Aquino to the presidency, with the help of breakaway reformist elements of the Philippine Armed Forces and millions of Filipinos who heeded the call of the country's Roman Catholic primate to take to the streets in their support, was a rare victory for democracy. In a world where popular revolutions have tended in recent years to catapult religious zealots or Marxists to power, Aquino's triumph in ousting one of the world's most durable dictators infused that heretofore moribund slice of the ideological spectrum—the political center—with new dynamism.

II

Credit for the virtually bloodless uprising against President Ferdinand Marcos belongs to the Filipino people, who were jolted out of long indifference to the loss of their freedoms under martial law by their outrage over the assassination on August 21, 1983, of the president's chief rival and most popular potential successor, former Senator Benigno Aquino, Jr. Nearly two million mourners joined Aquino's funeral procession, and for the next three years the streets of major cities echoed with the chants of anti-Marcos demonstrators.

The Reagan Administration had stood squarely behind Marcos through successful negotiations to renew the bilateral agreement assuring continued operation on Philippine soil of America's largest overseas military bases. Suddenly it was faced with a major policy dilemma. In September 1983 President Reagan canceled a planned visit to Manila, albeit reluctantly. The State Department scrambled to reinforce the efforts of the non-

[1]Reprint of an article by Sandra Burton, a correspondent for *Time* magazine. *Foreign Affairs* 65: 524–537, 1987. Copyright © 1987, Sandra Burton. Reprinted by permission.

communist Philippine political opposition to resist a communist-led boycott of the May 1984 National Assembly election and to establish an independent citizens' organization to police the polls against anticipated fraud on the part of Marcos' party, the New Society Movement.

The failure of the boycott to diminish nationwide voter turn-out significantly, and the success of the moderate oppositionists in winning one third of the seats in the legislative body, indicated to U.S. policymakers that the vast majority of Filipinos still believed that change was possible through democratic means. Accordingly, Washington intensified its efforts to prepare for the post-Marcos period by pressuring the regime to democratize repressive institutions and by broadening contacts with newly victorious opposition leaders, disenchanted military officers and increasingly politicized members of the business and professional communities.

In late 1984 a National Security Decision Directive drafted by the Department of State formalized those efforts. In the first comprehensive redefinition of U.S. policy since martial law was declared in 1972, the U.S. government clearly targeted the enemy as the Communist Party of the Philippines, together with its military and political wings, the New People's Army and the National Democratic Front. Containment of the insurgency, rather than human rights violations or other shortcomings of the Marcos regime, thus became the consistent justification for the reforms pressed on Marcos by the Reagan Administration. However, a careful distinction was made by the United States between true communist sympathizers and those anti-Marcos nationalists whom Marcos routinely accused of being subversives. The latter were regularly invited to luncheons at the residence of U.S. Ambassador Stephen Bosworth and included on the agendas of visiting officials from Washington, to the considerable annoyance of, for one, Imelda Marcos, the ambitious wife of the president.

While the State Department blueprint identified the ailing and increasingly isolated Marcos as part of the problem, its authors were loath to repeat the mistakes made by the Carter Administration in Iran. Thus, they took care not to suggest his ouster as long as Imelda Marcos and the blindly loyal armed forces chief of staff, General Fabian Ver, were positioned to seize power during the chaos that would inevitably follow his downfall.

The process of setting the stage for the succession was not yet complete by November 1985, when Marcos made the fatal mistake of calling a snap presidential election more than one year ahead of schedule. Partly in response to U.S. prodding, a revitalized political opposition had been set up and mechanisms designed to select a common candidate. Meanwhile, the military reform movement, which official U.S. visitors never failed to praise in Marcos' presence, had gained a toehold inside the Armed Forces of the Philippines. It was these two groups, supported by the most powerful nongovernmental institution in the republic—the Roman Catholic Church—that would ultimately accept Marcos' electoral challenge and wrest a fraudulent victory from him.

This was one of those rare occasions when a U.S. policy composed in the midst of an ongoing crisis was able to draw strong support from both sides of the congressional aisle and from the Pentagon. Its implementation was entrusted to diplomats and bureaucrats who were thoroughly familiar with the country, its problems and the key players. Together they issued criteria for what would constitute free and fair elections and dispatched a team of official American observers to monitor the polling of votes. At first President Reagan was unprepared to acknowledge the glaring anomalies of intimidation and fraud perpetrated by the Marcos forces on election day, February 7, 1986, and in the subsequent counting of the ballots. He was quickly set straight by on-the-spot reports from diplomats and intelligence sources in the Philippines, as well as congressional and State Department emissaries fresh from the scene. "Once the administration moved to support Cory Aquino, it received the strongest bipartisan support in a foreign policy crisis in the past decade," said Richard Holbrooke, former assistant secretary of state for Asian and Pacific affairs, after Marcos had been airlifted from his besieged palace and transported to Hawaii by the U.S. military.

III

Corazon Aquino came to power not only because she was the widow of Benigno "Ninoy" Aquino, but also because she was not a professional politician. From the moment her husband was slain, she became a symbol of protest against the crimes of the Marcos regime. Because she was perceived as but a simple housewife, she became a figure around whom the ambitious and ideologically incompatible leaders of the fragmented anti-Marcos movement could rally. Fortunately, as she proved once she became the common presidential candidate of the opposition, she was up to the job. A fearless campaigner, inspiring speaker and determined consensus-builder, she was blessed with nerves of steel, an innate sense of confidence in the people from whom she drew her strength, sharp political instincts and a superb sense of timing.

Her campaign against Marcos was viewed both inside and outside the Philippines as a modern Third World morality play, pitting the forces of justice and freedom against those of graft and repression. The only charge lobbed by Marcos which seemed to find its mark was that she was soft on communism. Doubts about whether she was tough enough to deal with the guerrillas grew to the point where the powerful Roman Catholic Church was drawn into the electoral fray to remind the faithful that her piety, like that of the Filipino people, rendered her impervious to the blandishments of a godless ideology.

When she was robbed of probable victory in the counting of the ballots, the Catholic Bishops Conference of the Philippines convened to assess the election. One week after the election the churchmen rendered their judgment that a "government that assumes or retains power through fraud has no moral basis to govern." When computer operators engaged by the government Commission on Elections to tabulate returns walked out, protesting that votes for Aquino were not being tallied, they were extended protection by the Archbishop of Manila, Jaime Cardinal Sin, and by reformist military officers. Then, on February 22, Defense Minister Juan Ponce Enrile and Acting Armed Forces Chief of Staff Lieutenant General Fidel Ramos staged a revolt against Marcos. This rescued the election for Aquino, and many hailed it as a victory for both might and right.

Auspicious as the advent of the Aquino government was, however, the fact remained that the so-called four-day revolution neither kicked out all the rascals nor vested the new leaders with the wisdom to rebuild quickly an economy saddled with a $26-billion foreign deficit or bring an end to the 17-year-old communist insurgency that affected the lives of Filipinos in 20 percent of towns and villages throughout the archipelago. Given the magnitude of the problems and the lack of experience of the woman who was expected to solve them, American policymakers wisely tried to cap their expectations. They knew that the hard part lay ahead, though there was once again at least some room for hope. "With Marcos we had only an end," said a U.S. embassy official in Manila. "With these people we have a beginning."

Aquino arrived in office with what was not so much a platform as a set of beliefs. One was her religious conviction but the other, just as strong, was a belief that people who are free to choose what is best for them will choose peace and freedom and democracy over communism. At the same time, she knew that those who live in poverty, as some 60 percent of her countrymen do, or under threat from guerrillas, as is the case in almost all of the nation's 73 provinces, are not free to choose. Therefore, economic assistance and pacification of the countryside were just as essential to the viability of her recovery programs as the restoration of human rights, the one area in which her administration has already succeeded.

She entered public life not as the leader of a strong party with a mandate to implement specific programs, but as the unifying force within an unlikely coalition of center-to-left parties and cause-oriented groups, which was joined at the eleventh hour by defectors from Marcos' military, led by Enrile and Ramos. Deprived of a transition period by the suddenness of Marcos' departure, the new government, not surprisingly, lacked a clear and coherent plan of attack on the problems with which it was confronted.

Had the largely psychological war between rebel officers and Marcos loyalists lasted longer than four days, Ramos and Enrile might well have wielded considerably greater influence over the transitional government which they urged Aquino to establish. But the tables were turned on them when Marcos was airlifted out of his besieged palace the very night that Aquino was inaugurated. The civilian leadership moved quickly and shrewdly to begin fulfilling its campaign promises to release political prisoners and restore the writ of habeas corpus—hardly top priorities of the new Armed Forces of the Philippines.

Before objections could be raised, President Aquino had taken charge and named a cabinet. Although it was primarily moderate in composition, important portfolios were given to several left-leaning human rights lawyers who had supported and defended Ninoy Aquino when he was Marcos' most prominent political prisoner, and Ramos and Enrile were the prime enforcers of martial law. The military and civilian elements of the de facto coalition government were bound to clash eventually, given their adversarial roles in the past and their dual claims of credit for the overthrow of Marcos.

IV

The hotline linking Enrile and the office of the president went cold by summer. The military found itself reacting to memos sent not by Aquino but by her executive secretary, Joker Arroyo, a human rights lawyer who had represented numerous victims of military abuse in the past. The top brass resented what was regarded as his anti-military bias and objected to being shut out of discussions about preliminary peace negotiations with the communist insurgents.

The smoldering bitterness between the military and leftist ministers flared into the open following the aborted Manila Hotel coup on July 6, 1986, when Marcos' vice-presidential running mate Arturo Tolentino attempted to establish an alternative government. President Aquino's closest advisers accused Enrile of having advance knowledge of dissident troop movements. Shortly thereafter Enrile began to criticize publicly the competence of the civilians named to explore peace talks with the communists and even to question the legitimacy of the Aquino government, which had abolished the 1973 constitution fashioned by Marcos and appointed a committee to draft a new one.

For the next four months the jockeying for influence between the military and civilian components of the Aquino government dominated the news in the newly unfettered press. The power struggle that was played out on the nation's front pages drained energy and diverted attention that might better have been focused on the monumental tasks of reducing the gap between rich and poor—the widest in Southeast Asia—and moving decisively to stem the only expanding communist guerrilla movement in the region. Highly publicized rumors of an imminent coup by frustrated officers identified with Minister Enrile also frightened investors away from channeling badly needed foreign exchange into the ravaged economy.

The talk of a coup built toward a climax in early November, on the eve of the president's state visit to Japan. Before she left,

Aquino declared, "I shall oppose any attempt from any quarter to interfere with or dictate to my government." She threatened to call her supporters into the streets in a second display of "people power" if necessary. In an effort to defuse the crisis, General Ramos urged disgruntled officers to present their grievances to the president in writing and give her an appropriate period of time to respond. They agreed, and immediately upon her return from Tokyo Ramos forwarded a respectful but pointed bill of particulars calling for replacement of certain of her ministers, restoration of a central role to the military in drafting the strategy to be used against the communists, and the setting of deadlines for cease-fire talks with the rebels.

With coup rumors still making headlines, Aquino met privately with each of the service commanders to try to gauge the depth of their discontent and to discuss what should be done. Then she summoned General Ramos for a long meeting, which she termed "the frankest" they had ever had. The two apparently agreed on measures to pacify the military and bring an end to the infighting so that the government could speak with one voice as it prepared to begin peace talks with the rebels.

The following day, November 22, Ramos acted on the pretext that Enrile was planning to lead a group of former pro-Marcos assemblymen to occupy the National Assembly and declare the Aquino government illegitimate. He set up roadblocks around the National Assembly building in a remote area of the capital and ordered troops to ignore commands issued by Enrile. On Sunday morning, November 23, Aquino asked for the resignations of her entire cabinet and pointedly accepted Enrile's. She subsequently balanced the ouster of her outspoken defense minister with the firings of four ministers targeted by the military for corruption and leftist sympathies.

Aquino's well-timed action was widely applauded. Her coalition government was now less broadly based, but it was more stable without some of its most controversial members. Enrile was now free to move into open opposition, and Aquino was free to continue with two major initiatives: a truce with the communist insurgents and a campaign to gain approval of the new constitution in a national referendum. After Enrile's ouster, the new defense minister, Rafael Ileto, told a group of Manila businessmen: "We will endeavor to observe only one policy line in matters of national security." He added that the military "fully supports the peace initiatives of President Aquino" and promised to "always uphold civilian supremacy."

Nonetheless, the military's direct intervention in civilian affairs for the second time since February 1986 signaled a new balance between the military and the civilian government. By working quietly behind the scenes, the inscrutable Ramos had achieved what the flamboyant Enrile had vainly sought: veto power, albeit limited, over the president. One reformist officer identified with Enrile called the turn of events "a new precedent for military intervention in civilian affairs." Ramos, a military professional and a political pragmatist, was known to share some of the plotters' complaints, but he also appreciated the value of a popular leader like Aquino and therefore was determined to effect a compromise. Said Edgardo Angara, president of the University of the Philippines and a middleman in earlier efforts to effect a reconciliation between Aquino and Enrile: "The military will have a more influential voice in government."

V

On November 27, four days after replacing Enrile, Aquino seized the initiative by concluding a 60-day cease-fire with representatives of the rebels. Formal talks to reach a truce had begun in August between Philippine government negotiators Ramon Mitra, Jose Diokno and Teofisto Guingona, and National Democratic Front leaders Satur Ocampo and Antonio Zumel. The cease-fire began on December 10, to run two months, through the referendum on the constitution. On December 23, the government and the communists' representatives began substantive peace talks. At year-end the truce, though shaky, was holding.

A 47-member constitutional commission set up by Aquino in June had approved its final version of the new constitution, which will be submitted to a national plebiscite on February 2. The first landmark along the road to long-hoped-for stability, the plebiscite has been turned into a vote of confidence in President Aquino, who would serve a full six-year term if the charter is ratified. The new constitution establishes a U.S.-style system of government while greatly reducing the presidential powers that Marcos had decreed for himself. A second landmark will follow in May 1987, when elections for a bicameral legislature will be held. A third will be reached in August, when thousands of provincial governors and local mayors will be elected to fill positions currently held by highly controversial Aquino loyalists, who were appointed as "officers-in-charge" to replace the pro-Marcos officials who were in office when the government changed.

On both the issue of the new constitution and the issue of negotiating with the insurgents, Enrile will lead the challenge to the Aquino government as the de facto leader of the new political opposition. He is likely to exploit pockets of discontent in northern Luzon, home of both himself and Marcos, and on the embattled island of Mindanao, where Christians and Muslims alike oppose the charter's provision for granting only limited autonomy to predominantly Muslim provinces.

"Now we shall see who are the fascists," commented Enrile, as he launched his campaign against the constitution and prolonged negotiations with the communists in a series of public rallies across the country. Although Enrile's own presidential aspirations tend to color his credibility in criticizing Aquino, a serious issue lies at the heart of his dissent over government handling of national security matters. That is the question of how much time should be allowed to pass before the cease-fire talks reach what most observers foresee as their inevitable breakdown and the military is called upon to resume fighting the insurgents.

He fears that if the government and the National Democratic Front negotiators seek to string out the peace talks until after the upcoming elections, the seeds of a de facto coalition government will already have been sown, because local politicians in communist-infiltrated areas will have to obtain the support of the rebels to win office. He argues for a resumption of military action now, "while our resources are still capable of dealing with the situation without depending too much on the U.S." He adds, "We do not want to place ourselves in the position of Vietnam, Laos and Cambodia, to the point where they became involved in the politics of the U.S. and then when it was no longer tenable for the American government to support them, it pulled out and they were captured by the Marxist movement."

The government has already acted to meet that argument by declaring the rebel negotiators' demand for a coalition government "non-negotiable" and by separating the upcoming congressional election from the local contests, in which communist gains in areas of heavy infiltration are more to be feared. The prospect for renewing the current cease-fire after it has lapsed in February appears dim.

Given the seemingly irreconcilable differences between the two sides, it is more likely that the current round of talking will be followed by a resumption of shooting, at least in certain regions. Ileto has intimated that he is considering the same sort of divide-and-conquer strategy against the rebels as was employed against the Huks in the 1950s and the Muslims in the 1970s, stating that the government is prepared to grant regional cease-fires if the nationwide peace cannot be maintained. Meanwhile, Ileto, a highly respected West Pointer who is known for his expertise in counterinsurgency, pleads for patience and good faith. "The cease-fire is a test of our faith in democracy and the potential success of the Aquino leadership to build a just society and attain an honorable peace," he says.

VI

Just as important a test for the government is its ability to pre-empt the insurgents' promises of nationalized industry and radical redistribution of land and wealth, which have fallen on fertile ground, especially in the rural areas where 70 percent of Filipinos live. Aquino's technocrats have drafted a blueprint for economic recovery entitled "Policy Agenda for People-Powered Development," which proposes to harness the forces of capitalism to raise rural incomes, provide jobs and rekindle consumer demand that would eventually stimulate a revival of flagging industry.

As the year ended, the government was preparing to launch its long-delayed program of economic development measures and rehabilitation centers designed to spark economic recovery and give non-hardcore members of the New People's Army incentive to surrender their firearms and shift their struggle from the hills to the political arena. The attendant infusion of resources into the countryside only weeks before the February 2 referendum on the new constitution prompted charges that the program was nothing but the old-fashioned political pork barrel, which was by tradition served up to voters on election eves.

During the last years of the Marcos regime and the early months of the new government, the Philippine economy had shrunk by 12 percent, as investment dried up and annual service on the country's $26-billion deficit consumed 37 percent of its foreign currency earnings. As thousands of jobs were lost in ur-

ban industry, many of the unemployed returned to their family
homes in the provinces, where incomes were already suffering
from depressed world prices of Philippine commodities like sugar
and coconuts. The first update on family income to be published
in ten years revealed that 60 percent of all families are living below the poverty line of $120 per month.

Taking an opposite tack from the export-driven growth strategy that was so successfully pursued by the Philippines' East and
Southeast Asian neighbor states but failed when applied by Marcos, the country's new economic planners are counting on a $200-
million program of public spending to create one million jobs by
the end of 1987. They propose such labor-intensive development
projects as schools, irrigation projects and roads, primarily in the
rebel-infested countryside. Regional Development Councils are
being established to identify, implement and monitor these projects and to channel foreign investment into small and medium
agriculture-based industries capable of competing in export markets.

While the economy registered some gains in 1986, anticipated foreign investment was not forthcoming. Japanese, American
and European businessmen responded positively to the government's debt-equity swap program, unveiled in August 1986, to
sell off millions of dollars of government holdings in bankrupt
state corporations. But investors were waiting for the chaotic political and national security situation to stabilize before injecting
new money or bringing back capital that had flowed out during
the turbulent last years of Marcos. Meanwhile, a delay by the
country's 483 foreign commercial creditors in the rescheduling
of $6–$9 billion of private commercial debt due to mature between 1987 and 1991 threatened to sharpen differences within
the Aquino cabinet over debt repayment terms.

VII

As the Aquino government completes its first year in power,
the stakes are rising. The honeymoon it enjoyed for much of
1986 is already over, and it will become even harder for the president to impose her will on her quibbling cabinet and her restless
constituents once the checks and balances enshrined in the new
constitution are put in place. A lot is riding on the ability of the
new government to bring about by democratic and capitalist

means the critical changes that are necessary in the Philippines if the political center is to remain relevant. "This may be the last chance for the political center to make good the promise of a free economy," wrote the *Far Eastern Economic Review*.

Indeed, Corazon Aquino has become the best advertisement for the democratic alternative in years. But as she reminded the U.S. Congress with just a touch of bitterness during her moving speech to a joint session last September, the resulting assistance forthcoming from the industrialized democracies had not been "commensurate with the calamity that has been visited on us." Arguing for more U.S. aid and private investment, she told an adoring audience, "You have spent many lives and much treasure to bring freedom to lands that were reluctant to receive it. And here you have a people who won it by themselves and need only the help to preserve it."

If the revival of democracy in the Philippines were to falter and the communists to gain the initiative in the strategically located archipelago, acknowledges a U.S. official, "our inability to do something about it would be regarded as another example of American impotence." Thus, the United States has good reason to do all within its power to help the new government through this perilous period before recovery takes hold—without, however, trying to dictate the terms to a proud nation or become deeply involved in the internal rivalries that have long characterized the culturally and ethnically diverse archipelago.

That means budgeting the full amount of security owed the Philippines in return for the U.S. military facilities, the Gramm-Rudman law notwithstanding, offering the best possible trading terms on export quotas for such products as sugar and textiles, encouraging private investment, and helping to broker a settlement on the "hidden wealth" of President Marcos. It also means not falling prey to the seasonal longing for an advance guarantee that U.S. military bases on Philippine soil will be retained beyond expiration of the U.S.-Philippine Military Bases Agreement in 1991. No government can responsibly provide such assurance prior to the formal review process, which will begin in 1988.

Emmanuel Pelaez, a former foreign minister who is currently Philippine ambassador to Washington, points out that President Marcos' assurances to that effect were useless, given the fact that he was overthrown before the expiration date. Moreover, by accepting Marcos' guarantees, the United States opened itself up to manipulation by the Philippine leader. "Marcos was motivated by the obsession to remain in power for life," says Pelaez, "for which he needed U.S. assistance and support."

Precisely because sentiment against the bases runs high in the ranks of the left-of-center nationalist groups that support Aquino and because closure of the American bases is a condition for a political settlement set by the Communist Party of the Philippines, it is important not to whip up emotions over the subject prematurely. President Aquino has pledged to honor the current agreement for the length of its life and to keep all her options open after that with regard to renewing it or letting it lapse. While she, like most Filipinos, would prefer that Philippine sovereignty not be diminished by the presence of any foreign facility, she is aware that the U.S. military bases are her country's third-largest employer, and that the other free-market countries in the area consider the continued presence of the bases critical to regional security. On the issue of renewing the bases agreement, Michael Armacost, under secretary of state for political affairs and a former ambassador to Manila, said: "We can afford to let this issue lie for the meanwhile. I am personally confident that our security relationship will endure beyond 1991."

The best guarantee of the future of the bases is a stable and prosperous Philippines with a leader who is responsive to the needs of the people and thus able to deliver on whatever agreement is ultimately reached between the two countries. The committee that wrote the new constitution rejected a provision that would have barred foreign bases from the Philippines. The final draft of the constitution gives the president a free hand to renegotiate an agreement, subject to legislative approval. The controversial subject may also be put to a plebiscite.

VIII

With so many question marks on the political page in the Philippines, President Aquino's greatest gift may be her ability to exude optimism that problems can be solved and confidence that they will be. Shortly after the cease-fire took effect, she spoke with satisfaction about her new, smoother relationship with the armed forces. She feared neither its influence nor the seductive powers of the communists, she said, because she had faith that the Filipino people were sophisticated enough to make the right choices. "I am so convinced that this country of ours has become so conservative," she said. "Anything in the extreme is very upsetting to a great number. At the same time, people are not going to let the military rule it over them. We have gone through so much controversy and division that people would like officials who won't divide them."

If President Aquino spent most of her first year in office favoring the left wing of her unruly coalition, as the military, with some justification, feels she did, it would appear that she has recently swung back toward the right to assure that the military is with her during the highly sensitive period ahead, whether it is one of peace negotiations or renewed hostilities. Though such support-building maneuvers are necessary to keep her government together in the near term, her aim remains to wind up back in the center. In the longer term, however, she must expand the center over the years ahead to include more of those on the left and the right. Only then can democracy ultimately prove workable in the Philippines.

DEMOCRACY IN THE PHILIPPINES[2]

Philippine President Corazon Aquino is halfway into her six-year term. Her late husband, Benigno Aquino, predicted that anybody who succeeded President Ferdinand Marcos would be ousted in six months. Thus Aquino's ability to survive is remarkable. But she has not had an easy transition, and while her administration has achieved a measure of political stability, it continues to be plagued by Communist and Muslim insurgencies, creeping militarism, human rights violations, social unrest, general poverty, government corruption and the Marcos factor. Two other major problems—land reform and the foreign debt—pose considerable difficulties for the Aquino government. And when Aquino begins winding down her term in the early 1990's, she will face the contentious issue of continuing the United States military bases on Philippine soil.

[2]Reprint of an article by Belinda A. Aquino, associate professor of political science, University of Hawaii at Manoa. Reprinted with permission from *Current History*, April 1989. Copyright © *Current History* 1989.

Since the stunning overthrow of Marcos in the 1986 "people power revolution" at Epifanio de los Santos Avenue (ESDA), Aquino's greatest achievements have been in the area of redemocratization, particularly restoring the basic freedoms and civil liberties of Filipinos. She immediately embarked on a course of political liberalization, abolishing the repressive decrees of Marcos and his rubber-stamp legislature, cleaning out the judiciary, releasing political prisoners and naming a commission that would draft a new constitution to be ratified in a nationwide plebiscite. Most of all, as the moral symbol of the revolution, Aquino generally restored the people's faith in the incoming government. And before her first year was out, Aquino had made significant trips to Singapore, Indonesia and Japan to try to establish closer links with her country's neighbors in Asia.

Her first year in office was stormy, but she overcame a military attempt to unseat her in a plan code-named "God Save the Queen," in November, 1986. She had hastily put together a multiclass coalition that included Juan Ponce Enrile, an ex-Marcos defense minister who had played a central role in the ESDA revolution. As in all political honeymoons, however, the coalition had begun to falter as Enrile became increasingly strident and critical of Aquino's policy initiatives. Aquino deftly maneuvered to have Enrile ousted from the Cabinet when it became evident that he was involved in the coup, "God Save the Queen." The attempt was masterminded by Colonel Gregorio "Gringo" Honasan, Enrile's chief security aide and close ally, who had earlier organized the Reform the Armed Forces (RAM) movement. It would have strained credulity to assume Enrile had nothing to do with the plot to make Aquino a figurehead, somewhat like a ceremonial queen.

If 1986 was a difficult year, 1987 was even more difficult, because it was Aquino's first real test of political survival. It opened with another military attempt to destabilize her government, as more than 500 military officers and enlisted men took over Channel 7 in Quezon City and struck Villamor Air Base and Sangley Air Station outside Manila. It was believed that this effort was supported by Marcos, operating from his exile in Honolulu. The deposed dictator had kept in close touch with his loyalists in the Philippine military. In fact, Marcos had planned to leave Hawaii the day the coup was taking place in Manila, but the Philippine consul in Honolulu, Tomas Gomez 3d, foiled the escape plan.

That incident is now the object of a grand jury investigation in Honolulu.

But it was the coup attempt led by Honasan on August 28, 1987, that shook the very foundations of the fledgling Aquino government. It came at a time when the government had become somewhat stable and ready to function. The new constitution had been ratified overwhelmingly the previous February. The Congress, moribund for nearly 14 years, had been reestablished, with a national election for 24 Senators and close to 200 Representatives. The congressional leadership in both the House and the Senate had been chosen. The general public had not shown any real support or enthusiasm for the military "misadventurism" of Honasan and company. But it had happened, and a shaken President Aquino, whose son had been seriously injured in the abortive coup, promised the plotters punishment under the fullest measure of the law. In the end, loyal forces under Chief of Staff Fidel Ramos aborted the coup that had killed 53 people and wounded several others.

Although the August coup failed, the military continued to be a serious force in the country's political system. The military had acquired a taste for power during the Marcos regime, when it was the main pillar of the dictatorship. Under a redemocratized system, it was not easy to send the military back to the barracks at the beck and call of civilian authority. The genie would not go back in the bottle. The legacy of the Marcos years had become a specter to the successor regime; witness the political assassinations that marked 1987 and 1988. The politicization of the military under Marcos is apparently directly correlated with the politically motivated killings of elements associated with left-of-center groups.

Human Rights Violations

Despite the government's attempts to reverse the pattern of human rights violations of the previous regime, there has been a reemergence of mysterious killings of politically oriented Filipinos, killings that are often attributed to government or government-backed forces. The Philippine military argues that there are also killings perpetrated by the New People's Army (NPA). Although this argument has some validity, it is a separate issue and should not be used as a rationalization for the human rights excesses of some elements in the government's military establishment.

Amnesty International (AI) commissioned three missions—in May and December, 1986, and in July, 1987—to assess the human rights situation in the Philippines. The missions collected information, including notarized affidavits, court documents and press and media reports. They also interviewed government officials, human rights advocates, and the victims of human rights abuses. During the Marcos regime, AI sent missions to the Philippines in 1975 and 1981. Both missions found that the Marcos regime had a brazen and brutal human rights record. A similar finding was filed by another mission from the International Commission of Jurists in 1977.

Because denial of human rights was one of the basic issues charged against Marcos, Aquino placed it high on her agenda when she assumed power. The new constitution had several provisions ensuring the protection of human rights and curtailing military arbitrariness. One of Aquino's early executive orders created a Presidential Commission on Human Rights (PCHR), which was initially headed by the late Senator and human rights activist José Diokno.

The two AI missions in 1986 upheld the Aquino government's commitment to human rights and found little evidence of the systematic abuses that had marked the previous regime. The missions found almost no "incommunicado" detentions, which had been prevalent under martial law. There were few "extrajudicial executions" ("salvaging" was the term used in the Marcos regime), but one murder—that of *Kilusang Mayo Uno* (May First Movement, or KMU) leader Rolando Olalia—was linked to the military.

The third mission found another picture. As AI puts it:

By the time of Amnesty International's third mission in July, 1987, there had been a sharp escalation in political violence, and the government appeared increasingly unwilling or unable to persuade its security forces to respect the safeguards it had promoted so vigorously a year earlier, particularly when the members of the military and police were targets of the NPA assassination squads.

A pattern of widespread human rights violations had developed by 1987. Well-known activist Leandro Alejandro of the left-wing *Bagong Alyansang Makabayan* (New Nationalist Alliance, or BAYAN) had been murdered that year. The suspicion again fell on the military. And in June, leading figures of another left-wing political party, the *Partido ng Bayan* (People's party), like former NPA head Bernabe Buscayno, better known as *Kumander* Dante, were ambushed in a blast of gunfire from men riding on motorcycles. Dante survived but two in his party, including University of the Philippines political science instructor Dan Sibal, were killed.

Several other killings were reported during 1987 and 1988. Human rights lawyers, journalists and captured NPA rebels were either murdered, harassed or assaulted by military or paramilitary forces. The situation had become so alarming by mid-1988 that, for the first time since the ESDA revolution, the Catholic Church called on the Aquino government to respect human rights and asked the military to stop plotting coups. The country's 100 Roman Catholic bishops made their appeal in a pastoral letter read in Manila churches. They admonished the government and the military to "remember that peace and order cannot be achieved if respect for the law and human rights are ignored." Then, addressing the rebels "from the left and right," the bishops warned that the "killings of the Filipinos and grabbing power are not ways of democracy."

Why the escalation in human rights abuses? In a sense, many military officers believe that the Aquino government has been soft on Communists and that it has offered amnesty to NPA rebels while calling for the prosecution of military and paramilitary personnel accused of abuses. The hard-liners in the military establishment have always opposed Aquino's peace initiatives toward the left. They objected to her release of political prisoners, especially José Maria Sison, founder of the Communist party of the Philippines (CCP), and *Kumander* Dante. Similarly, they denounced the cease-fire negotiations with leaders of the National Democratic Front (NDF), which began in December, 1986. The negotiations collapsed anyway in February of the following year. The talks gave the general public an idea of the goals of the NDF and its constituencies, notably the CCP and NPA. But the military charged the media with glamorizing the Communists. Some military brass admitted that they were losing the "propaganda war."

Another reason for human rights abuse is the military's perception that preoccupation with human rights impedes the government's counterinsurgency program. Military leaders see human rights and a counterinsurgency program as "mutually

exclusive." This attitude was exemplified by the then spokesper-
son of the military, Colonel (now Brigadier General) Honesto Is-
leta, who asked for emergency powers for the military in its drive
against the insurgents.

Rise of Vigilante Groups

Part of the government's counterinsurgency effort is the encouragement of civilian "self-defense units," which have become
more popularly known as "vigilantes." It is estimated that there
are close to 200 such groups around the country, particularly in
the Visayas and Mindanao. Most are staunchly anti-Communist.

The ostensible reason for the proliferation of these vigilante
organizations is to counter the activities of the NPA, especially
the collection of "revolutionary taxes" and harassment or killing
of local officials or suspected government informers. The *Alsa
Masa* is credited with wiping out the NPA in Davao City. The
commander of the Philippine Constabulary assigned there virtually directed the *Alsa Masa* operations, which included nonstop
commentaries against the NPA and its supporters over the local
radio station.

While the connection cannot be fully established, it is interest-
ing to note that the rise in vigilantism in late 1986 and early 1987
coincided with the presence in the country of right-wing figures
and avowed anti-Communists of the United States like General
(ret.) John K. Singlaub, whose support for the Nicaraguan con-
tras and El Salvador "death squads" was well known. Singlaub's
"cover" was the Nippon Star, a registered company that he set up
in Makati to hunt for the "Yamashita treasure" that the Japanese
were reported to have buried in the Philippines. In reality, according to a National Security official in Manila, Singlaub was
"setting up a well-organized anti-Communist movement with
front organizations which can be used for all sorts of purposes."

At the same time, religious fundamentalist groups were
mushrooming in many parts of the country, representing the various sects in the United States—the Campus Crusade for Christ,
the 700 Club, Assemblies of God, World Vision International,
and the Billy Graham Evangelistic Association. A combination of
political and religious right-wing activity has apparently foment-
ed a "Red Scare" in the Philippines, similar to the scare that has
developed in some Latin American countries. It is not unreason-

able to assume that the right-wing organizations have been instrumental in forming or encouraging some of the vigilante groups that have burgeoned in recent years. In turn, the NPA has unleashed its liquidation agents, called "Sparrows," to assassinate abusive law enforcement and other public officials. The Alex Boncayao Brigade is believed to be responsible for several of the killings that have occurred in Metro Manila in the last three years.

Aquino's Burden

The Aquino government has acknowledged that human rights violations exist. Adding to the violence is a pattern of disappearances, including 82 that were reported in the first six months of 1988 alone. The Task Force Detainees of the Philippines (TFDP), the church-based organization that has documented the disappearances, claims that the government should be held morally responsible because the military has once again resorted to the repressive practices of the Marcos regime. The TFDP has also engaged in a systematic campaign to link activist groups like BAYAN, KMU, GABRIELA (a coalition of radical women's groups), and other left-of-center organizations to the underground Communist party. It has charged that Congress has been infiltrated by "Communist cadres," a charge that Senate President Jovito Salonga and Speaker Ramon Mitra have vigorously denied.

Unfortunately, the military is unwilling or unable, or both, to make distinctions about "communism." The military treats all "Communists" alike, and attacks the members of the "legal left," who are not necessarily calling for armed struggle and are willing to participate in the "democratic space" restored by Aquino. It is ovious that the military needs a drastic reexamination of its simplistic approach to the insurgency and to leftist politics in society. Otherwise the political polarization will be exacerbated.

It is disappointing that the government has not convicted a single human rights violator worthy of note. In this connection, even the most celebrated case—the murder of Benigno Aquino—remains unsolved more than five years after his assassination. If this is the fate of the most blatant murder under Marcos, what can we expect of less well-known cases? Because of the vulnerability of the judicial system to the manipulation of powerful elements, the current leadership apparently lacks conviction in implementing the human rights mandates that the President has enunciated. It is also ironic that the most notorious human rights violator in the Marcos era, Colonel Rolando Abadilla, has been cleared of charges by a military court and returned to government service. The government needs firmer policy enforcement.

Meanwhile, the CPP-NPA–led insurgency continues to bedevil and befuddle the government. However, it is difficult to secure a clear picture of the real strength of the Communist threat. The most often cited figure is 23,000 Communists, sometimes 24,000. The NPA is said to control 20 percent of the country's 40,000 *barangays* (village units). But these might be exaggerated figures designed to justify a heavy-handed approach by the government's defense establishment and to give weight to requests for more sophisticated equipment of the counterinsurgency.

The NDF itself, according to an experienced journalist, has confirmed that the actual number of Communist armed regulars is 12,500, or half the figure the military has claimed. Former Nueva Ecija officer-in-charge Emmanuel Santos offers an even lower estimate: 7,500.

Because many of the top NPA leaders have been captured, the strength of the movement should be reevaluated. Internal dissension may have weakened the party. It is well known that, as in every struggle, the party has differing factions advocating hard-line or moderate views. Among the more contentious issues being debated by the left wing are the continuing validity of armed revolution and how to deal with the Aquino government—a liberal democracy obviously backed by the United States. Ultimately, the issue will be how long the party's strategy of "protracted war" can last.

Along these lines, it is instructive to cite the CPP situation in Negros Occidental, a hotbed of social unrest. Nemesio Dimafiles, a senior member of the party's regional leadership, resigned after devoting 18 years of his life to the cause. He questioned the party's "protracted war" strategy, its policies on "revolutionary taxation," and the role of the New People's Army. His resignation was followed by the defection of 25 others.

Still, the armed left is one of the more serious problems of the Aquino regime. As Walden Bello puts it, the left's most effective weapon is not arms but a political message. "The appeal of the

NPA comes mainly from its program of thoroughgoing land reform and its commitment to ending the dominant United States military and economic presence." To undercut the left's political attraction, the government would have to embark on a genuine program of land reform that could lead toward a more equitable distribution of power and wealth. Congress has passed a law incorporating Aquino's Comprehensive Agrarian Reform Program (CARP), which is designed to benefit 2 million farmers. But its meaningful implementation is another matter. About $16.6 million is needed to implement the law. Finally, the government must make a dent in the conditions of poverty and inequality that stalk about 70 percent of the Philippine population. The Aquino performance in this area is at best ambiguous. Aquino must articulate a clearer vision and direction, and must demonstrate bolder initiatives.

No mention of land reform is complete without an evaluation of the larger economy of the country and the Aquino administration's program to revitalize it after the plunder of the previous regime. In 1987, the economy grew at the rate of 5.7 percent, and it grew at 7.6 percent in the first quarter of 1988. These impressive gains barely make up for the 10 percent contraction in the economy during the last two Marcos years. It was Aquino's misfortune to inherit the disaster. To hasten economic recovery, the Philippine government has accepted massive amounts of assistance from a "Marshall Plan" organized by the United States and its allies. Up to $10 billion is being raised to energize the devastated economy. President Aquino has made official trips to the United States, Switzerland, Italy and Brunei, partly to negotiate loans and assistance packages for the Philippines.

The biggest drain on the economy is the huge external debt incurred by the predatory Marcos and his cronies. The economy cannot grow if it continues to remit billions of dollars to pay off the gargantuan debt. The country has paid $5 billion to its creditors since Aquino took power, and by 1992, when her term ends, debt payments will have totaled a staggering $20 billion.

The debt crisis is compounded by fundamental disagreements among Aquino's top economic advisers—Economic Planning Secretary Solita Monsod, Central Bank Governor José Fernandez and Finance Secretary Vicente Jayme—on an appropriate strategy. Monsod has argued for a "selective repudiation" of the debt. The absence of a consensus on debt management has been over-

taken by legislative action. The Philippine Senate has passed Bill
535, putting a limit on the annual debt service of the country, a
limit that has alarmed more conservative sectors who fear that
this action will cut the availability of new loans. In any case, the
Senate has proposed to establish a Foreign Debt Commission to
try to consolidate a national consensus on the pesky debt question.

The New Military Bases Agreement

Another lingering externally related issue that confronts the
Aquino government is the future of the American military bases
in the Philippines. The original Military Bases Agreement (MBA)
was signed in 1947, and is due to expire in 1991, after more than
50 amendments over the years. During the administrations of
United States Presidents Jimmy Carter and Ronald Reagan, the
United States and the Philippines entered into five-year agreements: the current agreement expires in 1989. In July, 1988, the
governments started discussions designed to work out the details
of the last two years of the MBA, not the use of the bases beyond
their expiration in 1991.

On October 18, Philippine Foreign Secretary Raul
Manglapus and United States Secretary of State George Shultz
signed an agreement allowing the continuing use of the American bases until 1991, at a cost to the United States of $1.46 bil-
lion.

The "hard" cash, amounting to $471 million, includes the so-
called Economic Support Fund (ESF) of $160 million. The "soft"
components, amounting to $305 million, will go to housing in-
vestment schemes and the procurement of Philippine goods and
materials. A debt-reduction scheme is included and the estimated
"savings" will be of between $390 million and $480 million. And
the Philippine Base Command will receive an assistance fund of
$4 million.

Predictably, the nationalist groups are unhappy with the renewed agreement. They have always demanded unconditional
withdrawal of the bases, which they consider an affront to Philippine sovereignty that makes the country a pawn in the United
States global game. The nuclear issue has been a bone of contention, especially in light of the provision in the new constitution
that the Philippines, consistent with the national interest, adopts

and pursues a policy of freedom from nuclear weapons on its territory. The social costs of the bases in terms of prostitution, gun-running, smuggling, violence and other forms of criminality are also part of the nationalist argument.

But the political question of sovereignty rankles most sharply. "In fact, [the] continued existence [of the bases] on Philippine territory hinders the pursuit of an independent course of action in all matters of national interest, from foreign relations to political and economic development." The bases are seen as offensive "vestiges of colonial rule."

And as good as it sounds the debt-reduction scheme will not reduce the Philippine debt significantly, according to Professor Leonor Briones of the University of the Philippines, who is also vice president of the Freedom from Debt Coalition (FDC). This is because the Philippines will be incurring new debts "due to the bonds that will be issued in exchange." The FDC has proposed three minimum demands, namely: 1) the declaration of a moratorium while negotiating with creditors for better terms, including write-offs; 2) the imposition of a ceiling on debt service payments; and 3) selective disengagement from debts that are tainted with graft and corruption.

An Independent Foreign Policy

In spite of polls showing that a majority of Filipinos favor the retention of the bases, there is an emerging consensus according to Senator Leticia Ramos Shahani, chairperson of the Senate Foreign Relations Committee, that eventually the United States bases will have to go. And Shahani noted that in anticipation of the MBA's termination in 1991, the Senate has passed a resolution allocating $7.5 billion to implement programs for alternative use of the bases.

Among current Filipino officials, Shahani is the foremost supporter of an independent foreign policy, based on mutual respect and on the concept of multipolar diplomacy that is "no longer fettered by cold war political rigidities." She exhorts her fellow Filipinos to look beyond the bases, which means looking forward "to a Philippines that shall no longer be a passive object of the major powers' strategic calculations but a key player in the Century of the Pacific."

In advocating a more independent foreign policy posture, Shahani calls for a more fundamental change; i.e., she asks Filipinos to forget the "neocolonial psyche" that has made them subservient to the United States over the years through the World Bank, the International Monetary Fund and the American Chamber of Commerce. Filipinos should also be aware of the rapidly changing geopolitical picture in the Asian-Pacific region, which has tremendous implications for the future.

It is imperative, not just important, for United States decisionmakers to realize that the demand to end the Philippine-American "special relationship" is growing stronger and is not confined to left-leaning groups. Senator Shahani does not have a leftist perspective; she takes a moderate but no less nationalistic stand on the need to recast Philippine-American relations. Otherwise, the United States will continue to repeat disastrous blunders.

Conclusion

Official corruption, the Muslim insurgency, labor strife, the urban crisis, the still expanding population, the lack of social services and the destruction of the environment are also continuing problems. In dealing with these and other problems cited earlier, Aquino faces a major dilemma. For all the criticism heaped on her administration (some of which is unreasonable), Aquino can claim with pride that she has restored and stabilized democratic institutions and turned the economy around. But political stability and economic growth often clash with issues of equity and redistribution.

The government has set in motion certain populist measures, apparently to counter the criticism that it has moved to the right in areas like the counterinsurgency program and land reform. Populist measures or policies include the rollback in oil prices, free high school education, the sale of generic drugs, low-interest home loans for the lower and middle income classes and the Comprehensive Agrarian Reform Program (CARP). Of these, the last is seen as lacking in teeth and conviction, essentially because it was crafted by a conservative Congress (particularly the lower house). In its final form, CARP is "certainly not the drastic social reform that can immediately transform the power structure in the countryside. It must become more decisive. But given the present political culture and social structure, this may well be impossible.

Speculation has turned to Aquino's political future, particularly the question of whether she will run again. There is reason to believe that she will not run. But there may well be forces that will persuade her to seek reelection. One of these is the challenge of transforming the current liberal elitist political system into a genuine popular democracy. Aquino must become more aggressive and tougher in applying a combination of state power and moral leadership if she is to control corruption, purge the bureaucracy of its venalities, instill discipline in the military, handle insurgent groups effectively and deal with the United States more forcefully. Above all, Corazon Aquino needs to become an activist President who will not only lead but will force the Philippines to a real democratic revolution.

"TOTAL WAR" IN THE PHILIPPINES[3]

A women's organization reports on the arrest of its campaigners for breast-feeding. Commuters whisper about a bus halted at a military checkpoint where passengers wearing the *tubao* (head scarf) are detained. Community activists are furious over the demolition by soldiers of a water-powered rice thresher. Workers tally the number of trade unionists found dead, hogtied and mutilated, in the cogon grass. A woman calmly recounts that, after a meal at a Chinese restaurant, she's arrested by the police, sexually molested and jailed for months. The amazing thing is that such stories are hardly considered news, so inured to the bizarre has Philippine society become since 1986.

On the other hand, a returning resident is besieged by queries as to what kind of car he's brought home (by executive order, he's allowed this) and is offered payment in hard cash. Luxury cars are in demand—B.M.W.s, Mercedes-Benzes and Porsches—which has meant profit for some officers of the Asian Development

[3]Reprint of an article by Ninotchka Rosca, author of the novel *State of War* and a nonfiction report, *Endgame: The Fall of Marcos. The Nation*, June 19, 1989, pp. 839-842. Reprinted by permission from *The Nation* magazine/The Nation Company, Inc. Copyright © *The Nation* 1989.

Bank, who bring them in duty-free. Also brought in from over-seas are apples and grapes, perfumes and cosmetics, chocolate bars and even underwear. And at any time, a ball for a simpering debutante is likely to be in progress at a five-star hotel to the tune of a million pesos (about $50,000).

Equally amazing is the fact that such stories are hardly consid-ered news, so shameless has Philippine society become in its con-spicuous consumption since 1986.

With the fall of the twenty-year regime of Ferdinand Marcos in February 1986, the chronic crisis in the Philippine archipelago abated dramatically. The new head of state, President Corazon Aquino, having made a point during the electoral campaign of being "unlike" Marcos, embarked rapidly on a "liberalization program." Political prisoners were released; negotiations with the underground revolutionary forces were started; a new Constitu-tion was drafted with the help of a few radical elements; and assets seized by Marcos and his cronies were returned to private hands. But five coup attempts by splinter military factions since then have altered the scene dramatically once again—and there are those who say that the coups (or the "shows détat") were indeed staged to bring about the current situation.

A number of realities seem to coexist in Aquino's new "democratic" dispensation, none of them with any relation to de-mocracy itself. Two of them correspond to two phrases constant-ly used by government: economic recovery and counter-insurgency. The two are both goal and process, manifesting themselves in various guises within the different universes of the 7,100-island archipelago. On a larger scale, the two are linked, being components of an all-encompassing strategy to depoliticize Philippine society.

"If the truth be told, 1986 frightened the ruling elite," says a political science professor. "Bear in mind that though factions within the elite quarrel, they're united in: one, that they should control the country—economically, politically and socially; and two, that links with the United States should not be severed. That's their soup kitchen, you know."

According to the professor, the first step to such a depolitic-ization was the removal from center stage of the "people power revolution," and of those issues that created the strongest and most sustained activism during the time of Ferdinand Marcos. Such issues as agrárian reform, labor rights, women's rights and housing, not to mention consumer prices. In their place, an alternative reality was installed, hallucinatory to a degree, of "economic recovery." The how and the for whom of such a recovery was never discussed, leaving government free to pursue whatever means it deemed necessary, even if they were inimical to the general population. The current prosperity is artificial, fueled largely by loans. Although the government claims that the economy grew at 6.7 percent in 1988, the balance-of-payments deficit was $922 million.

The need to maintain appearances ties the Aquino government in knots when it comes to overseas handouts. In March, the President signed a letter of intent with the International Monetary Fund for an additional $1.3 billion loan. The I.M.F. conditions include currency devaluation, value added taxes, government "streamlining" (i.e., firing employees) and ending subsidies for rice and corn—measures that, in Marcos's time, would have been called draconian.

In the United States, the Philippine Embassy has launched a campaign to get resident Filipinos behind a so-called Multilateral Aid Initiative sponsored by Representative Stephen Solarz. The first $200 million appropriation for this is now before the U.S. Congress. Having accepted the M.A.I., the Philippines estops itself from (a) not renewing the U.S.-Philippine Military Bases Treaty, which expires in 1992; (b) refusing to pay full interest on the $30 billion foreign debt; and (c) repudiating loans fraudulently obtained by Marcos and his cronies.

Such heavy borrowing and begging overseas assail Filipinos with *déjà vu*. Since 1946, begging and borrowing have been the mainstay of all government economic programs, with the sole exception of former President Carlos Garcia's "Filipino First" policy of the mid-1950s. But the muffled despair that greeted the I.M.F. letter of intent did not break out into protest. The leadership of the opposition movement that stalemated the Marcos regime has been dispersed. One faction works in government, at minor positions; another has fled into private life, bribed into silence by multiple corporate directorships; and a third, the most organized and most consistent, is hard-pressed to survive.

To recap the record of the past two years: The head of the largest labor center was assassinated; the secretary general of the biggest cause-oriented coalition was assassinated; more than two dozen members of a youth organization were assassinated; a dozen trade unionists were assassinated; about two dozen demonstrating peasants were gunned down and their leader charged with subversion; a university president was twice ambushed and left for dead; a half-dozen human rights lawyers were assassinated; and at the moment, a campaign of assassination is being carried out against socially active religious leaders, both Protestant and Catholic.

Asked what their constituents can do in defense of their rights without incurring harassment (arrest, detention, subversion charges) or suppression (physical attacks of every severity, up to and including murder), lawyers for organizations of labor, the urban poor, women, peasants and students readily answer: nothing. Brinksmanship underlies any advocacy for the poor. The ante has been upped, and what's at stake is not even one's legal rights but the right to live.

Meanwhile, the statistics of poverty remain the same. An estimated 10 million are homeless (per the government's National Economic Development Authority figures); more than 80 percent of urban households live below the poverty line (per the Catholic Bishops Conference's figure) while four-fifths of rural households are below the poverty line (per the National Statistics Office figure); and an estimated 40 percent of the labor force remains unemployed.

None of the measures ostensibly designed to redress these social inequities are being implemented with full political will. CARP, the country's forty-third land reform program, has enabled even the President's own sugar plantation to escape untouched—though Aquino herself had vowed while campaigning to make her *hacienda* a model of agrarian reform. An increase in the minimum wage is still being debated, while onerous decrees against trade unions, passed by Marcos, are still in operation. Squatting, or summary occupation of even idle lands, remains a criminal act under Marcos-era laws, and military tribunals are still the exclusive arbiters of cases against enlisted men. To cap it all, basic services—potable water, electricity, garbage disposal, etc. —have failed to improve, not because of lack of resources but because of indifference. In Nonoc Island, for instance, where the local nickel refinery uses only 30 percent of the electric power it generates, the surrounding barrios cannot tap the excess power for lack of a grid.

Such concerns have been effectively shoved to the wings, principally as a result of the intense and concerted suppression of legal, cause-oriented organizations. This suppression is justified by the armed forces as "depriving" the revolutionary National Democratic Front (N.D.F.) of its infrastructure. But the end result is depriving the majority of the population of its voice and lobbying groups. When Defense Under Secretary Fortunato Abat spoke rather candidly of the need to "outlaw" seven organizations, he was in effect proposing the disenfranchisement of women, teachers, students, workers, peasants, youth and their allied professionals. What this really means can be gleaned from one police officer's nonchalant joke that 10 million might have to be killed to insure peace and order.

Hair-splitting as to what's legal and what's not, says a military source, is not tolerable under conditions of war—which, he maintains, is what the situation is. The right of the state to protect itself is the dominant principle here; there are no ethical or moral considerations, simply the goal of remaining in power so that the socioeconomic system may remain unchanged.

From the military's point of view, the principal objective is maintaining the status quo even though it has been proven untenable. Since 1910, when U.S. control of the Philippines was consolidated, the country has had three large-scale rebellions of the poor, with a half-dozen smaller ones in between. The military informant is aware of this, and says it is the reason top officials of the Philippine armed forces no longer speak of "eradicating" the insurgency but of "containing" it—an admission that the system breeds its own enemy. "Perhaps the N.D.F. forces can be weakened to a level where the insurgency can be efficiently contained," he says.

Perhaps. But a recent release from the New People's Army (N.P.A.), the N.D.F.'s armed component, shows an increase in the number of full-time guerrillas, from 25,000 two years ago to 30,000 now. The rate of tactical offensives by the guerrillas remains the same, but new types of warfare and new targets have appeared. River ambushes in Bulacan and Laguna; a paramilitary base overrun in Sorsogon; six soldiers shot dead in an encounter in Iloilo; two Presidential Security Group members shot dead in Manila; a U.S. communications antenna bombed and U.S. Army Col. James Rowe shot dead in Manila.

It is fashionable to explain away the vigor of the N.P.A. as "desperation" or as "attention-grabbing." Which raises the eyebrows of N.D.F. members. "If there's anything anyone should have learned in the past decade," says one, "it is this: We mean what we say." He is referring to an N.D.F. advisory last year warning that U.S. personnel involved in the counterinsurgency program would be included in the N.P.A.'s order of battle. The N.D.F. believes, rightly or wrongly, that Rowe was responsible for the establishment of the notorious paramilitary unit Cafgu (Citizen Armed Forces Geographical Units).

"The Americans have taken control of the government's counterinsurgency operations," says one N.D.F. member. "Orders and politics are no longer funneled through the A.F.P. [Armed Forces of the Philippines] bureaucracy and command. U.S. personnel, particularly C.I.A. agents, are directly involved. Bodily involved."

Independent observers say, however, that the war's intensity has little to do with the magnitude of the threat that the N.P.A. represents. After all, the armed forces number a quarter-million, fully supplied with high-powered weapons and backed by planes and helicopter gunships (which a U.S. Embassy official once characterized as "invitations to indiscriminate slaughter"). Such observers point to the deadline the military has given itself—containment before 1992. "That's when the President's term expires," says a human rights activist, "and that's when the bases treaty comes up for renewal." Seen in this context, the underlying rationale becomes that of dismantling possible overt and legal opposition to the presence of bases. "I think Mrs. Aquino will declare herself in favor of renewal before then," he says. The President has said she'll keep her "options open" (though in one silly instance, she did threaten the bases if no accommodation was reached in the matter of a friend of hers currently being tried by a California court).

Contrary to conventional wisdom, which holds that the bases constitute a "Manila intellectual issue," Filipinos elsewhere do worry about the U.S. presence. First, because the bases constitute an excuse for the United States to continue meddling in Philippine affairs; second, the bases are a locus for infectious mendicancy and subservience at a time when the country needs to "know itself"; and third, the bases are "a doorway" for pernicious health hazards, including AIDS (see Saundra Sturdevant, "The Bar Girls of Subic Bay," *The Nation*, April 3). "One has only to look at the communities surrounding Clark Air Base and Subic Bay Naval Base to understand this," says an antinuclear activist. "A nuclear attack can be considered a *vague* threat, compared to what we're facing right now in terms of our health."

To such activists, the "total war" policy of the Aquino government serves the dual purpose of insuring minimal opposition to the bases treaty and only marginal challenge to the power of the landed oligarchy, of which the President herself is a member. By lumping an activist organization together with the N.D.F., the Communist Party of the Philippines (C.P.P.) and the N.P.A., the military manages not only to scare away prospective supporters but also to mark members as open targets.

It can happen to almost anyone. To dissuade workers from joining the militant Kilusang Mayo Uno (May First Movement) and steer them toward the A.F.L.-C.I.O.-supported Trade Union Center of the Philippines (T.U.C.P.), which used to support Marcos staunchly, military special operations teams visit factories in Bulacan and Rizal, giving lectures on alleged "Communist penetration of the trade union movement." Such teams also go house to house in barrios suspected of being sympathetic to the N.D.F. Photographs of supposedly "starving children in socialist countries" are shown and a doctored tape of alleged C.P.P. founder José Ma. Sison's voice is played, ostensibly naming the largest cause-oriented groups as "C.P.P. fronts." To this propaganda war the U.S.-based Heritage Foundation contributes its periodic "reports" and "lists." In an interview, one visiting Heritage Foundation honcho insisted on referring to Antonio Fortich, the Emeritus Bishop of Bacolod, as "Commander Tony"—the honorific being the N.P.A. officers' only title.

The most dangerous effect of this "lumping" process is that it makes any advocacy for the poor into something disreputable; community or social activism is something to be extirpated. Even the Catholic Church–backed Task Force Detainees of the Philippines, which valiantly chronicled human rights violations during Marcos's time in power, has had its credibility assailed at home and overseas. The head of a nonideological foundation seeking to stop logging in Palawan Island's rain forest has received death threats.

None of which, says an N.D.F. member, alters the under-ground's pace of work. The Provisional Revolutionary Government, which the N.D.F. sees as a precursor to the full victory of the revolutionary forces and whose establishment is a principal objective over the next three years, is being built slowly, region by region. The newest regional P.R.G. was set up in March, in the Central Cordillera—the Philippines' largest and highest mountain range, from which comes 70 percent of the country's gold production and where seven major U.S. banks have heavy investments.

By closing legal avenues for the redress of grievances, the Aquino government and the military are driving the aggrieved straight into the arms of the N.D.F.—a strategy of dubious value if the objective is to maintain the status quo. As "illegals," opponents of the government can then be dealt with militarily—in other words, exterminated. "Or so they think," says the N.D.F. member. "This is not Jakarta 1965. We have the capability to defend ourselves." The government's tactic, he points out, actually helps to hammer home the revolutionary truth: that within the system, there can be no salvation. Government-backed social action groups concentrate largely on charity and do nothing with regard to empowerment of their constituency. "If you want empowerment of the majority, for genuine democracy," he goes on, "you'll have to come to us."

Thus ricocheting between contradictory interests and assumptions, the Philippines slouches toward 1992, its path strewn with an accretion of corpses, its way attended by violence. One can only wonder what strange beast will be born by then.

IV. CAMBODIA

EDITOR'S INTRODUCTION

The situation in Cambodia, the country disrupted by spillover from the Vietnam War and which became the "killing fields" of the 1970s, is at another critical juncture. With the pullout of the Vietnamese occupying troops, efforts to seize power from the Hanoi-supported government will doubtless ensue. In the first article in this section, "Efforts toward a Cambodian Settlement," Vernon A. Walters, U.S. Permanent Representative to the United Nations, outlined the U.S. policy position as regards Cambodia—Vietnamese soldiers out, no return to power of Pol Pot or any other faction of the once genocidal Khmer Rouge, Sihanouk preferably to be the leader of a future coalition government, and ASEAN support for Cambodian self-determination. This article also includes the text of UN General Assembly Resolution 43/19, similar in its essentials, which carried overwhelmingly. In the other article in this section, "The Endless War: The Return of the Khmer Rouge," Steven Erlanger, the Southeast Asia correspondent for the *New York Times*, describes the different factions jockeying to gain power in Cambodia, as well as the new strides achieved by Vietnamese-supported leader Hun Sen in his attempt to stabilize the country. According to Erlanger, Washington's new bottom line is: The Vietnamese out; the Khmer Rouge kept out of power.

EFFORTS TOWARD A CAMBODIAN SETTLEMENT
[statement and text
of UN General Assembly Resolution,
November 3, 1988][1]

AMBASSADOR WALTERS' STATEMENT

For the first time in nearly 10 years, there is reason for cautious optimism regarding Cambodia's future. During the past 6 months, there has been considerable diplomatic activity surrounding the Cambodian conflict and some signs of progress. This activity includes the Vietnamese announcement in May that they will withdraw 50,000 troops from Cambodia by the end of 1988, the Jakarta informal meeting at the end of July, and the special talks on Cambodia between the Soviet and Chinese Vice Foreign Ministers held in Beijing at the end of August.

In addition, other avenues for further progress toward a Cambodian settlement are being vigorously pursued. These include the discussion of the Association of the South East Asian Nations' (ASEAN) revised "Situation in Kampuchea" resolution here at the General Assembly, the Jakarta informal meeting working group which met in Jakarta earlier this month and continues to explore ways of achieving lasting peace for this war ravaged land, and the upcoming meeting in Paris between [Cambodian] Prince Sihanouk and Hun Sen—the so-called prime minister of Vietnam's puppet regime in Phnom Penh.

An acceptable settlement of this tragic conflict must permit the Cambodian people to determine their own future without internal or external manipulation or intimidation. It should be based on the complete withdrawal of all Vietnamese troops from Cambodia so that this foreign occupation is brought to an end as soon as possible. We strongly hope Hanoi will follow through on its pledge to undertake a partial withdrawal in the remaining weeks of this year. There have, however, been few concrete signs up to this time of major movement of Vietnamese forces out of

[1]Reprint of a statement by U.S. Permanent Representative to the United Nations Vernon A. Walters in the UN General Assembly on November 3, 1988, and the text of UN General Assembly Resolution 43/19 of November 3, 1988.

Cambodia. We must ensure as well that Hanoi's withdrawal will not lead to the return to power of the Khmer Rouge, a contingency to which the United States and the international community are unalterably opposed.

H. J. Res. 602 and Other Measures

Recently, my government approved a Joint Resolution of the Congress on Cambodia [H. J. Res. 602], and it was signed by President Reagan. It reflects the overwhelming bipartisan sentiment in the United States for a total withdrawal of Vietnamese forces and for the prevention of a Khmer Rouge return to power. The resolution calls on all parties to "respect the territorial integrity of Cambodia" and to "deny safe haven to Khmer Rouge forces seeking the overthrow of a newly formed sovereign Cambodian Government." It urges that the international community "use all appropriate means available to prevent a return to power of Pol Pot, the top echelon of the Khmer Rouge, and their armed forces, so that the Cambodian people might genuinely be free to pursue self-determination without the spectre of the coercion, intimidation, and torture that are known elements of the Khmer Rouge ideology." Finally, it asks that those nations providing aid, support, and sanctuary to the Khmer Rouge, especially arms and military equipment, cease doing so.

Along with these principles, which we believe must govern any comprehensive settlement of the tragic situation in Cambodia, there are a number of possible measures concerning the Khmer Rouge which warrant serious and urgent consideration. These include the holding of internationally supervised elections. We cannot imagine that the Cambodian people would willingly vote for the return of the Khmer Rouge. Another essential element is the removal of Pol Pot and other senior Khmer Rouge leaders most responsible for crimes against the Cambodian people and violations of basic human rights on a massive scale. A third is the dispatch of some form of international monitoring and peacekeeping force. Another basic element should be provisions for the disarming of all the factions under international monitoring. Finally, measures should be developed to provide for the cutoff of arms aid from the outside in a balanced and symmetrical manner. We believe some combination of these or other approaches can prove effective. Following the implementation of

these measures, the international community should stand ready
to assist the Cambodian people in the resettlement of refugees
and the reconstruction of their war ravaged country.

The United States believes that the best course for the international community is to continue to support Prince Sihanouk
and the noncommunist resistance forces in their valiant struggle
for a free and independent Cambodia. Because they constitute an
increasingly viable alternative to both the Vietnamese and the
Khmer Rouge, they can and must play a key role in a settlement
which will serve the best interests of the Cambodian people. We
view Prince Sihanouk as the indispensable leader of any future
coalition government in Cambodia.

Vietnamese Occupation

It is vital that all peace-loving nations continue to stand firm
in opposition to Vietnam's occupation of Cambodia. We believe
that the international effort to ostracize Vietnam has, over the
years, helped to bring home to Hanoi the cost of its action and
that the recent, although inconclusive, signs of change in Vietnam's approach attest to its effectiveness. Under current conditions, Vietnam cannot and should not participate fully in the
world's economic and diplomatic activities. One result has been
that as the economies of other nations in Southeast Asia thrive,
Vietnam's has disintegrated. Until Vietnam withdraws from
Cambodia, it cannot hope to seriously address its social and economic malaise. Thus, not only Cambodians but also Vietnamese
continue to suffer from the folly of Hanoi's military adventurism.

Unquestionably, Vietnam's illegal occupation remains the
root cause of the conflict in Cambodia today, and the expeditious
withdrawal of all of the Vietnamese troops—we believe that
more than 100,000 are still in country—is the key to resolving
this tragic situation. The United States has joined with the vast
majority of the nations of the world in condemning Vietnam's occupation and has called for Hanoi to withdraw its forces and to
negotiate a settlement acceptable to all sides. We believe that only
through a political solution can the suffering of the Cambodian
people be brought to an end and regional stability be restored.
Our goal is a free and independent Cambodia which is not a
threat to its neighbors.

Today, despite a series of announcements by Hanoi over the years that its troops would soon withdraw, the Cambodian people continue to endure the pain and humiliation of the Vietnamese occupation of their homeland. The influence and control of Vietnam permeates all aspects of Cambodian life and society. Vietnamese personnel, euphemistically referred to as "advisers," can be found at almost every level of government in Phnom Penh and are assigned as watchdogs to all Cambodian military units. There are also disturbing reports of attempts by Hanoi to bring about demographic change in Cambodia through the establishment of a number of Vietnamese settlements.

Nevertheless, Vietnam, like oppressors from time immemorial, has found it impossible to suppress the indomitable spirit of the courageous Cambodian people. Rather than submit meekly to Hanoi's attempt to seize hegemony over Cambodia, thousands of resistance fighters have flocked to the banners of the noncommunist resistance, seeking to drive the invaders from their country. This effort has been fueled by the widespread popular dissatisfaction with the puppet Heng Samrin regime.

In addition to its impact on Cambodia and its people, the Vietnamese invasion and continuing occupation of that country constitute a direct threat to the security of Thailand, a long-time friend and treaty ally of the United States, and to the stability of the entire region. ASEAN has responded to this danger with vigor and effectiveness. It has marshaled international opposition to Vietnam's occupation of Cambodia and has fostered the growth of the Cambodian noncommunist resistance into a viable military and political force in the struggle for a free and independent Cambodia.

The United States has noted with interest Hanoi's frequent announcements of its intention to withdraw 50,000 troops by the end of 1988 and the remainder of its troops by 1990 without regard to the political, economic, or military situation existing at that time. We hope Vietnam will meet and preferably beat these deadlines, and we will be watching. In another positive step, Hanoi has recently reiterated its willingness to allow foreign observers into Cambodia to verify its announced 50,000 troop withdrawal. Despite these encouraging signs, however, fundamental uncertainties remain. Even if Hanoi were to withdraw 50,000 soldiers, the continued presence of an estimated 70,000 troops in Cambodia would preclude genuine national reconciliation. Moreover, the United States remains skeptical of Vietnam's promise to depart Cambodia by 1990 in light of past announced troop withdrawals which later proved to be no more than troop rotations. The international community has the right to expect the act of actual withdrawal to follow the words of Vietnam's promise.

U.S. and International Support

In closing, I would like to offer several important points for your consideration.

• First, the United States will continue to support the efforts of ASEAN to achieve a negotiated solution to this tragedy. Since the beginning of the conflict, ASEAN has been in the forefront of the search for peace. By focusing international attention on Cambodia, it has functioned as our conscience, ensuring that the world does not forget.

• Second, the United States also strongly supports UNGA Resolution 43/19 now before us. We believe that the newly drafted language better reflects the current situation in Cambodia while maintaining as the world's priority the need for the Vietnamese to withdraw their forces. The resolution is in harmony with my own government's twin goals for Cambodia: first, immediate, unconditional, and total withdrawal of Vietnam's forces in Cambodia; and, second, a nonreturn to power of Pol Pot and those closely associated with him in the Khmer Rouge.

• Third, the invasion and occupation of Cambodia by Vietnam are illegal. This assembly has overwhelmingly and repeatedly demanded that Vietnam withdraw from Cambodia. We should do so again with the hope that our combined voices may persuade Vietnam to follow up its conciliatory words with action. In this way, our votes here can contribute to the achievement of a peaceful settlement in Cambodia.

• Fourth, it is the Cambodian people themselves who must determine their own future course. We are certain that for this eminently reasonable and humane objective to be realized, there must be workable measures to assure that the Khmer Rouge can never again exercise control over that country's destiny. Complete Vietnamese withdrawal, however, remains the first step toward resolution of this conflict.

The Cambodian people have suffered long enough. They deserve the right to determine their own form of government, free from outside interference. They are entitled to our best effort. The international community, which has come to equate the name Cambodia with tragedy, should do everything possible to ensure that Cambodia becomes once again a gentle land, independent and free from conflict.

GENERAL ASSEMBLY RESOLUTION 43/19

Recalling its resolutions 34/22 of 14 November 1979, 35/6 of 22 October 1980, 36/5 of 21 October 1981, 37/6 of 28 October 1982, 38/3 of 27 October 1983, 39/5 of 30 October 1984, 40/7 of 5 November 1985, 41/6 of 21 October 1986 and 42/3 of 14 October 1987,

Recalling further the Declaration on Kampuchea and resolution 1(I) adopted by the International Conference on Kampuchea,

Taking note of the report of the Secretary-General on the implementation of General Assembly resolution 42/3,

Deploring that foreign armed intervention and occupation continue and that foreign forces still remain in Kampuchea, thus causing continuing hostilities in that country and seriously threatening international peace and security,

Noting the continued and effective struggle waged against foreign occupation by the Kampuchean forces under the leadership of Samdech Norodom Sihanouk,

Taking note of Economic and Social Council decision 1988/143 of 27 May 1988 on the right of peoples to self-determination and its application to peoples under colonial or alien domination or foreign occupation,

Greatly disturbed that the continued fighting and instability in Kampuchea have forced an additional large number of Kampucheans to flee to the Thai-Kampuchean border in search of food and safety,

Recognizing that the assistance extended by the international community has continued to reduce the food shortages and health problems of the Kampuchean people,

Emphasizing that it is the inalienable right of the Kampuchean people who have sought refuge in neighbouring countries to return safely to their homeland,

Emphasizing further that no effective solution to the humanitarian problems can be achieved without a comprehensive political settlement of the Kampuchean conflict,

Seriously concerned about reported demographic changes being imposed in Kampuchea by foreign occupation forces,

Convinced that, to bring about lasting peace in South-East Asia and reduce the threat to international peace and security, there is an urgent need for the international community to find a comprehensive political solution to the Kampuchean problem, with effective guarantees, that will provide for the withdrawal of all foreign forces from Kampuchea under effective international supervision and control, the creation of an interim administering authority, the promotion of national reconciliation among all Kampucheans under the leadership of Samdech Norodom Sihanouk, the non-return to the universally condemned policies and practices of a recent past and ensure respect for the sovereignty, independence, territorial integrity and neutral and non-aligned status of Kampuchea, as well as the right of the Kampuchean people to self-determination free from outside interference,

Recognizing that the Jakarta Informal Meeting in Bogor, Indonesia, held from 25 to 28 July 1988 was a significant development, which marked for the first time the participation of the parties directly involved and other concerned countries,

Reiterating its conviction that, after the comprehensive political settlement of the Kampuchean question through peaceful means, the countries of the South-East Asian region can pursue efforts to establish a zone of peace, freedom and neutrality in South-East Asia so as to lessen international tensions and to achieve lasting peace in the region,

Reaffirming the need for all States to adhere strictly to the principles of the Charter of the United Nations, which call for respect for the national independence, sovereignty and territorial integrity of all States, non-intervention and non-interference in the internal affairs of States, non-recourse to the threat or use of force and peaceful settlement of disputes,

1. *Reaffirms* its resolutions 34/22, 35/6, 37/6, 38/3, 39/5, 40/7, 41/6 and 42/3 and calls for their full implementation;

2. *Reiterates its conviction* that the withdrawal of all foreign forces from Kampuchea under effective international supervi-

sion and control, the creation of an interim administering authority, the promotion of national reconciliation among all Kampucheans under the leadership of Samdech Norodom Sihanouk, the non-return to the universally condemned policies and practices of a recent past, the restoration and preservation of its independence, sovereignty, territorial integrity and neutral and non-aligned status of Kampuchea, the reaffirmation of the right of Kampuchean people to determine their own destiny and the commitment by all States to non-interference and non-intervention in the internal affairs of Kampuchea, with effective guarantees, are the principal components of any just and lasting resolution of the Kampuchean problem;

3. *Takes note with appreciation* of the report of the *Ad Hoc* Committee of the International Conference on Kmapuchea on its activities during 1987–1988 and requests that the Committee continue its work, pending the reconvening of the Conference;

4. *Authorizes* the *Ad Hoc* Committee to convene when necessary and to carry out the tasks entrusted to it in its mandate;

5. *Reaffirms* its commitment to reconvene the Conference at an appropriate time, in accordance with Conference resolution 1(I), and its readiness to support any other conference of an international nature under the auspices of the Secretary-General;

6. *Requests* the Secretary-General to continue to consult with and assist the Conference and the *Ad Hoc* Committee and to provide them on a regular basis with the necessary facilities to carry out their functions;

7. *Expresses its appreciation once again* to the Secretary-General for taking appropriate steps in following the situation closely and requests him to continue to do so and to exercise his good offices in order to contribute to a comprehensive political settlement;

8. *Expresses its deep appreciation once again* to donor countries, the United Nations and its agencies and other humanitarian organizations, national and international, that have rendered relief assistance to the Kampuchean people, and appeals to them to continue to provide emergency assistance to those Kampucheans who are still in need, especially along the Thai-Kampuchean border and in the various encampments in Thailand;

9. *Reiterates its deep appreciation* to the Secretary-General for his efforts in coordinating humanitarian relief assistance and in monitoring its distribution, and requests him to intensify such efforts as necessary;

10. *Urges* the States of South-East Asia, once a comprehensive political solution to the Kampuchean conflict is achieved, to exert renewed efforts to establish a zone of peace, freedom and neutrality in South-East Asia;

11. *Reiterates the hope* that, following a comprehensive political solution, an intergovernmental committee will be established to consider a programme of assistance to Kampuchea for the reconstruction of its economy and for the economic and social development of all States in the region;

12. *Requests* the Secretary-General to report to the General Assembly at its forty-fourth session on the implementation of the present resolution;

13. *Decides* to include in the provisional agenda of its forty-fourth session the item entitled "The situation in Kampuchea."

NOTE: Adopted by a vote of 122 (U.S.) to 19, with 13 abstentions.

THE ENDLESS WAR:
THE RETURN OF THE KHMER ROUGE[2]

At dusk, when all the Western relief workers have left for the day, blue Chinese-made trucks drive up to Site 8. Nudging the Thai-Cambodian border, Site 8 is run by the Khmer Rouge. Soldiers in green Chinese-made fatigues supervise the loading and unloading of the sullen cargo—men and women compelled under guard to carry Chinese ammunition, weapons and mines to Khmer Rouge forces fighting inside Cambodia.

Site 8 is a "civilian" camp for Cambodians displaced by a decade-long civil war and is monitored by the United Nations Border Relief Operation, other international aid agencies and units of the Thai Army. But within the camp, the Khmer Rouge does much as it pleases, recognizing no distinction between civilian and military. It has been waging a war against Vietnamese soldiers who have occupied Cambodia since 1979. Now that Hanoi

[2]Reprint of an article by Steven Erlanger, the Southeast Asia correspondent for the *New York Times. New York Times Magazine*, March 5, 1989, pp. 25, 27, 50, 51, 52. Copyright © 1989 by The New York Times Company. Reprinted by permission.

is gradually pulling out, the Khmer Rouge's main enemy has become the Phnom Penh Government installed by Hanoi.

The border region is malarial, the narrow paths through it strewn with plastic land mines, fragmentation grenades and claymores. In Site 8 alone, 1,500 of the 35,800 inhabitants are maimed. According to Son Song Hak, director of the camp's Khmer Handicap Association, 75 percent of the handicapped are "fighters." It is, he says, "a war of mines."

If those who live in Site 8 refuse to carry ammunition, their food rations are cut. They are summoned to sessions of political "re-education." Sometimes they are beaten, sometimes imprisoned. Sometimes they disappear. Few refuse to do what they are told. The Khmer Rouge—which turned Cambodia into a charnel house when it ruled from 1975 through 1978, and which is once more making a bid for power—has a reputation.

Today, at least 350,000 Cambodians live in holding camps of bamboo-and-thatch tract housing just inside Thailand, within the sound, the range and sometimes the reach of Vietnamese shells. The Thais and the United Nations have decided they are not refugees but people displaced by war, and thus ineligible to settle in any other country. Most have had no choice in selecting the camps in which they live. Of the 100,000 or so under Khmer Rouge control, the majority either took a wrong turn crossing the border or chose the wrong guide into Thailand. Others, who ended up in the camps run by the two other resistance factions, fare somewhat better.

The camps in Thailand for Cambodians displaced by a 10-year civil war are governed by three factions united against Vietnam, whose troops invaded Cambodia in late 1978, and against the Hanoi-backed Government in the Cambodian capital, Phnom Penh. Together, the factions form the United Nations–recognized Coalition Government of Democratic Kampuchea—the name for Cambodia in the Khmer language.

Prince Norodom Sihanouk, Cambodia's former god-king, leads Funcinpec (a French acronym for National United Front for an Independent, Neutral, Peaceful and Cooperative Cambodia), which is concentrated in Site B, a relatively well-run camp of about 60,000 people.

Son Sann, once Prime Minister under Sihanouk, is the nominal head of the hopelessly divided and corrupt Khmer People's National Liberation Front, whose various warlords control a sprawling collection of camps called Site 2 (with a total population of 179,000) as well as a smaller camp in the south of Thailand, Sok Sann (population: about 9,000).

The Communist Party of Kampuchea, which Sihanouk long ago labeled the Khmer Rouge, or Red Khmer, and which is led by Pol Pot, is the best-armed, best-trained and most disciplined group in the coalition. During its years in power, between 1975 and 1978, the Khmer Rouge transformed the country into a Maoist, highly xenophobic, peasant-dominated land. A fifth of the population of about seven million died from overwork, starvation, disease or execution. The Khmer Rouge camps are Site 8, Borai, Ta Luan and O'Trao. There are also an unknown number of secret military camps, such as V. 4. About 100,000 people live in these camps.

Ten years ago, the Khmer Rouge was on its knees. Weakened by ferocious internal purges and a wrecked economy, it fled from the Vietnamese invaders toward the Thai border. "One more considered push [by the Vietnamese] and the Khmer Rouge would have been finished," says an Asian diplomat. "Instead, they were resurrected."

For China, rivalry with the Soviet Union and long enmity with Vietnam made the humiliation of its ally, the Khmer Rouge, unacceptable—whatever its crimes. While the Soviets supported Vietnam, the Chinese revived the Khmer Rouge as the best way to harass Hanoi and Moscow. Thailand, always fearful of Vietnam's expansionist ambitions, facilitated Chinese aid to the Khmer Rouge, happy to take a cut and to have a buffer of Khmer Rouge soldiers and Cambodian civilians between itself and Vietnam. The United States, traumatized by its military defeat in Indochina and preferring improved relations with China over those with Vietnam, sided with the Chinese and thus, ironically, with the Khmer Rouge.

Chinese policy worked, helped by slackening Soviet aid to Vietnam as well as Hanoi's own economic ineptitude. Vietnam has decided to pull out of Cambodia, even though Hanoi continues to support its client, Hun Sen, Prime Minister of what is called the People's Republic of Kampuchea, the Khmer word for Cambodia. But Hanoi's decision has kindled fears that the Khmer Rouge will regain power once the Vietnamese leave.

In a series of peace talks among the warring factions—the most recent late last month in Jakarta, Indonesia—some progress has been made on a timetable for Vietnamese withdrawal and a parallel cessation of military aid to the resistance. But the Cambodian factions remain deeply divided over the nature of an interim administration that would oversee new elections.

Their quarrels are easy to understand. In the past 20 years, Cambodia has known betrayal, invasion and genocide. Even now, the tragedies result in twisted alliances. Pressured by the Chinese, Prince Norodom Sihanouk, Cambodia's former monarch, has forged an uneasy coalition of convenience with the Khmer People's National Liberation Front, made up largely of rightists who overthrew him in 1970, and with the Khmer Rouge, which he detests but whose military strength he needs in fighting the Vietnamese and their ally in Phnom Penh.

But even if, in a future settlement, the Chinese cut off aid to the Khmer Rouge and the Thais shut down the border camps that have protected and nurtured it, the Khmer Rouge will remain a formidable force. American intelligence estimates of Khmer Rouge strength vary from 28,000 to nearly 60,000, with the usual interagency compromise cited officially by diplomats as "30,000 to 40,000."

"The fact is, nobody really knows," says a senior American diplomat. "I tend to err on the high side, because it would be imprudent not to do so." Part of what is unclear is the size of the core, he says, the committed party members and fighters. But there the little question that in terms of men and matériel, the Khmer Rouge forces dwarf those of Sihanouk and Son Sann. Some 16,000 soldiers are loyal to the Prince, and 11,000, to Son Sann's Khmer People's National Liberation Front.

The Americans also believe the Khmer Rouge has stored up to two years' worth of arms and ammunition. And few expect aid to the Khmer Rouge to be cut off entirely. The Khmer Rouge is China's only insurance in Cambodia, and it would cost Beijing little to maintain a covert channel for resupply. Nor are the Thais eager to have a suddenly desperate Khmer Rouge raiding Thai villages for money, guns and rice.

Wedged against the foot of the mountains that stretch from Thailand into Cambodia, Site 8—the only Khmer Rouge camp open to the press—is a stage set of devastating cynicism. When it ruled Cambodia, the Khmer Rouge forced everyone to wear black; here, the clothes are vermilion, fuschia, bright green, gold. Religion was banned and many monks executed by the Khmer Rouge; here, a pagoda flourishes. Money and private property were abolished; here, a market does a brisk business in Thai and Chinese goods. Schooling was forbidden and teachers eviscerated; here, near the Site 8 Teacher Training Center, which opened in 1986, is an Orwellian sign: "Education Is Growth."

Arguing that the government-in-exile is legitimate, the Thais have not applied their own laws within the camps, leaving justice to be meted out by Cambodians running them. In Site 8, the Thais are training some Cambodians to function as an internal police force. The training includes weapons handling and lectures on the intricacies of the rocket launcher. Asked why, the Thais say that the camp has been attacked in the past by bandits with grenade launchers.

Seng Sok, who holds the title of administrator at Site 8, will say nothing of his life under the Khmer Rouge leader Pol Pot. "It's not important," he says. He provides the standard, soothing Khmer Rouge line: Communism has been "spoiled," he says. "Everyone is a capitalist now." He wears the marks of a Khmer Rouge of rank: a row of pens in the pocket of his military-style shirt, and on his wrist, a chunky, steel-banded watch.

Asked if Ta (Grandfather) Mok—the most ruthless of the Khmer Rouge commanders—considers himself a capitalist, Seng Sok says, "If we remain Communist, how could we unite with other forces?" Then he laughs.

Everything, he insists, has changed. Khmer Rouge, he says, "is not our name"; the Communist Party abolished itself in 1981; Pol Pot "retired" in 1985. He laughs again. There is just Democratic Kampuchea now, he says, the coalition government recognized by the United Nations.

Doesn't the Khmer Rouge intend to take power again? After Vietnamese troops withdraw, he says, "We should have elections to choose who will be President." He himself would vote for Sihanouk, with Son Sann as Prime Minister.

"Seng Sok is a stupid man," says a Western relief official. "The camp is controlled by other people. It is as with everything in the Khmer Rouge: everything is hidden. You never meet the people in charge."

The other three Khmer Rouge camps in Thailand open to the United Nations and other international agencies—Borai, Ta Luan and O'Trao—are off-limits to journalists. Even the international agencies, which are responsible for feeding and protecting the rights of the inhabitants, have limited access. Few in these camps, according to those who have escaped, have any idea that anyone other than the Khmer Rouge feeds them.

A relief worker describes the three camps as "resistance outposts in the woods." The women have the same short haircuts and wear black or blue; the men are in uniform. The isolation of these people is maintained through disinformation, propaganda sessions, fear and retribution. Food and medical care are not given; they must be earned. Contact with Westerners—even for medical attention—is discouraged. Last Christmas, unhappy with the large number of people in O'Trao seeking Western medical care, the Khmer Rouge torched the camp's only hospital.

For the Khmer Rouge, secrecy is not only a virtue, but an obsession. After taking power in 1975, the Khmer Rouge hid behind the name Angka, meaning organization, and said that Sihanouk, actually under house arrest, was running the country. It was two years before Angka was officially revealed to be the Khmer Rouge; it was a year before a "new" government was announced, with Pol Pot as Prime Minister. He was sometimes called "Brother No. 1," and he occasionally referred to himself by his code name "No. 870." Since the Vietnamese occupation, he has been signing his messages "No. 87." He has never acknowledged that his given name is Saloth Sar.

The Khmer Rouge's predilection for secrecy is most evident in its military camps, just inside Thailand, where perhaps as many as 50,000 live. No outsider has access to these camps, and even the Thai Army—a conduit for Chinese arms to the Khmer Rouge—rarely ventures there.

This is "the hidden border." Here, by all accounts, the Khmer Rouge has hardly changed at all.

Sam Vuth, a veteran of the hidden border, is nervous. It is his wedding day. The Handicap Association Band is playing, the guests moving to the rock music in a traditional Cambodian dance. Sam Vuth has on a shirt and tie, but he also wears the customary lipstick and makeup of a Cambodian bridegroom, which are creased by the sweat from his malaria. When he must lift his

17-year-old bride to the ceiling to retrieve their wedding gifts—money in airmail envelopes tied by a ribbon above each table of guests—he can barely do it.

Last fall, Sam Vuth defected and went to a non-Communist camp, Site 2. Since the Khmer Rouge kills its defectors, Sam Vuth has all the skittishness of a hunted man.

He had been a Khmer Rouge soldier since 1973, when he was 16; in 1984, he became a battalion commander in charge of 80 to 100 soldiers fighting the Vietnamese. Like Seng Sok, he will not describe his activities while the Khmer Rouge was in power. Nor will he describe why he chose to defect. He simply says he was tired of fighting.

Sam Vuth has been debriefed by Thai, American and United Nations officials, and his account of life along the hidden border is confirmed by other Cambodians who have spent time in those camps. Until last September, he lived in a camp called V.4, in Thailand's Trat Province, near the border of Cambodia's Koh Kong Province.

According to Sam Vuth, Pol Pot lived a half-hour away by truck, just inside the Thai border, with his second wife, whom he married in 1986, and their young daughter. (Pol Pot's first wife, who suffers from mental illness, is believed to be living in Beijing.) Nuon Chea, Pol Pot's loyal deputy and No. 2 in the hierarchy, lived nearby. Ieng Sary, the Foreign Minister of Pol Pot's Government, and Khieu Samphan, the official head of the Khmer Rouge, would come at least once a month for consultations, sometimes more. Son Sen, the commander in chief, and regional commanders like Ta Mok would come at least once a year.

V.4 held about 4,000 people. It was a place where battalion and other senior commanders went to study and rest. Pol Pot would lecture about tactics and strategy. "The commanders obey him and regard him as the leader," Sam Vuth says.

In a lecture in early September, at which Sam Vuth was present, Pol Pot told his battalion commanders to prepare to occupy half of Cambodia's Battambang Province once Vietnamese troops pulled out, and then to move in civilians behind them. It was important, he said, to show the world that it was the Khmer Rouge who had fought hardest against the Vietnamese, so its interests could not be ignored.

In the months since, the Khmer Rouge has moved thousands of civilians out of camps, especially from Ta Luan in the south and O'Trao in the northeast, to so-called "repatriation villages" closer to the border, where no outsider has any access. With heavy shelling along the border, causing hundreds of casualties, the Vietnamese have thus far repulsed efforts to occupy signifi- cant areas inside Cambodia. But Vietnamese troops are leaving, and the soldiers of their ally in Phnom Penh are only modestly equipped and largely untested.

Sam Vuth sees "no good future" for Cambodia. Of course, the Khmer Rouge intends to take sole power again in Cambodia— the very question seems to puzzle him.

Has the Khmer Rouge changes? "A little bit," he says. It has become more practical. There is less emphasis on Pol Pot's brand of Communism and more on driving out "the contemptible Vietnamese." Fewer violations of discipline are regarded as capi- tal offenses. Deserters are executed, but low-ranking soldiers who botch up tend to get a "re-education"—the euphemism for beat- ings, torture and prison.

Other Cambodians and international agency officials who regularly interview refugees fill out the picture of the secret camps. There is a command elite of party members who have ac- cess to the best of everything. For the others, food and medicine are rationed. Marriage is discouraged until men are 40 and wom- en 30, when their best fighting days are done. Able-bodied sol- diers who distinguish themselves are allowed to marry, especially to women who have distinguished themselves equally, either in combat or in the "women's transportation units," which haul am- munition and mines deep inside Cambodia. Girls as young as 12 are required to be porters—if they look old enough, they are.

There is, as well, a subclass, treated as subhuman, virtually as instruments or logistics. They include anyone without a party or military role, and they are kept isolated and illiterate. Some, like Oll Sophal, were Cambodians living in their own country who were captured as they wandered into ruby-mining areas that are controlled by the Khmer Rouge. These unfortunates are kept captive for years in secret camps, like one near V.4 called O'Lahong; usually after a year's captivity, they are trusted enough to carry ammunition.

"The Khmer Rouge killed my parents," says Oll Sophal. He was held in the O'Lahong camp for nearly two years, and had to carry ammunition and listen to political lectures before escaping to Thailand. He now lives in Site 2. "When the Vietnamese came, the Khmer Rouge escaped to the border. That's where they are today. The Khmer Rouge are the same people who killed my parents."

David P. Chandler, an American historian at Australia's Monash University who specializes in Cambodian history, likens the closed circle of loyalists and devotees around Pol Pot to the Baader-Meinhof gang, with its quasi-religious ethos of self-criticism and confession. "They regret nothing," Chandler says.

Their "disbanding" of the party in 1981 was simply a return to the secrecy they prefer, he says. The structures of the party remain in place. "The comical, ironical point is that the central committee claimed to abolish the party and turned out the lights. It's absurd. It was a completely pragmatic and crass gesture to help their image. Now they can call themselves the Coalition Government of Democratic Kampuchea, with a flag at the United Nations."

In a lengthy internal document dated Dec. 2, 1986, stolen by a defector and translated last year, the Khmer Rouge leadership provides guidelines to political officers on how to read its current circumstances and its temporary alliance with Sihanouk and Son Sann.

The paper is considered genuine, says a senior Western diplomat, pointing to its insularity, race consciousness and tortured syntax.

The paper describes "the 30-year struggle" this way:

"From non-existence of force to existence of force. From small to large force. From no state control to full state control. From struggle by political shadow to political struggle, to armed struggle, to five-year war, to control of the whole country and the establishment of socialism in Cambodia. And at the present time, we engage in a guerrilla war, fighting the contemptible Vietnamese enemy aggressors to defend our nation, protect our people and our Cambodian race so that it will last forever.

"In these struggles which follow one another, we use secret form, open act, half-open act, unlawful act, lawful act and half-lawful act; we fight and build forces in remote areas and cities according to the political slogan, 'National Democracy and Economy.' We use 'Economy' as a means to incite and mobilize people in the remote areas, 'Democracy' to mobilize people in the middle level such as students and intellectuals, and 'Nation' to mobilize front forces in the upper level."

The paper acknowledges past "excesses," "errors" and "faults," but ascribes them to the manipulations of Vietnamese agents, the inexperience with power of the "base people" (the ascendant Cambodian peasantry) and the limited period of the Khmer Rouge rule: "Three years was too short a time."

But "we have learned our lessons." In any event, these errors were grounded in "a spirit of patriotism and nationalism," and are minor compared with those of the Soviet Union, China, Vietnam and other Socialist countries.

"America, England, France, Australia, what are they?" the document asks. "Their true identities originally were land-swallowers, race killers, mega-colonialists."

The party history concludes with this claim: "Comparing those examples that truly exist in world history, we see that the true character and value of Democratic Kampuchea is far higher. Democratic Kampuchea has never violated or abused anybody."

At last month's conference in Jakarta, Khmer Rouge officials went out of their way to put on an affable face. The polished delegates sought out the press to describe their group as transformed, agreeable to power-sharing and willing even to ban notorious figures like Pol Pot and Ta Mok from any political involvement.

"Khmer Rouge tactics have shifted," says a Western diplomat, "but certainly not their goals. Anyone who believes they would be content to share power is living in cloud-cuckoo-land."

The continuing threat from the Khmer Rouge coincides with an improvement, albeit modest, within Cambodia. Prime Minister Hun Sen has attempted with some success to consolidate his support and distance himself from his former colleagues, the Khmer Rouge, and his patrons, the Vietnamese.

War weary and skeptical of anyone with two such hated affiliations, Cambodians are nevertheless responding favorably to his efforts, especially in the last two years, to moderate his brand of socialism. Land is being returned to individual farmers; private restaurants and shops have been allowed to open and flourish; pagodas have been reconstructed. Hun Sen has lately taken to traveling around the country, shaking hands like a politician, even bowing to monks and apologizing for "mistakes regarding religion."

Only 37 years old, Hun Sen has been transformed in the last 10 years from the shy, awkward Khmer Rouge commander who fled Pol Pot's purges of 1977–78 into a leader the Vietnamese believe stands a good chance of keeping his seat. Although Sihanouk calls him "a valet" of the Vietnamese, Hun Sen believes his Government has earned legitimacy through its efforts to rebuild the nation and defend it from the Khmer Rouge.

With the sometimes overbearing help of Vietnamese advisers (most of whom have returned to Hanoi) and Soviet advisers, the Hun Sen Government has made progress in recovering from the depredations of what is generally called "the Pol Pot time." Phnom Penh and other cities, once emptied and left to decay, have an undeniable life, their markets stocked with an extraordinary array of imported goods, most of them smuggled from Singapore and Thailand.

But if a bottle of French champagne is available for less than $5 in Phnom Penh, the water supply is intermittent and unsafe, the sewage-treatment plant is in disrepair. The new paint applied for the regime's 10th anniversary in January does little to disguise the poverty in the cities or the insecurity in the countryside, where few travel the roads much after noon, and never after dark.

The official line in Phnom Penh is that the Khmer Rouge is not only containable, but on the run. Hun Sen's army has 44,000 men in six divisions, and a militia of about another 100,000 men. But even after 10 years of occupation, the Vietnamese have not pacified the country. Western military experts believe that, at any given time, the Khmer Rouge has as many as 20,000 fighters inside Cambodia, harassing villages, killing village chiefs.

Shunned by much of the world, Hun Sen contends that if anyone can hold off the Khmer Rouge it is he and his army, and that if Sihanouk and Son Sann had any sense, they would make common cause with him. Instead of pretending that the Chinese formula of a four-party government and army—made up of his forces and those of the three guerrilla factions—can somehow coopt the Khmer Rouge, says Hun Sen, leave the Khmer Rouge in the forest and unite against it.

Internationally, Hun Sen's credibility appears to be growing. Breaking with its own decade-long foreign policy, Thailand hosted Hun Sen for three days in January, bolstering his reputation considerably and infuriating Sihanouk, who sees Hun Sen as a traitor.

"It is coming to the point, I'm afraid, that Sihanouk had better cut his best deal and go home," says one Asian diplomat. "And it's time that the West starts to tell him so." With the Prince as head of state, Hun Sen administering the country, a significant commitment of Western development aid and a sizable international peacekeeping force, he argues, the Khmer Rouge just might be contained over time. "Their morale is bound to suffer. With the Vietnamese gone, some of them aren't going to keep up the fight."

It is not impossible, says another diplomat, that the Khmer Rouge could be reduced to what it was before 1970: a dangerous group isolated in the forest that poses no real threat to central authority. "It is just possible," he continues, "but it would require the expenditure of great treasure and blood by those willing to do it."

And who would that be? "That's just it," he says. "You've got to be willing to fight. That's the big question with the non-Communist resistance, and with Hun Sen's army, too. The Khmer Rouge will fight."

The Khmer Rouge has significant vulnerabilities, he says. If the camps in Thailand are closed, the Khmer Rouge will be denied its prime source of sanctuary and supplies. If there is an international peacekeeping force in Cambodia, some of the young people who joined the Khmer Rouge after 1979 are bound to defect. With the Vietnamese gone, Cambodians like Sam Vuth, who have fought since they were teen-agers, might tire of the endless war. Not the least of the Khmer Rouge's weaknesses, of course, is the hatred in which it is held.

Nonetheless, says a former diplomat and an authority on the Khmer Rouge, it is a mistake to think the guerrillas have no political, nationalist or class support in the countryside. Under Pol Pot, the urban bourgeoisie suffered more than the peasantry. The Khmer Rouge has regenerated itself with new recruits, and not merely from intimidation. "They are, after all," says the former diplomat, "the only Cambodians really fighting the Vietnamese."

A Western diplomat points out that American policy has recently undergone a shift toward more realism. "The Vietnamese out and the Khmer Rouge out of power is the new bottom line," he says. "And if it means a solution more on Hun Sen's terms than Sihanouk or Washington would like, at least there's a fair chance of pulling it off."

Son Song Hak, director of the Khmer Handicap Association of Site 8, lost his leg above the knee in October 1980, from a land mine. "I was a soldier then," he says. "I became a soldier in 1979, when the Vietnamese aggressor came to my country. The only person who led us to fight against the Vietnamese was Pol Pot."

Son Song Hak is 31 years old and behaves like a trusted party member; he has the easy confidence of an articulate man. He says he taught himself English by listening to the Voice of America and the BBC. Before 1979, he "drove a tractor on a collective farm" in Battambang Province.

What went wrong? "If something crumbled between 1975 and 1978," he says smoothly, "we can fault both Pol Pot and the Vietnamese, who started their aggression long ago. Pol Pot made revolution because he wanted to do something good for the country. Perhaps he was confused about the nature of Communism."

The party has reformed, he says. Things are much improved—just look around. "You couldn't see children at school then," he says. "You couldn't see handicapped at school. You couldn't see people walking and smiling. You couldn't see people wearing different colored clothing—now people can wear what they want."

It is time for Cambodians to settle their differences and unite. Words are a problem. "Sometimes even close friends don't talk clearly to one another. Words sometimes make people understand each other very well, and sometimes words make people quarrel."

And sometimes people don't mean what they say?

Son Song Hak smiles broadly. "Yes," he says. "Even I, sometimes."

V. MALAYSIA

EDITOR'S INTRODUCTION

Since confederation in 1963, the multiracial society of Malaysia has suffered intermittent ethnic conflict, culminating in major riots in 1969 that took 200 lives. More recently, political deals have been struck that maintain ethnic balance and defuse tensions. In the first article in this section, "Malaysia's Premier Jails 'Hotheads' to Buy Time," reprinted from *U.S. News & World Report*, Walter A. Taylor, correspondent in Kuala Lumpur, describes the threat of resurgent conflict over shrinking wealth in a time of economic downturn. In response, Prime Minister Mahathir Mohamad used internal-security laws to jail activists of all stripes he considered to be disruptive of his "extreme brand of affirmative action for the majority" government, in which Malay economic and cultural ascendancy is maintained in the face of superior Chinese and Indian economic prowess in exchange for preservation of certain minority rights and an enforced peace. The next article, "The Politics of Ethnicity in Malaysia," written by Gordon P. Means, a professor of political science at McMaster University in Canada and reprinted from *Current History*, details the mechanics of this majority-entitlements policy, the NEP (New Economic Policy), initiated in 1971, as well as various aspects of Malaysian politics and foreign relations. The third article, "Asia's Regional Hopes," reprinted from *World Press Review*, consists of an interview, written in a question-and-answer format, with Munir Majid, group editor-in-chief of *New Straits Times* of Kuala Lumpur. Majid regards his government as strong, even though the economy is bad; mentions Malaysia's residual British ties; describes "development journalism" and government censorship; and asserts that his greatest worry is over potential superpower conflict. Finally, in "Developments in Malaysia," reprinted from the *Department of State Bulletin*, David F. Lambertson, Deputy Assistant Secretary for East Asian and Pacific Affairs, analyzes recent developments in Malaysia and discusses resulting U.S. government concerns.

MALAYSIA'S PREMIER JAILS "HOTHEADS" TO BUY TIME[1]

For three decades, while ethnic conflicts festered and frequently exploded in much of South and Southeast Asia, one nation with its own sharp ethnic divisions—Malaysia—somehow managed to keep the lid on communal tensions and to prosper. Now, the unhappy collision of an economic downturn, Islamic fundamentalism and a hard-line Malay nationalist Prime Minister threatens to shatter Malaysia's uneasy peace.

Declaring that he was acting "to save the country from disastrous riots" late last month, Prime Minister Mahathir Mohamad invoked harsh internal-security laws to jail nearly 100 prominent political and social activists, shut down three outspoken newspapers and ban all political gatherings. The police roundup cut cleanly across partisan and ethnic lines. Swept into indefinite detention without trial were Malays, Chinese and Indians, opposition politicians as well as members of Mahathir's own ruling Malay-Chinese coalition.

Civil libertarians, opposition groups and even the leading government-controlled paper denounced the Prime Minister's actions. The father of modern Malaysia, former Prime Minister Tunku Abdul Rahman, charged that Mahathir had put the nation "on the road to dictatorship" and added pointedly: "This is not the way we agreed and promised to form this country as a democracy." Still, some welcomed the arrests as averting a repeat of a racial outburst that took 200 lives in 1969. One Western diplomat declared, "The situation was out of hand and heading fast to flash point; the only way out was to get the hotheads off the street for a while."

Call to Arms

The crackdown, the most sweeping since the crushing of a Communist insurgency in the early 1960s, was timed to head off

[1]Reprint of a magazine article by Walter A. Taylor, correspondent in Kuala Lumpur. *U.S. News & World Report*, November 16, 1987. Reprinted by permission. Copyright © November 16, 1987, *U.S. News & World Report*.

a huge public meeting organized by the Prime Minister's own party, the United Malays National Organization. At an UMNO youth rally last month, speakers called for "extermination" of Malaysia's economically dominant Chinese minority.

Since the 1969 riots, there has been a gentlemen's agreement whereby the Malays run the government and protect the cultural diversity, if not the equal rights, of the Chinese and Indian minorities. Moslem Malays total barely half of the country's 16 million people, ethnic Chinese 33 percent and ethnic Indians about 10 percent. Both are descendants of immigrant laborers brought in by the British colonial masters to work on rubber plantations.

In six years in office, Mahathir has been much more vigorous than his predecessors in promoting preferential treatment for ethnic Malays. His Malay-first drive has been reinforced by pressures from a growing Islamic-fundamentalist movement. Minorities are excluded from many government jobs and economic programs designed to give the mostly rural, easygoing Malays a 30 percent slice of the country's economic wealth by 1990. Today, that share is 18 percent compared with 66 percent for the Chinese and Indians.

The theory was that Malays could claim the fruits of economic growth without taking anything away from their hard-working neighbors. So long as Malaysia's economy was booming, as it did for a decade, minority worries over discrimination were mostly masked. But collapsing prices for Malaysia's main exports of rubber, tin and copra put an end to the boom two years ago, and early this year, former Deputy Prime Minister Musa Hitam warned that the "shrinking economic cake" could reawaken old animosities.

Shrugging aside such warnings, the government pushed its extreme brand of affirmative action for the majority into sensitive areas, announcing plans to dub all programs on government television in Malay and suggesting that the basic education laws, which protect minority-language schools, be revised. Chinese anger welled up when the government attempted to put non-Chinese-speaking administrators in charge of schools that teach the Chinese, in Chinese.

One final ingredient in the bubbling stew: The weakened position of Mahathir himself. Often described as stiff, cold and arrogant, the 61-year-old country doctor barely survived a leadership struggle earlier this year—winning a new term as UMNO leader

and, thus, as Prime Minister, by a margin of only 43 votes out of
1,500 amid charges of economic mismanagement and rampant
corruption. His victory was Pyrrhic, splitting UMNO and the coalition. "With Mahathir wounded, every politician is out to try to
enhance his own future," says one of Mahathir's supporters.
Prime Minister Mahathir was taking a well-worn route to the
same end when he clapped his opponents and rivals in jail.

THE POLITICS OF ETHNICITY IN MALAYSIA[2]

During 1986, Prime Minister Datuk Seri Dr. Mahathir Mohamad entered his sixth year in office. Although he renewed his
mandate with a decisive victory at the polls, Mahathir faces a faltering economy, a vocal opposition, and intensified ethnic conflict. The New Economic Policy (NEP), which was initiated in
1971, established an elaborate system of Malay and other
Bumiputra [Bumiputra are the ethnic Malays and non-Malayan
indigenous groups who make up a majority (54 percent) of Malaysia's population.] privileges and quotas in education, jobs and
other economic benefits designed to raise the wealth and occupa-
tional status of the Bumiputra to assure 30 percent Malay ownership and participation in all industrial and commercial activities
by 1990. Although this target is within reach in many sectors, the
issue of the continuation or expansion of Malay ethnic privileges
is extremely contentious. The economy is not expanding, yet the
political demands of ethnically mobilized constituencies are in-
tensifying in anticipation of a major policy review. The crisis in
ethnic relations will come when the NEP policies are reviewed
and new policies are devised for the post-1990 period. In these
circumstances, the Mahathir regime has been resorting to coercive measures to stifle criticism and intimidate opponents. Increasingly, the processes of public policy making and evaluation
have been centralized and cloaked in secrecy.

[2]Reprint of an article by Gordon P. Means, a professor of political science at
McMaster University, Hamilton, Ontario. Reprinted with permission from *Current
History*, April 1987. Copyright © *Current History* 1987.

For three decades, Malaysia has experienced dramatic economic growth, with an average increase in per capita gross national product (GNP) of 6.5 percent between 1960 and 1970 and 7.9 percent between 1970 and 1978. This economic vitality has been led by petroleum and liquid natural gas exports, which together accounted for 29.6 percent of exports in 1985 and provide approximately 26 percent of all government revenues. Over the past decade, palm oil has expanded to 10.4 percent of exports, surpassing Malaysia's traditional export commodities of rubber (7.5 percent) and tin (4.2 percent). Malaysia's New Economic Policy was funded in large part by the revenues from foreign oil sales.

The expanding economy provided the resources to cushion the ethnic conflicts and grievances that have plagued the country since its independence. These favorable circumstances began to change in 1984, when Malaysia felt the impact of the world economic recession. Oil prices dropped from US$34 per barrel in 1982 to $15 per barrel in 1986. The tin market also collapsed in 1984 when the International Tin Agreement (ITA) failed to sustain minimum prices. The price of tin fell from M$30.15 per tonne in October, 1983, to a low of M$14.12 per tonne in October, 1986. The drop in price has resulted in the closure of over half of Malaysia's tin mines. Similarly, rubber prices fell from M$2.60 per kilogram (kg) in 1984 to below M$1.80/kg in 1986; the International Rubber Agreement failed to protect a minimum price for that commodity. A similar fate befell palm oil, which had a price of M$1,600 per tonne in April, 1984, but fell to less than M$650 per tonne by November, 1985. The government learned the hard way that commodity cartels provide little protection in the event of depressed world markets.

The drastic losses in foreign exchange resulted in a decline in real economic growth of 8.1 percent for 1986 and a drop in per capita GNP from M$4,937 in 1984 to M$4,327 in 1986. The lower earnings led to a rapid rise in external debt to over M$50 billion and to severe debt repayment problems. In 1985, the public debt increased to M$62.4 billion or about 86 percent of the nation's GNP. In these circumstances, the government has had to devise policies to cut government expenditures, to attract greater foreign investment, and at the same time to manage escalating ethnic demands with fewer resources and benefits to distribute.

The cornerstone of government policy has been the New Economic Policy (NEP). Although it has been the basis for most economic and social policy since 1971, it has come under increasing scrutiny and criticism. Under its policy of Malay ethnic preferences, the system was expanded from the public services and education to private commercial and industrial enterprises. Government-funded quasi-public corporations were created as "trust agencies" that were designed to increase Malay participation in business and Malay ownership of share capital. However, too many of these Bumiputra trust agencies were inefficient and operated at a loss. Bumiputra financial institutions made too many unsecured loans with high default rates, and some became the victims of blatant corruption and fraud. The largest losses were incurred by Bumiputra Malaysia Finance (BMF), a subsidiary of Bank Bumiputra. BMF had invested heavily in Hong Kong property and lost US$960 million in bad loans and fraudulent operations. To cover the losses, Bank Bumiputra was taken over by Petronas, the government-owned oil corporation. Many other enterprises encountered serious difficulties during the economic recession, leading to new credit controls.

As foreign investments dwindled, the government responded to the criticism of investors and United Nations consultants concerning the economic costs of the NEP. Finally, Mahathir stated that the NEP "will be held in abeyance, more or less, except in areas where there is growth." This policy shift, while viewed as temporary, was deemed necessary in order to attract foreign investment and to allow "market forces" to operate.

The "Look East" policy, which had been enunciated by Mahathir in 1982 as a means to increase Japanese and Korean investment, technology transfer and the work ethic, had resulted in rising investment but little in the way of high-technology transfers. Nor had the policy made much change in the Malaysian work ethic. As its prestige project, Mahathir's policy focused on the manufacture of the Proton Saga, the Malaysian-made automobile. The first vehicle was completed in September, 1985, and by mid-1986 arrangements had been made for sales in five Asian countries. The car was manufactured by the government's Heavy Industries Corporation, in a joint venture with Japan's Mitsubishi. To support a mass consumption market, Mahathir announced that Malaysians should raise the country's annual population growth rate from its present 2.3 percent to 3.2 percent so that the population would increase from 15.7 million to 70 million by 2100. The proposal to increase birthrates appeared to be directed to the Malays, who already have higher birthrates than non-Malays.

Mahathir's much publicized "privatization policy" proposed to sell many government agencies and corporate bodies to the private sector. After the public sale of stock in the Malaysian Airlines System (MAS), that policy seemed to have been put on hold. The sale of shares in MAS left its management and control in the hands of government-appointed managers, so the enthusiasm of domestic investors has waned.

Islam

Tight government control is maintained over Islamic institutions, Muslim law and the definition of orthodox Islamic doctrine. The government wants to proscribe deviant Islamic sects and doctrines, which have been challenged by militant fundamentalists and by liberal "modern secularists." Increasingly, government policies are cloaked in an Islamic idiom. Malay leaders invoke Islam to justify public policy and to exhort the public on issues of morality and behavior. Official policy aims to "infuse Islamic values" into society, explaining "Islamic values" to non-Muslims for emulation, and enforcing these values more strictly in law and policy for Muslims. The incorporation of Islam into more aspects of public policy has meant that greater efforts have been placed on the suppression of various Islamic "deviations."

Issues of human rights have generated increasing domestic controversy and foreign criticism. Under the Internal Security Act (ISA) and the Essential (Security Cases) Regulations (ESCAR), the government has wide powers of summary arrest; many offenses are tried by a judge without a jury, and conviction leads to the mandatory death penalty. Previously, most of such convictions had to do with possession of arms or seditious activities. However, in 1984 the Dangerous Drugs Act provided a mandatory death sentence for drug traffickers. By 1986, 72 drug dealers had been hanged; 200 more are on death row. Two Australians who attempted to smuggle drugs out of the country were hanged after appeals for clemency from a number of foreign governments were rejected.

Foreign Relations

Because 1986 was an election year, much of the government's energy was devoted to domestic issues. However, Mahathir did visit China at the end of 1985, attempting to normalize relations and increase trade while also raising the difficult issue of China's sympathies for the outlawed Malayan Communist party. Earlier, at the Commonwealth meetings, Mahathir had taken a strong stand for economic sanctions against South Africa and had proposed the internationalization of the Antarctic. When the Commonwealth Games were held in Britain, Malaysia led a boycott as a protest against Britain's mild sanctions policy.

Two issues of border security have arisen, with the Philippines and with Thailand. Over the years, about 250,000 Muslims arrived in Sabah from the Philippines and Indonesia, most of them illegal immigrants. In October, 1985, there were some Filipino "pirate raids" in Sabah, and Malaysian troops chased the attackers back to Philippine territory. Near Thai boundary waters, the Malaysian navy arrested many Thai fishing boats for fishing in Malaysian waters. To avoid further conflict, agreements regarding piracy and territorial waters were finally reached between the governments involved.

The 1986 Elections

Despite its problems, the Mahathir administration began preparations for a general election one year before its mandate expired in April, 1987.

Since Malayan independence in 1957, the dominant party in the ruling Barisan Nasional (BN) coalition has been the United Malay National Organization (UMNO). At the party's annual general assembly in September, 1985, Prime Minister Mahathir received the unanimous support of the delegates. Mahathir stressed the main theme of UMNO unity and a dedication to "the Malay struggle." Indirect warnings about involvement in politics by the Malay rulers hinted that the 1983 constitutional crisis over the role of the monarchy might still be simmering. Rumors of a rift between Mahathir and Deputy Prime Minister Musa Hitam were denied by both men. Yet five months later Musa Hitam suddenly resigned. Musa said he resigned because Mahathir had questioned his loyalty. He explained that he was tired of "money politics" and the abuse of power in UMNO. This may have been an oblique way of objecting to the growing influence of "money brokers" and the web of political patronage that was centralized in Mahathir's hands. Originally elected by a free vote of UMNO, Musa Hitam was viewed as having some independence from Mahathir. He had objected to the centralization of policy around a small kitchen cabinet composed of Finance Minister Daim Zainuddin, Agriculture Minister Anwar Ibrahim and Minister of National and Rural Development Sanusi Junid. Although press reports speculated that Musa Hitam might challenge Mahathir's leadership, he kept a low political profile. Mahathir appointed UMNO vice president Ghaffar Baba as the new Deputy Prime Minister and moved his protégé, Anwar Ibrahim, from the Agriculture to the Education ministry. Thus Mahathir further consolidated power in the hands of those who were dependent on him for political support.

In the Barisan Nasional, the political instability within the Malaysian Chinese Association (MCA) is a recurring problem. For several years, the MCA was split between two factions, one led by Neo Yee Pan and the other by Tan Koon Swan. The controversy involved political representation in the Cabinet and the BN councils and control of a large portfolio of investments operated by Multi-Purpose Holdings (MPH), a holding company that had been formed by Tan Koon Swan to channel the savings of MCA members into growth sectors of the economy and to increase the political-economic leverage of the Chinese in public affairs. The prolonged and bitter struggle involved complicated court litigation over "padded" membership lists and the expulsion of Tan Koon Swan and his supporters from the MCA. During the struggle, UMNO leaders had threatened the MCA with expulsion from the Barisan Nasional government, and both Musa Hitam and Mahathir made unsuccessful attempts to resolve the dispute. Finally, at the MCA general assembly in November, 1985, Tan Koon Swan and his faction were able to wrest control of the MCA from Neo's faction by a vote of 2,715 to 809.

Tan Koon Swan's decisive victory at the MCA general assembly appeared to stabilize the MCA as a viable partner in the BN coalition. However, it was not long before another controversy erupted over his involvement in shady and speculative stock market maneuvers as the managing director of MPH, which in turn controlled a network of allied companies in most sectors of the economy. With large numbers of Chinese in MCA holding MPH shares, any mismanagement or major losses would reflect on Tan Koon Swan's political leadership. Within a week of his elections as MCA president, the Pan-Electric Company collapsed, unable to repay S$75 million in credit (Tan Koon Swan held a controlling stake). Pan-Electric's stock was suspended and both the Singapore and Kuala Lumpur stock exchanges were closed for four days to prevent a domino effect of bankruptcies and to enable the government of Singapore to intervene to organize a rescue package. Apparently, too many investors had engaged in reckless "forward dealings." While in Singapore to deal with the Pan-Electric collapse, Tan Koon Swan was arrested and charged with criminal breach of trust. He pleaded guilty and was sentenced to two years' imprisonment and a fine of S$500,000. As a result of his sentence, he resigned from the MCA, and the office of MCA president was assumed by deputy president Lim Liong Sik, who was minister of transport in the post-1986 election BN government. The storm surrounding Tan Koon Swan's business dealings certainly weakened the party during the 1986 campaign.

Gerakan Rakyat Malaysia (GRM), a member of the Barisan Nasional coalition, claimed to be a noncommunal party, but it contested the claim of the MCA to be the primary spokesman for Chinese interests in the Barisan Nasional coalition. The GRM, which held five seats in Parliament, has its political base in Penang, with its large Chinese constituency. In 1985, the GRM and the MCA held talks that explored the possibility of a merger between the two BN partners, but the extended leadership crisis in the MCA and old rivalries prevented it. As the 1986 elections approached, each party agreed to defend its traditional constituencies, which depended primarily on Chinese voters.

The Malayan Indian Congress (MIC) represents the Indian ethnic component of Malaysia's population in the Barisan Nasional. The MIC has chafed at being so junior a partner as to be almost ignored. In a pattern similar to that of MCA's Multi-Purpose Holdings, the MIC formed Maika Holdings to promote Indian investment and to strengthen the economic power of the Indian community. MIC president Samy Vellu publicly criticized the New Economic Policy for not giving the Indians their fair share; this criticism violated the unwritten rule of the Barisan Nasional that member parties do not criticize the government publicly. Thereafter, Samy Vellu promised to "present the case in a more acceptable forum," meaning through Cabinet channels.

The Opposition

Parti Islam Se Malaysia (PAS, formerly the Pan-Malayan Islamic party) was viewed by the government as its most dangerous opposition, primarily because both PAS and UMNO competed for the Malay vote and resorted to similar religious and ethnic appeals. PAS had a dedicated following in areas where Malay majorities were overwhelming, particularly in the eastern and northern Malay states of Kelantan, Trengganu, Kedah and Perlis. After years of PAS-UMNO contests for power in these states, PAS was admitted as a member of the BN coalition in the years between 1972 and 1977, but withdrew from the BN when PAS leader Datuk Asri bin Haji Muda was overthrown by a more militant faction led by Haji Yusof Rawa, who espoused a more uncompromising position on Islamic issues.

In the 1982 elections, PAS won five parliamentary seats and garnered about 16 percent of the vote. PAS accused the government of not upholding Islamic principles, and at the village level it challenged the authority of government-appointed imams (mosque leaders) with their own orthodox and devout PAS imams. Many Malay villages were torn by the contest for power and legitimacy between PAS and UMNO. The government's concern over the activities of the "extremists" in PAS was presented in a White Paper of 1984 entitled "Threat to Muslim Unity and National Security."

The Democratic Action party (DAP) was the largest opposition party, having gained nine paliamentary seats, six from peninsular Malaysia and three from the Borneo states. Just as PAS was the core of the Malay opposition to the government, DAP was the opposition spokesman for non-Malay interests. Over the years, DAP politicians have skirted close to the limits placed by the government on raising in public "sensitive issues" that are deemed to be likely to lead to ethnic hostilities. As a result, DAP has tended to concentrate on holding the government's performances to stated promises and goals.

Although DAP could not threaten the core support of the government, which was based on the Malay electorate, it expanded its support base in 1982 to Sarawak and Sabah, being the only peninsular Malaysian party to do so. From this perspective, DAP was viewed as a formidable opponent, particularly for the Chinese-based BN parties—the MCA and Gerakan.

The Barisan Nasional had the usual internal conflicts over the allocation of seats among member parties. Berjasa, a small Kelantan-based Islamic party, withdrew from the BN when Hamim was allowed to enter the BN. Hamim was composed of the moderate faction expelled from PAS and led by Datuk Asri, who was viewed as an important symbolic counter to PAS. The People's Progressive party, based in Ipoh, decided to stay in BN although it was given no parliamentary seats. Because the number of seats in Parliament had been increased by 17, all the major BN parties were given more seats. Even so, many intra-BN disputes erupted. In the end, all decisions on seat allocation were left to Mahathir for final resolution.

Parliament was dissolved on July 18; and nomination day was set for July 24, with elections set for August 2 and 3. Although the campaign period was only nine days, most parties had begun canvassing earlier in anticipation of elections.

The biggest problem facing the opposition was whether it could form a united front to maximize its potential in Malaysia's single-member constituency system. PAS decided to make the establishment of an Islamic state its primary plank, claiming that nationalism and ethnic divisions were contrary to Islam's "universalism." It also attempted to widen its appeal by forming a Chinese Consultative Committee (CCC), which promised that PAS would abolish Malay special rights; some Chinese and Indian Muslims were selected as PAS candidates.

With this shift in stragegy, PAS hoped to forge an opposition front. However, such a front was difficult to establish because of policy differences among opposition parties. Eventually, a minimal "front" was forged with three minor, ostensibly "multiethnic" opposition parties—the Social Democratic party (SDP), Partai Sosialis Rakyat Malaysia (PSRM) and Parti Nasionalis Malaysia (Nasma). The agreement avoided policy matters but divided constituencies to avoid opposition parties contesting against one another. DAP refused to join any opposition front unless PAS would abandon its goal of an Islamic state.

The BN depicted the opposition front as an unholy alliance of extremists seeking contradictory objectives. In particular, the BN attempted to draw out the meaning and implication of an "Islamic state." Various PAS candidates and party leaders were pressed for explanation, and eventually some acknowledged that in an Islamic state neither non-Muslims nor women would be allowed to vote. Embarrassed by the PAS stand, state SDP branches disavowed the opposition pact and there were defections from the CCC.

Claiming to provide "unity, prosperity and harmony," the Barisan Nasional stated that it needed a two-thirds majority in Parliament to insure stability in Malaysia's multiethnic setting. The argument was made that the constitution might require amendment in an emergency without the threat of partisan veto. When the votes were finally counted on August 3, the Barisan Nasional had won its two-thirds majority and much more; although its proportion of the popular vote had dropped from 60.4 percent in 1982 to 55.8 percent in 1986, it commanded 83 percent of the parliamentary seats. However, the largest proportionate increase in seats went to DAP, which had avoided the opposition front and had campaigned on a platform of equality for all races and programs to alleviate poverty regardless of race.

This appeal was targeted on non-Malay constituencies, and it resulted in an increase of DAP seats from 9 to 24, 5 of which were won in the Borneo states. In peninsular Malaysia, DAP gains were made largely at the expense of BN seats contested by MCA candidates. The most dramatic and surprising results involved PAS, which captured only one parliamentary seat, even though its percentage of the total vote dropped by only 0.8 percent from its 1982 showing. Many of its losses were by narrow margins, but the BN celebrated its decisive victory as a dramatic repudiation of the PAS program for an Islamic state.

Postelection Politics

A postelection crisis emerged in Penang, which had a party distribution of UMNO, 12, Gerakan (Parti Gerakan Rakyat Malaysia), 9, MCA, 2, and DAP, 10. With the largest bloc of seats in the state assembly, UMNO demanded that it control the chief minister's post, even though the state is overwhelmingly Chinese. The Gerakan leader and former chief minister, Lim Chong Eu, threatened to join the opposition DAP to control the state. In the circumstances, Lim Chong Eu became chief minister and Penang remained the only state in Malaysia with a Chinese chief minister. Any other arrangement would have created a racially explosive atmosphere.

The elections confirmed UMNO's dominant power and the results prompted some party officials to warn non-Malays that the Malaysian political system is founded on Malay dominance, and that those who challenge the special rights of the Malays and Malay privileges are "playing with fire." Mahathir acknowledged these sentiments in a speech to the UMNO assembly, stating: "We do not wish to rob other people of their rights. But let no one try to rob us of our rights." When Parliament convened, the King's speech from the throne warned against discussing issues in terms of racial sentiments. However, as the parliamentary sessions got under way, DAP objected to the division of Malaysians between "first class and second class citizens." As the debate intensified between those defending and those opposing special Malay rights, some began referring to non-Malays as *orang pendatang* (immigrants or foreigners). When DAP began asking parliamentary questions on the current status of ethnic target goals of the NEP, the standing orders of Parliament were amended to disallow questions seeking information on racial distribution.

Apparently, even the issue of whether the NEP had reached its 1990 target goals was deemed to be a matter of secrecy and "national security." Malay politicians seemed more determined than ever to extend Malay rights and privileges under the NEP, while DAP and many non-Malays argued that most NEP targets had been met and that the NEP should be considered a remedial "affirmative action" program, subject to revision and gradual conversion to more equalitarian policies. Political differences over this fundamental issue were likely to reach crisis proportions sometime before the 1990 NEP target date.

ASIA'S REGIONAL HOPES[3]

This *World Press* dialogue was conducted by editorial director Alfred Balk with Munir Majid, group editor in chief of the conservative *New Straits Times* Sendiran Berhad of Kuala Lumpur, Malaysia.

How serious are Malaysia's ethnic problems?
Potentially very serious. When the tin market collapsed and

[3]Reprint of excerpts from an interview with Munir Majid, group editor-in-chief of *New Straits Times* of Kuala Lumpur. *World Press Review*, 33:28–30, May 1986. Reprinted by permission.

the mines closed, almost all their workers were thrown out of work. They were from Chinese enclaves—and there was a lot of political canvassing. Such agitation can snowball into a chauvinistic show of strength or despair and lead to a dangerous social disturbance.

If Malay rubber workers were thrown out of their jobs, or receiving only a quarter of their previous miserable wages, their lives would be unbearable, and they would be receptive to a political party that said, "The material world is not the right world, and this government's policies lead to this kind of despair. We must have an Islamic government." That might manifest itself in the next election. That's democracy.

When is the next election?

It must be held by April, 1987. The chances are that it will be held this year. The government should emphasize the grave political consequences of creating three or four Islamic-governed states and one or two Chinese-governed states—even if the central government continues to be by the ruling coalition. There would be many problems.

Could this threaten the nation's unity?

No. There would be no secessionist tendencies, but the society would be polarized. Then the Communists or Islamic extremists would go to work.

How much of your population is Moslem?

About 51 per cent. One fifth of this population supports the Islamic Party—which, since the revival of Islam, has become rather extreme. It wants an Islamic government. There is a lot of Khomeini-style rhetoric, which is disturbing. And the Islamic Party is ready to take advantage of any situation.

How strong is Malaysia's government?

Very strong. It has been in power since independence in 1957. It consists of a broad National Front coalition of eleven parties designed to insure a consensus, which is how Malaysian politics works. It includes Chinese, Indian, and Malay parties. This coalition was formed in 1971 after the race riots of 1969, which were sparked by the Chinese community's economic dominance and challenge to the Malay political position.

Is your prime minister popular?

We have had four prime ministers since independence. Our present one, Datuk Seri Mahathir bin Mohamad, has been in office since 1981. He is assertive and forceful, and sometimes rubs people the wrong way. We have become more nationalistic under his leadership. He says he wants to change Malaysians from self-effacing to aggressive.

In trying to create this New Malaysian, he has introduced many new policies. He has asked civil servants to punch time-clocks. He hammers at them: "You get paid, and you must work." He says "Look East!"—which shocks many people who have reservations about the Japanese dating to World War II.

But his main point is: What can we learn from the Japanese? Why are they so successful? His "Look East!" does not mean that we should turn away from the West. This is one of Malaysia's most fascinating and innovative administrations.

What remains of your colonial ties to Britain?

Almost nothing. Our Prime Minister has had a long-running battle with the British because they increased fees for our students who were studying in Britain, and he urges us not to buy British products if we can find better deals elsewhere. He is trying to tell Malaysians, "Snap out of your colonial hangover. Let's show what we can do on our own."

What is your population?

About 15.5 million, half of whom live in the cities. Our population has been growing steadily. We are not interested in population control; we believe we should have a larger population base. We have a large land area and tremendous resources. We want to build up our domestic demand base; we now depend too much on world trade.

Our long-range aim is to achieve a stable society based on a degree of income equalization. One of the main causes of racial conflict in our country has been the unequal distribution of wealth. The Chinese have had an inordinately large share, and the Malayans are low-income peasants.

Tell us about your paper.

My group publishes four dailies. Our flagship, the English-language *New Straits Times*, has a circulation of 200,000. Our Malay-language *Berita Harian*, with about 230,000, has overtaken our English-language paper in circulation although not, by far, in advertising revenue.

That reflects our educational policies; Malay is now the national language. We have a regional English-language daily, the *Malay Mail*, that sells about 70,000. Our national daily *Business Times* sells 10,000. We have three Sunday papers and a Sunday tabloid. We also publish magazines and books. We are the largest media house in Malaysia.

There are hundreds of papers in Malaysia. Our literacy rate is 70 per cent, and we are trying to raise it.

How free is the press?

Not as free as in the U.S. Because of our nation's fragility, we have some restrictive laws. They are not specifically applicable to the press; they apply to everyone. We have an Internal Security Act, a Sedition Act, an Official Secrets Act, and a Printing Presses Act that applies specifically to the media. It specifies that you have to get a license every year to print and publish. This may sound like anathema, but we have not had problems and no newspaper has been denied this license.

Our approach to reporting the news is different from American journalists' adversarial approach. We emphasize development journalism. My paper, for instance, tries to play a role in the schools. We produce a computer supplement once a week so that students can acquire some familiarity with the new technology.

Do you criticize government?

Yes. Americans probably may recall a controversy in 1984 involving the New York Philharmonic. It was scheduled to play a concert in Kuala Lumpur that included *Schelomo*, by the Jewish composer Ernest Bloch. The government insisted that it be removed from the program, and the orchestra canceled the concert. We questioned the government's position and asked it not to confuse anti-Zionism on the one hand with anti-Semitism on the other.

What is Malaysia's greatest concern?

We are worried about the U.S.-Soviet standoff. We think that President Reagan's arms position is counterproductive and unrealistic. We wonder why he does not take high-profile positions on trade and development issues.

Americans should realize that they are militarily superior to the Soviets. You can give Moscow a bloody nose. But if you are not realistic about priorities and resources there is a point at which everyone gets a bloody nose.

DEVELOPMENTS IN MALAYSIA[4]

Thank you for this opportunity to discuss recent developments in Malaysia and Singapore. I would like to begin with some remarks on Malaysia.

People and Government

Malaysia is a multiracial society in which ethnic Malays comprise a bare majority of the population. Chinese make up approximately 33% of the population, Indians 10%, and there are several smaller minority groups.

Since independence in 1957, Malaysia has had a parliamentary system of government based on free elections contested by several parties, almost all of which are racially based. The ruling National Front (composed of three major and several minor parties and dominated by ethnic Malays) has won a two-thirds or better majority in the federal parliament in all seven general elections since 1957, but opposition parties are active and vocal participants in the political system and occasionally hold power at the state level.

[4]Reprint of a statement before the Subcommittee on Human Rights and International Organizations of the House Foreign Affairs Committee on September 22, 1988, by David F. Lambertson, Deputy Assistant Secretary for East Asian and Pacific Affairs. *Department of State Bulletin*, November 1988, pp. 23-25.

Economy

A strong free market economy, abundant natural resources, and a relatively small population (17 million) have helped Malaysia become one of the most prosperous of the developing countries.

Shared Interests

The United States and Malaysia enjoy very good relations grounded on mutual interests in the fields of trade and investment and regional stability. We cooperate smoothly on a range of shared concerns, including defense, the fight against narcotics, the continuing refugee crisis in Southeast Asia, and education. In the field of education, for example, more than 20,000 Malaysian students are now enrolled in American universities—the second largest foreign student population in the United States.

Our economic ties with Malaysia are solid. The United States is Malaysia's second largest trading partner after Japan. We take one-sixth of Malaysia's exports and supply nearly one-fifth of its imports. For 1987 U.S.-Malaysia trade reached approximately $4.4 billion, while U.S. direct investment in Malaysia is estimated at $4 billion. More than 20 major U.S. electronics firms have established factories in Malaysia, and further expansion in this and other industrial areas is likely.

To facilitate the further development of economic relations, our two countries have ongoing discussions in a number of areas, including copyright and bilateral investment agreements.

Regional Stability

Beyond economic cooperation, Malaysia and the United States have strong mutual interests in regional security and stability. Strategically located on the Malacca Strait, Malaysia's continued political stability and economic development are important to U.S. interests in Southeast Asia. Confronted with the Vietnamese occupation of Cambodia and a major Soviet base at Cam Ranh Bay, Malaysia has been in the forefront of the Association of South East Asian Nations (ASEAN) strategy to bring about a withdrawal of Vietnamese forces from Cambodia and secure a negotiated settlement ensuring genuine self-determination for the

Cambodian people. Malaysia and its ASEAN partners have done an effective job in working for a just settlement in Cambodia, and the United States will continue to support their efforts.

Malaysia's geographic location has also made it a key player in the ongoing tragedy of Indochinese refugees. Since 1975 Malaysia has generously provided first asylum to more than 200,000 Vietnamese refugees. At present there are more than 13,000 refugees in Malaysian refugee camps, and it is significant that many of those granted asylum in Malaysia this year had been turned away by other countries in the region. The United States deeply appreciates Malaysia's commitment to the principle of first asylum, and we look forward to continued close cooperation on this humanitarian issue.

While the United States and Malaysia do not participate in a formal security alliance, we share an appreciation of the threats which jeopardize the area's peace and freedom. One example of our rapport in this area is Prime Minister Mahathir's public support for U.S. military facilities in the Philippines. A stable parliamentary democracy, Malaysia is nonaligned but staunchly anticommunist. Still emerging from its first economic recession since independent, Malaysia has expressed its appreciation of the small international military education and training (IMET) program grant, which represents the only form of aid it now receives from the United States. In FY 1988, that grant totaled $900,000.

Internal Security Situation

Internal security in Malaysia has been seriously threatened twice: first, by a major communist insurrection which began in 1948 and peaked in the early 1950s and which still smolders in a few border areas; second, by intercommunal rioting following the 1969 national elections, in which several hundred persons reportedly died.

In addition, since 1983 the government has explicitly classified the country's serious drug problem as a threat to national security. The remnants of the communist insurgency, the possibility of renewed communal conflict, and widespread drug abuse are cited by the Government of Malaysia as justification for laws allowing, in conformity with the constitution, preventive detention of persons suspected of subversive activity or of other activities, including drug crimes. Other laws empower the government to restrict the right to free expression and association. These laws, though seldom used, were strengthened by amendment in December 1987.

Prime Minister Mahathir's Administration has been relatively restrained in its use of Malaysia's Internal Security Act legislation to deal with political offenses. By mid-October of last year, the number detained under the Internal Security Act had been sharply reduced to at most 27 from about 500 when Mahathir took office in 1981. However, in late October and early November, in an effort it said was necessary to avoid serious racial strife, the government detained 106 persons under the Internal Security Act. Among those detained were opposition and government politicians, social critics, environmentalists, religious activists, and academics.

Shortly after the arrests began on October 27, our Embassy in Kuala Lumpur told the Malaysian Government of our concern over the detention without trial of opposition politicians and social activists and conveyed to the government our hope that those detained would be afforded every right and consideration under Malaysian law. Secretary Shultz raised the issue of Internal Security Act detentions with Prime Minister Mahathir during their July 9 meeting in Kuala Lumpur. In a news conference following the meeting, Secretary Shultz said he had been assured by the Prime Minister and other Malaysian Government officials that "those remaining under detention would be afforded full statutory and constitutional rights and that as time went on we would see them dealt with properly. So the subject was discussed in, I think, fundamentally a satisfactory way." Both before and after the Secretary's meeting with Prime Minister Mahathir, other representatives of the U.S. Government, including Assistant Secretary [for East Asian and Pacific Affairs] Gaston Sigur, Deputy Assistant Secretary [for Human Rights and Humanitarian Affairs Robert W.] Farrand, and myself, have reiterated our concerns to the Government of Malaysia.

To date the Government of Malaysia has released 85 of the 106 persons detained under the Internal Security Act. Orders permitting detention for up to 2 years have been issued for the remaining 21 persons. Under the Internal Security Act, the government is not required to bring detainees to trial. However, it must present each detainee with the grounds for detention and appoint an advisory board which reviews each case every 6 months. The board has no power to order release of a detainee. We have welcomed the Malaysian Government's release of 85 detainees and urged the government to release the remaining detainees as expeditiously as possible.

At the time of the Internal Security Act arrests last year, the government suspended three newspapers and banned all public assemblies. Shortly after this decision, and on several occasions since that time, we told the Malaysian Government of our concern over this action. Our approaches emphasized America's longstanding tradition of support for freedom of the press and expressed the hope that the newspapers which had their publishing licenses revoked would be permitted to resume publication as soon as possible. Both the suspensions and the ban on assembly were lifted earlier this year. However, parliament has enacted legislation further strengthening the government's already substantial control over the press and public assembly. We are encouraged that the publishing licenses of the opposition Democratic Action Party and Parti Islam have been renewed and would note also that the official publications of these opposition parties continue to freely criticize the Government of Malaysia. We are also pleased that the social awareness group, Aliran, has continued to publish its monthly newsletter. In addition, the important Malay language paper *Watan*, which was a weekly before the crackdown, now publishes three issues a week and carries extensive coverage of dissident activity. It is clear, however, that the inhibiting effect of the government's recent actions on the climate of press freedom is likely to continue for some time to come.

The Department has also been following closely recent controversial events in Malaysia involving the judiciary, the Prime Minister, and parliament. In response to what the Prime Minister viewed as unwarranted interference by the judiciary, the parliament has passed legislation limiting the role of the judiciary in reviewing executive acts. Parliament also amended the constitution in a manner which appears to limit the judiciary's independent authority. In turn many senior judicial figures reacted critically to what they viewed as an attack on their independence. The heightened stress between the two branches of government ultimately led to the removal of the Lord President of Malaysia's Supreme Court. In addition, five Supreme Court judges were later suspended and are awaiting the decision of a tribunal appointed by the King to examine the propriety of the actions they took in connection with the case that resulted in the removal of the Lord President.

While from an American perspective we find these trends disquieting, we believe it would be premature to draw conclusions about their ultimate impact on the historically independent Malaysian judiciary. We will continue to monitor these events closely and make our views known to the Government of Malaysia as appropriate.

VI. SRI LANKA

EDITOR'S INTRODUCTION

Located off the southeast coast of India, the island nation of
Sri Lanka once boasted one of the most vigorous democratic governments in the Third World. In recent years, however, violent
ethnic conflict between the Sinhalese majority and Tamil minority has seriously undermined the democratic process in the former
British colony of Ceylon. In the first article in this section,
"Tension and Conflict in Sri Lanka," reprinted from *Current
History*, Robert N. Kearney, a professor of political science at Syracuse University, traces the history of this ethnic tension. In the
following article, "Sri Lanka's Ethnic Conflict: The Indo-Lanka
Peace Accord," which appeared in *Asian Survey*, two Sri Lankan
scholars, Ralph R. Premdas and S. W. R. de A. Samarasinghe, examine the Indian-mediated peace accord of 1987, which attempted to end the conflict. Next, in "The Roots of Conflict in Sri
Lanka," from *Christian Century*, Victoria A. Rebeck, assistant editor of the *Christian Century*, describes the process by which, under
the British, the Tamil minority tended to gain proportionately
greater educational and job advantages, thus adding to the ethnic
tension. She also mentions the efforts of an interreligious group
with the slogan "Tell the People the Truth" to promote peace
and suggests that the small Christian community in Sri Lanka
may be able to play a unique role in achieving ethnic reconciliation. Finally, in "Resolving the Sri Lankan Conflict," taken from
the *Department of State Bulletin*, Robert A. Peck, Deputy Assistant
Secretary for Near Eastern and South Asian Affairs, discusses the
conflict in this strife-torn island and asserts U.S. government support for a negotiated solution.

TENSION AND CONFLICT IN SRI LANKA[1]

The past decade has been a period of contention and violence for Sri Lanka. Growing communal violence accompanied demands for a separate state for the Sri Lankan Tamil ethnic minority; in 1983, the violence triggered probably the most brutal and destructive communal riots in the nation's history and produced increasingly frequent clashes between armed bands of separatist guerrillas and the government's military and police forces. The mounting communal tensions in the early 1980's were underlined by controversial political developments that appeared to jolt the democratic political processes of which the nation was understandably proud. Sri Lanka had boasted one of the most vigorous and liveliest democratic systems of government in the third world, capable of repeated orderly transfers of power between partisan rivals as a result of popular elections characterized by very high levels of voter participation.

Political confrontation between the Sinhalese ethnic majority and the Sri Lankan Tamil minority assumed a prominent position in the politics of Sri Lanka (then Ceylon) in the 1950's, only a few years after the nation's independence from British colonial rule. In 1956, Sinhalese (or Sinhala), the language of the majority community, was recognized as the official language of the nation. In the same year, the first Sinhalese-Tamil communal riots broke out, followed two years later by more widespread and more deadly rioting. In addition to the official language question, Tamil grievances have centered on the government's sponsorship of migration by Sinhalese into areas viewed by Tamils as their ancestral homeland, the special status accorded Buddhism and alleged official discrimination in education and public employment.

Sinhalese, who are predominantly Buddhist, constituted 74 percent of the nation's population in the 1981 census. Sri Lanka's Tamils, who speak the Tamil language and are largely Hindu, comprised nearly 13 percent. Sri Lankan Tamils are a majority in the districts in the north of the island and on and near the Jaffna peninsula; they are also numerous on the east coast. Sharing

[1]Reprint of an article by Robert N. Kearney, a professor of political science at Syracuse University. Reprinted with permission from *Current History*, March 1986. Copyright © *Current History* 1986.

the Tamil language and Hindu religion but socially and territori-
ally separate from the Sri Lankan Tamils are members of an ethnic group known as Indian Tamils, so designated because their
ancestors came to the island from south India in the nineteenth
century or later. The Indian Tamils, most of whom live in the tea-
growing areas of the central highlands, accounted for slightly less
than 6 percent of the 1981 population. A Muslim community
known as Sri Lankan Moors formed 7 percent, with smaller ethnic groups making up the balance of the population.

Demands began to emerge in the early 1970's for a separate
Tamil state that would include the northern and eastern regions
in which Sri Lankan Tamils have lived since antiquity. In 1972,
the major Tamil political organizations banded together to form
a Tamil United Front, later renamed the Tamil United Liberation Front (TULF). The organization contested the 1977 parliamentary election, asking the Tamil people for a mandate to seek
a separate independent state, to be called Eelam. Although the
TULF captured only 18 out of 168 parliamentary seats, the party's candidate won every constituency on the island with a Sri
Lankan Tamil majority except one.

In addition, in the early 1970's an underground separatist
group composed mostly of Tamil youths began to engage in assassinations and robberies and other acts of violence. Described vari-
ously as "terrorists," "guerrillas" or "freedom fighters," the
underground came to be known collectively as the Tiger Movement. Before the end of the decade, the movement had split into
several separate and often antagonistic organizations.

The separatist movement has been essentially confined to the
Sri Lankan Tamil community. Indian Tamils, most of whom do
not live in areas included within or contiguous to the proposed
Tamil state, have on the whole remained aloof from the movement.

Elections and Constitutional Changes

The parliamentary election of 1977 produced the most recent of six consecutive transfers of government power between
the major rival political parties, the United National party (UNP)
and the Sri Lanka Freedom party (SLFP). The UNP won a massive parliamentary majority, capturing 51 percent of the total
popular vote; this was the first time a single party had collected

an absolute majority of all votes cast. Sri Lanka's plurality electoral system based mostly on single-member districts magnified the
UNP victory into an overwhelming 83 percent of the seats in Parliament. The SLFP, which had been in power since 1970, captured 30 percent of the popular vote but won only about 5
percent of the parliamentary seats. Among the contestants was
the TULF, which won only slightly more than 6 percent of the
vote nationally but scored impressively in the Tamil-majority areas of the north and east.

Immediately after the election, there was brutal communal rioting, the first major outburst of communal violence in 19 years.
The 1977 riots were explained in terms of Sinhalese reaction to
Tamil separatist demands, terrorist acts committed in the name
of separatism, and anti-Sinhalese statements allegedly made by
Tamil politicians in the course of the campaign. It was estimated
that about 300 individuals lost their lives.

A constitution that drastically altered the nation's political institutions was adopted in 1978. The new constitution replaced a
constitution adopted in 1972, when the government was controlled by a united front consisting of the SLFP and two smaller
parties, the Lanka Sama Samaja party and the Communist party.
The 1978 constitution embodied the long-cherished objectives of
UNP leader J. R. Jayewardene and was expected to favor the
UNP. Not surprisingly, the SLFP leadership soon announced
that, when the SLFP returned to power, the 1978 constitution
would be scrapped and the nation would return to the constitution of 1972. Sri Lanka thus seems to face the prospect of constitutional change each time control of the government passes from
one party to another.

Among the principal innovations introduced by the 1978
constitution was the replacement of the parliamentary system of
government following the British model by a presidential system
in which executive power is concentrated in the hands of a President elected for a six-year term. The office of Prime Minister and
a Cabinet drawn from the Parliament were retained but were
clearly subordinated to the President. Jayewardene, the first
President under the new constitution, was selected by Parliament; thereafter the President was to be chosen by direct popular
vote.

Another radical departure came with the introduction in the
1978 constitution of the closed list system of proportional repre-

sentation. Proportional representation was expected to dampen
the wide swings in the electoral fortunes of the major parties that
had resulted from the plurality electoral system. The UNP appeared likely to benefit from the change, because in parliamentary elections that party had generally received a slightly larger and
more consistent percentage of the popular vote than had its rival,
the SLFP. (It can be argued, based on past voting patterns, that
the new electoral system would make it virtually impossible for
the SLFP to return to power without assistance from smaller allied parties.)

Smaller parties presumably would be disadvantaged by a provision that a party's list had to receive at least one-eighth of the
total vote in an electoral district to be awarded any seats from the
district. Also working to the detriment of smaller parties was the
novel provision of a bonus seat for the party list winning the largest number of votes in the district before the seats were allotted
on a proportional basis. Outside the north, it was expected that
the bonus seats would be won by the UNP or the SLFP.

The adoption of proportional representation raised the prospect that the 1978 constitution might be virtually immune to
amendment, since no party was likely to obtain the two-thirds majority in Parliament required for amendment. This possibility
soon appeared to have major political consequences.

The first popular presidential election was held in October,
1982. Originally scheduled for early 1984, the election was
moved forward after a constitutional amendment was adopted allowing a first-term President to seek reelection any time after the
first four years of his term. Presumably, the move was designed
to take advantage of the disunity and demoralization of the opposition. The SLFP was at the time undergoing a battle for party
leadership. President Jayewardene defeated the candidate of the
SLFP and four other candidates, winning 53 percent of the votes
cast, a plurality of every electoral district except Jaffna in the far
north. The candidate of the divided SLFP trailed with 39 percent
of the vote.

The TULF declined to contest the presidential election or en-
dorse any candidate, but the leader of the small Tamil Congress
entered the race with a call for a separate Tamil state. The Tamil
Congress had recently been reestablished as a separate political
party after merging into the TULF in the early 1970's. The Tamil Congress candidate won a plurality of the votes, 40 percent, in

Jaffna district, and in the Tamil-majority district of Batticaloa on the east coast his proportion of the votes came within 1 percent of those cast for Jayewardene. It is perhaps indicative of the estrangement of the voters of the north that the incumbent President was not only outpolled by the Tamil Congress candidate but finished behind the SLFP candidate; the north was the only district in which the SLFP attracted more votes than did the UNP.

The candidates of three small leftist parties collectively received slightly more than 5 percent of the vote. A minor surprise was the dismal performance of the Lanka Sama Samaja party (LSSP), long the premier party of the Sri Lankan left. The LSSP candidate received only 1 percent of the vote and did not win more than 2 percent in any electoral district. In 1977, the LSSP failed to win a seat in the legislature for the first time in four decades. The party's performance in the presidential contest, following its 1977 debacle, suggested the decline or perhaps the collapse of the left as a force in electoral politics. An additional leftist party, the Communist party, supported the candidate of the SLFP.

Soon after the election, President Jayewardene suggested that a referendum be held asking the voters to approve the continuation of the Parliament elected in 1977 for an additional six-year term instead of holding new parliamentary elections as expected by the middle of 1983. The controversial proposal was justified on the grounds that an ultra-left plot to assassinate government leaders and foment disorder had been uncovered. The new system of proportional representation, UNP spokesmen claimed, would allow extremists to obtain sizable representation in Parliament and would jeopardize the nation's political stability. More plausible was the strong probability that in a parliamentary election the UNP, although a likely winner, would no longer hold a more than two-thirds majority in Parliament and would thus lose the ability to amend the constitution at will.

The 1982 Referendum

The referendum held in December, 1982, was reportedly approved by 55 percent of the voters. The proposal was defeated in seven electoral districts, of which four were in the north and east. In Jaffna district, 91 percent of the votes cast were negative. The balloting results, however, were clouded by reports of widespread voter intimidation and ballot tampering, as well as by the government's detention of opposition leaders during the campaign. Despite highly competitive contests, Sri Lankan elections had remained strikingly free of scandal for 50 years after the introduction of universal adult suffrage in 1931.

Claims of local instances of voter intimidation or impersonation were not uncommon, particularly in the elections soon after independence, but the balloting and counting procedures had not been called into question until a 1981 election for newly established district development councils. In Jaffna, the 1981 balloting was preceded by an eruption of communal violence and followed by reports of ballot-box stuffing and the mishandling of ballots. In 1982, the allegations of irregularities in the referendum balloting far exceeded those of 1981, posing a threat to the integrity of the electoral process.

The surprising actions of 1982 were followed by another highly unusual move, apparently in response to criticism that voters opposing the referendum were being deprived of their right to participate in parliamentary elections. Jayewardene had earlier secured undated letters of resignation from all UNP members of Parliament. Eighteen seats won by the UNP in 1977 were vacated when Jayewardene accepted the resignations of members of Parliament after their constituencies voted against the referendum. By-elections were held for the seats in 1983. The UNP retained 14 of the seats, but 10 were won with a reduced share of the votes, compared with the 1977 election. The SLFP won 3 seats and 1 seat was captured by a small party, the Mahajana Eksath Peramuna. The seats at stake were all in the southwest. More than nine-tenths of the voters in Jaffna district opposed the referendum. However, the UNP had won no seats in that district in 1977, so the arranged resignations and by-elections had no effect in the north.

If votes for the presidential candidates had been apportioned by district to party lists according to the procedures of the 1978 constitution, the UNP would have won 59 percent and the SLFP 37 percent of the seats in a 196-seat Parliament, with other parties winning about 4 percent. It is highly improbable that votes would have been cast for lists exactly as for presidential candidates. But even in very favorable circumstances the UNP would not have retained a two-thirds majority in Parliament. And the party would have been 16 members short of the 131 members required for a two-thirds majority.

Escalating Communal Violence

In July, 1983, the most deadly and destructive explosion of communal rioting in the history of Sri Lanka engulfed the nation. Starting in Colombo, a wave of incendiarism, looting and assault spread rapidly across the island. The death toll was reported to be 387, which may significantly understate the carnage. Some sources claimed a death toll in the thousands. Property damage was severe. Much of the commercial section of Colombo known as the Pettah was gutted. Tens of thousands of people were driven from their homes to seek shelter in grim refugee camps. In Colombo, there was apparently an element of organization and planning not recorded in earlier communal riots, allegedly perpetrated by employees of a government ministry armed with election lists by which Tamil property could be identified.

The riots of 1983 underscored the vicious circle of retaliation and counterretaliation that characterizes the island's ethnic conflict. The riots were seen as retaliation for the ambush killing of 13 Sinhalese soldiers on patrol in the north by Tamil Tigers pursuing the objective of a separate state. It has been claimed, in turn, that the ambush was a retaliation for the abduction and rape of several young Tamil women by Sinhalese soldiers in Jaffna district. In the perverse logic of the mob, riot victims included not only Sri Lankan Tamils but Indian Tamils and Indian nationals who had no ties with the north and no association with the separatist movement.

The riots surely heightened alienation among Tamil citizens and undermined their confidence in the ability or willingness of the government to protect their lives and property. Increased separatist militancy, in turn, probably heightens the prospect of violence against Tamils by Sinhalese mobs or security forces.

After some confusion, the government fixed blame for the 1983 riots on an unlikely combination of three small leftist political parties, the Janatha Vimukthi Peramuna, the Nava Sama Samaja party and the Communist party. The three parties, which were subsequently banned, shared little other than a general adherence to Marxism. The leader of the NSSP had contested the presidential election, urging that concessions be made to the Tamils, even allowing them to form a separate state if they so wished. Despite the fact that it was unlikely that three tiny leftist rivals had joined in a conspiracy to attack Tamils, the explanation neatly brought together the government's various opponents. President Jayewardene told the Parliament in early 1985:

The events of July [1983] not only smeared the name of Sri Lanka throughout the world, they also showed that all those in the North and the South who seek to overthrow an elected government by violence, by creation of communal and religious discord, by terrorism and other similar methods had joined hands.

The following year saw a rapid escalation in the level of violence associated with the separatist movement. Tiger operations shifted from attacks on individuals and government installations to pitched battles with military units and assaults on major police stations by heavily armed guerrillas. By late 1984, government leaders were predicting a major assault on security forces in Jaffna district by Tamil guerrillas trained and outfitted in bases in the southern Indian state of Tamilnadu.

Throughout 1984, the foreign press reported military and police excesses, mounting civilian casualties and the destruction of property in the Tamil areas. Sinhalese civilians also became targets of armed attack, presumably by one of the groups of the Tiger movement. The Sinhalese civilian victims were generally migrants to predominantly Tamil regions. A deadly attack was made on the ancient city of Anuradhapura, a center of Buddhist pilgrimage in a region largely populated by Sinhalese. As the devastation mounted, the economic dislocations and financial drain of the struggle became increasingly evident. Reiterating the need to defeat "terrorism," Jayewardene noted somberly that "we may have to equip ourselves to do so at the expense of development and social and economic welfare plans."

After the 1983 riots, India, Sri Lanka's giant neighbor, began to assume an increasing role in the communal discord on the island. The government of Sri Lanka charged that Tamil separatist guerrillas were being trained in bases in south India. There were incidents involving Indian fishing vessels because of Sri Lankan efforts to prevent movement between south India and northern Sri Lanka. In late 1984 and early 1985 strains in relations between the two governments were evident. New Delhi's repeated assurance of support for the political unity of Sri Lanka, combined with growing pressure on separatist groups to negotiate a settlement, however, seemed to restore cordiality between the two nations. India's role in pressing the militant separatists to the bargaining table became increasingly clear. Neither the separatists nor the government of Sri Lanka could ignore the proddings from New Delhi.

Attempts at Settlement

The search for a negotiated settlement began in early 1984, when President Jayewardene called an All Party Conference to "discuss the daily growing problems of the country in regard to ethnic affairs and terrorism and seek solutions." The all-party format for discussion was intended to rise above partisan contention, which had repeatedly frustrated earlier efforts. The TULF agreed to participate, but shortly after the dialogue began the SLFP withdrew, seriously compromising the nonpartisan nature of the discussions. The party delegations were soon joined by representatives of religious and cultural groups, in order to bring members of the influential *sangha* (Buddhist clergy) into the talks. In the past, some of the most impassioned opposition to government concessions to Tamil claims had come from clerical ranks.

The talks continued throughout the year. One long-standing ethnic problem was apparently resolved in the early sessions. Agreement was recorded on granting Sri Lankan citizenship to those members of the Indian Tamil community who did not possess either Sri Lankan or Indian citizenship and who remained in Sri Lanka. Soon after independence, Sri Lankan citizenship had been defined to exclude a large proportion of the Indian Tamil community. Most of those affected did not possess Indian citizenship and consequently became stateless. Several agreements were reached by New Delhi and Colombo under which some Indian Tamils departed for India and others received Sri Lankan citizenship. A residual group of stateless persons who did not wish to go to India had, however, remained. The 1984 accord seemed to assure Sri Lankan citizenship and permanent residence on the island for this group.

Once the question of the Indian Tamils was resolved, the all-party talks focused on questions of regional autonomy and the devolution of government power to local or regional public bodies. Despite what appeared to be a substantial narrowing of differences, the talks were adjourned at the end of the year and (to the surprise of some participants) were not resumed in 1985.

One problem of the All Party Conference was that, while almost every variety of political opinion among the Sinhalese was represented, the separatist guerrilla organizations had no direct voice in the talks, and the extent to which the TULF could secure separatist extremist acquiescence in any agreements was suspect. A renewal of large-scale violence occurred in 1985, including a rocket attack that destroyed a large police installation in Jaffna city. The violent confrontations between separatist guerrillas and security forces began to shift from the north to the east.

In June, however, a group of separatist organizations announced a cease-fire as a prelude to talks with the Sri Lankan government. The cease-fire and the willingness to negotiate were evidently the result of strong prodding by the government of India. Discussions were held in Thimpu, the capital of the tiny Himalayan state of Bhutan, in July and August. The talks were attended by spokesmen for the government of Sri Lanka, an alliance of four of the major separatist organizations called the Eelam Tamil Liberation Front, and the TULF.

Little public information was available. In the first sessions the Tamil separatist representatives apparently presented a set of four principles that were to serve as the basis for discussion of ethnic and territorial problems, to which the government of Sri Lanka responded in the August meeting. The four principles called for recognition of the Tamils of Sri Lanka as a "distinct nationality," the Tamil-populated areas as a Tamil "homeland," the right of self-determination for the Tamils, and the right to citizenship for all Tamils residing in Sri Lanka. The last of the principles presumably referred to the status of Indian Tamils resolved at the earlier All Party Conference.

The government response raised questions of definition of the terms employed in the first three principles and seemed to imply that agreements could be sought, provided they did not compromise the political and territorial integrity of the Sri Lankan state and did not create a special status for the Tamil community that was not recognized for other communities.

The negotiations were disrupted in September when the Eelam Tamil Liberation Front representatives walked out, charging security forces in Sri Lanka with atrocities against Tamil civilians. The cease-fire, however, was not repudiated, although numerous violations were reported, particularly in the vicinity of the east coast city of Trincomalee. Urged by the government of India, the two sides may well resume the dialogue. Although the intransigence and bitterness engendered by events of the past decade do not bode well for a swift or painless resolution of ethnic problems, the horrible costs of the struggle presumably offer both sides strong incentives to reach an accord.

Conclusion

The recent history of Sri Lanka has been rife with contention, conflict and violence. In the 1980's, a series of political moves suggested that constitutional and conventional practices were being manipulated for partisan advantage. The use of a referendum to avoid holding a scheduled parliamentary election in order to perpetuate the governing party's massive majority seems particularly detrimental to democratic practice. Charges of intimidation and ballot tampering added to the appearance of "political decay" in a once proud democracy.

Perhaps even more destructive to a free and orderly society is the mounting incidence of communal violence. The riots that convulsed the nation in 1977 and 1983 and the increasing tempo of armed clashes that in 1984 amounted almost to civil war in the north suggest a profound political malady, a spreading affliction that the nation's leaders seem incapable of arresting. Efforts to negotiate an end to the loss of life and property have not proved successful. The human cost of the communal conflict can probably never be calculated. The eventual social and political consequences may be equally difficult to gauge, but it seems certain that the polity will long bear the scars.

SRI LANKA'S ETHNIC CONFLICT: THE INDO-LANKA PEACE ACCORD[2]

On July 29, 1987, an Accord was signed in Colombo between Rajiv Gandhi of India and Junius Jayewardene of Sri Lanka

[2]Excerpted from an article by Ralph R. Premdas, a professor of political science at McGill University, and S. W. R. de A. Samarasinghe, associate director of the International Centre for Ethnic Studies in Kandy, Sri Lanka. Reprinted with permission from *Asian Survey* 28:676–690, June 1988. Copyright © 1988 by the Regents of the University of California.

bringing an end to four years of bloody civil strife between the Sinhalese and the Tamils in Sri Lanka. The internal war had devastated the Republic of Sri Lanka, causing at least 6,000 casualties, costing some 15 billion Sri Lankan rupees (US$500 million) annually, and creating in the populace a daily preoccupation with the war. If the majority Sinhalese were paying an astounding price to maintain a unified state, the minority Tamils were at least equally ravaged, their most densely populated areas in the north and east often reduced to free fire zones, their livelihoods nearly crippled, and many of their people turned into refugees.

At the time of the Accord, the political price of conducting the war by the central government had inflicted grievous wounds on Sri Lankan democracy. A veritable authoritarian state was established. A "Prevention of Terrorism Act," modeled on the draconian South African measure, had conferred arbitrary powers in the hands of the state and had harvested 6,000 to 8,000 "political" prisoners. Official censorship had become normal and domestic news, especially on the war, was dominated by government and separatist propaganda. The state of emergency, renewed perfunctorily by Parliament every month, had created an environment that constricted all civil liberties. Individual identity cards had to be produced on offical demand and personal searches became an unabridged state right. Abuses were inevitable, and the Sri Lankan state was fast acquiring an international image as a repressive regime.

The human cost was both brutal and subtle. On the Sinhalese side, some 600 civilians and 500 military and police deaths were recorded, and many more were wounded and rendered handicapped and unproductive for the rest of their lives. The Tamils paid more proportionately, with at least 5,000 killed and many more injured, losing thousands as political prisoners, and displacing more than 150,000 as refugees in India and elsewhere. Thousands of Sinhalese also became refugees in their own country, driven out by Tamil "militants" from numerous settlements, especially in the east. Uprooted and hopeless, Tamil despair was matched by growing Sinhalese fatalism at the interminable war. The rift between Tamil and Sinhalese grew wider daily; friendships became fewer and cross-communal voluntary associations lost their old intercultural vitality. The war continued with no end in sight; insecurity and fear had gradually been incorporated into life's routine as "normal."

The Sri Lankan economy became dramatically militarized, with 17% of the national budget allocated to defense by 1986 compared to 4% a decade earlier. Tourism, which at its peak had attracted over 400,000 visitors annually, generated about US$150 million in foreign exchange and provided about 64,000 jobs, contracted drastically. Foreign aid continued bringing in US$625 million from the aid consortium alone in 1987, but donors had signaled that their bounty was likely to be curtailed if the ethnic strife continued. The diversion of scarce resources for military expenditures and the loss of tourist dollars radically rearranged the country's development priorities, delaying project implementation and stunting growth potential. The currency was devalued from 21.32 rupees per US$1 in 1979 to 29.90 rupees in September 1987. Unemployment had been successfully reduced between 1978 and 1982, but was again on the increase and the number of jobless reached one million by mid-1987. The government's open economic strategy ran into serious difficulties, and as if all of this war-induced misfortune was not enough, the price of Sri Lankan raw materials on the international market remained depressed and drought ravaged the country throughout 1987.

Into this depressing social, political, and economic morass and especially in light of the deadlocked negotiations on the ethnic conflict, the Accord came as a sudden thunderbolt. In the months prior to the agreement, neither the Tamil militants—especially the paramount group, the Liberation Tigers of Tamil Eelam (LTTE)—nor the Sri Lankan government signaled any fundamental shift in their positions. Why then did the Accord come about? What changes in concessions and circumstances eventuated that led to the resumption of negotiations between India and Sri Lanka? In the following pages we first evaluated the salient political, military, and diplomatic features of the Accord. . . . Next we take up problems that have arisen in implementation of the Accord, and in the final section we analyze the adequacies and inadequacies of the agreement as the basis for a long-term solution to the Sinhala-Tamil conflict.

Major Political Exchanges in the Accord

The terms of the Accord contain protections for the fundamental vital interests of the Sri Lankan government, but while extracting concessions from India—acting on behalf of its own interests as well as those of the Tamils—Sri Lanka also incurred certain risks and costs. Gains and concessions were offset by direct and indirect costs and risks. To begin with, the Accord conceded "the unity, sovereignty, and territorial integrity of Sri Lanka," eliminating Tamil claims for a sovereign state (Eelam) and averting the threat of an Indian invasion. These gains were obtained by incurring certain commitments; specifically, the Sri Lankan government reaffirmed (Paragraph 1.2 of the Accord) that the state was multiethnic and multilingual and that "(1.3) . . . each ethnic group has a distinct cultural and linguistic identity which has to be carefully nurtured." It could be argued that this commitment was without cost since the Sri Lankan state had all along operated on the premise that it was multiethnic. To be sure, some early legislation and constitutional provisions, such as the 1956 "Sinhala only" official language law, had not "nurtured" these separate identities so much as challenged and even threatened them. Many Tamils would also argue that in employment practices, land settlement allocations, and university admissions, systematic state hostility was practiced and the idea of "nurture" was missing. They might even argue that the slow and steady erosion of their rights and opportunities since independence in 1948 amounted to an institutionalized undermining of their legitimate right to exist as free and equal citizens. In the present Accord, the real and imagined fears of the Tamil community are addressed: Tamils, as well as all other minorities, are explicitly recognized as an integral and legal part of Sri Lankan society, and further, their distinct cultural identities are to be "nurtured" by the state.

If in explicitly committing itself to a multiethnic state, the Sri Lankan government had merely made a symbolic gesture to the Tamils, the same could not be said about the concession to unify the Northern and Eastern provinces into a single politico-administrative unit. No other matter in the entire Accord has been more inflammatory to Sinhalese sensitivities, triggering even an assassination attempt on President Jayewardene's life. Indeed, in the past, it was the flat refusal of the Sinhalese negotiators to accede to the North-East amalgamation that, in part, frustrated the reaching of an agreement. Under the Accord, the Northern and Eastern provinces are provisionally unified for approximately a year at the end of which a referendum in the Eastern Province would determine whether it would remain in the merged unit. The merger posed a major hurdle in part because of the ethnic mix in the Eastern Province. The most recent (1981) census showed that Tamils constituted 42%, Muslims 32%, and Sinhalese 25% of the province's population. Despite this relatively balanced tripartite mixture, the Tamil militants claimed this region as well as the Northern Province as their traditional homeland in Sri Lanka. In the Accord, this Tamil argument was conceded temporarily and provisionally by the Sri Lankan government. The Accord admitted to "recognising that the Northern and Eastern provinces have been areas of historical habitation of Sri Lankan Tamil speaking peoples," but qualified this claim by conceding similar residential rights to other groups "who have at all times hitherto lived together in this territory." The important qualifier to the concession provides that, while the Northern and Eastern provinces were to be unified almost immediately and elections held to choose the new unit's political representatives, this arrangement was to be only temporary. By the end of 1988, at the discretion of the Sri Lankan president, a referendum would be held in the Eastern Province to determine whether its residents wanted it to remain a part of a combined North-East or to be a separate province with its own council.

In the projected referendum, the Accord states that political campaigns by individuals and parties would be free and open, following standard electoral campaign practices. The administration of the referendum itself would be overseen by observers from India and Sri Lanka. Both countries took a calculated gamble with this referendum, since it was not clear what the Tamil militants would do in the event the East voted against continued amalgamation of the provinces. The Tamils demanded as a precondition to any agreement that the Eastern Province be regarded as part of their traditional homeland. Should the referendum, in which President Jayewardene promised to campaign as a free citizen against continued merger, decide against continued unification, the new tensions are bound to be awakened. Should the Tamils win the referendum, Sinhalese feeling would be inflamed. On the day the Accord was signed, the wrath of the Sinhalese, who were disappointed over agreement on the provisional merger, was unleashed in fearsome riots that closed down Colombo for nearly a week. In the referendum and the fate of the Eastern Province resides much of the future of interethnic relations.

In conceding to India the temporary merger of the provinces, Sri Lanka incurred one additional major risk. By agreeing to a system of decentralized provincial government endowed with extensive powers, the central government could unwittingly be handing the Tamil militants the preliminary political tools for a final thrust at full independence. Would the provincial unification be a prelude to the full Eelam the autonomists claim? Put differently, the decentralization of the Sri Lankan polity was intended as a device to defuse secession sentiment, not encourage it. When elections are held for the amalgamated North and East provincial council, it is projected that a unified Tamil party will win most of the seats, since the Northern Province is around 92% and the Eastern about 42% Tamil. In the combined sectors, Tamils will make up about 69% of the population. Further, most Muslims in the Eastern Province are Tamil-speaking, and at least some of them may identify with certain Tamil interests. Together then, these figures suggest an arithmetic of Tamil victory in the combined council election which, if consolidated over time, will not only provide ample training to run a government, but under the right circumstances could stimulate demands for full autonomy and sovereignty.

Military Aspects of the Accord

Out of the Accord, the Sri Lankan government secured the cessation of hostilities, bringing the promise of peace to a war-weary population. It was stipulated that both sides would desist from military activities within 48 hours of the signing of the Accord, and within 72 hours of the cessation of hostilities, the Tamil militants were to turn their weapons over to Sri Lankan authorities at designated points. India undertook to prevent the continued use of its territory as a base from which to launch military operations into Sri Lanka, and it agreed to patrol the Palk Strait jointly with the Sri Lankan navy to intercept the flow of weapons from South India to the Jaffna peninsula. To end hostilities, Sri Lanka made several military concessions. First, troops in the North and East were confined to their barracks; second, the new bases built in the Vadamarachchi sector of the Jaffna peninsula, deep in Tiger territory and posing a direct threat to Jaffna city, were to be closed; third, the "homeguards" (villagers trained and armed by the government for self-defense) were to be disarmed;

and finally, over 5,000 Tamil detainees, mainly youths, were to be released.

India also undertook a major role in the military exchanges. It agreed to provide troops, on request by the Sri Lankan government, to enforce the agreement. The Accord used strong language to underscore India's responsibilities, stating that India agreed "to underwrite" the Accord and to offer troops as well as arms and military training to Sri Lanka. Simultaneous with its signing, the Sri Lankan government announced the entry of some 6,000 to 7,000 Indian troops into the Northern and later the Eastern province to assist in implementation of the military aspects of the Accord. By early 1988, over 60,000 Indian troops were in Sri Lanka to collect arms from the militants and to enforce general law and order. The most significant military undertaking by the Indian army was to ensure "the physical security and safety of all communities inhabiting the Northern and Eastern provinces." Rajiv Gandhi said at the time of the signing of the Accord in Colombo that it was security fears that caused the LTTE to be reluctant to cooperate. India undertook to provide that security, substituting itself for the Tamil militants. To have Indian troops on its soil meant that Sri Lanka made a major foreign policy concession to India, and this aroused the fears of many Sinhalese that their ancient anxieties over Indian invasion had become a reality through the ineptness or complicity of their own government.

It was clear that a mediating Indian military was indispensable for the surrender of Tamil arms and the cessation of hostilities. While President Jayewardene stated that Indian troops in Sri Lanka were ultimately under his direction, the fact remained that they had considerable autonomy. Indian troops, it seemed, would not leave willingly if their withdrawal meant a threat to Tamils by Sinhalese forces. In India, underwriting the Accord and guaranteeing the physical security of the Tamils gave the impression that an Indian presence in the dispute had become entrenched. Even though the Accord called for the eventual installation of normal civil and law enforcement administration in the North and East, the writ of the central government would always be qualified by the Accord's guarantee of Tamil security by Indian military might.

The Tamil militants, especially the LTTE, were most reluctant to relinquish control over their weapons. While the other

Tamil guerrilla groups agreed to comply with this provision, the Tigers' leader, Velupillai Prabakaran, openly argued that the loss of their weapons invited "genocide" of the Tamil people who would be left at the mercy of a Sinhalese administration. But Prabakaran had no choice. The Accord was to be executed by India with or without the Tigers' cooperation. Indeed, in agreeing to underwrite the Accord, India had explicitly undertaken to disarm the Tamil militants if they refused to surrender their weapons. At a mammoth open-air meeting in Jaffna, the LTTE leader announced his reluctant willingness to cooperate with India which, under the Accord, had agreed to "ensure the physical security and safety of all communities inhabiting the Northern and Eastern Provinces."

With India's guarantees to the Tigers, some of the arms slowly were surrendered to the Indian Peace Keeping Force (IPKF), but well beyond the initial 72-hour deadline. However, the cautious optimism of the Indian authorities that the Tigers would comply with the terms of the Accord soon proved to be wrong. By early October the Tigers were openly defying Indian authority, and the result was military confrontation between the two sides in the Jaffna peninsula. The Indian army won the battle, but both sides suffered heavy casualties. Civilian losses were even more severe and extensive damage was caused to property and infrastructure. Indeed, the Indian operation in the peninsula was a turning point in the war, not only because the Tigers lost their stronghold but also because the Indians, by the manner in which they conducted the military campaign, lost much of the goodwill they had with the Tamils in Jaffna.

Diplomatic Aspects of the Accord

The Accord also embodied exchanges with respect to the external relations and diplomatic requirements of both Sri Lanka and India, but lopsidedly in favor of the latter. Indeed, Rajiv Gandhi suggested at the signing ceremony in Colombo that the restoration of Sri Lanka's nonaligned posture underlaid the agreement, at least from India's perspective. For its role in terminating hostilities, India extracted broad undertakings from Sri Lanka to desist from entering into any military relations with India's adversaries. Sri Lanka, in frustration with India's role in arming and harboring the militants, had entered into countervailing security and military arrangements with Pakistan, the Peoples Republic of China (PRC), Israel, and the United States. From Pakistan, Sri Lanka procured training of its troops. From the PRC, it secured military equipment. From Israel, it got Mossad antiterrorist skills. From the United States, the Sri Lankan regime with its commitment to an open, free enterprise economy obtained easy access to aid and loans. In addition, Sri Lanka permitted American naval vessels access to its ports and leased some 1,000 acres for the construction of an enlarged relay facility for the Voice of America (VOA). India had alleged that the U.S. used its VOA facilities in Sri Lanka not only for broadcasting purposes but also for military surveillance.

In effect, Sri Lanka's countervailing relations with Pakistan, the PRC, Israel, and the United States had exposed India's southern flank. Already heavily preoccupied with security threats in its northeast and northwest from the Chinese and Pakistanis, respectively, and internally destabilized by the Sikhs and other secessionist movements, India was wary of opening yet another front to hostile penetration. India's strategic security needs then, as well as internal threats to its unity and stability, compelled it to seek the Accord with Sri Lanka. At least on the surface, Sri Lanka reaffirmed its commitment to a foreign policy of nonalignment and agreed not to permit the use of its territory by foreign military and intelligence agencies against Indian interests. On these matters, the relevant part of the Accord—an annexed letter from Gandhi to Jayewardene—should be cited in full:

Conscious of the friendship between our two countries stretching over two millennia and more, and recognizing the importance of nurturing this traditional friendships, it is imperative that both Sri Lanka and India reaffirm the decision not to allow our respective territories to be used for activities prejudicial to each other's unity, territorial integrity and security.

In this spirit, you had, during the course of our discussions, agreed to meet some of India's concerns as follows:
(i) Your Excellency and myself will reach an early understanding about the relevance and employment of foreign military and intelligence personnel with a view to ensuring that such presences will not prejudice Indo-Sri Lankan relations.
(ii) Trincomalee or any other ports in Sri Lanka will not be made available for military use by any country in a manner prejudicial to India's interests.
(iii) The work of restoring and operating the Trincomalee oil tank farm will be undertaken as a joint venture between India and Sri Lanka.
(iv) Sri Lanka's agreements with foreign broadcasting organizations will be reviewed to ensure that any facilities set up by them in Sri Lanka are

used solely as public broadcasting facilities and not for any military or intelligence purposes.

To fill the gap anticipated by Sri Lanka's loss of Pakistani and Chinese military aid, India undertook to provide Sri Lankan forces with military equipment and training. Two additional devices were built into the Accord to protect Indian interests. First, Indian personnel would participate in the anticipated project to restore the Trincomalee oil tank. Indirectly, this would permit Indian personnel on the premises of the port so they would be able to determine whether foreign agencies were present and misusing the base. Second, to review and monitor the implementation of the Accord, a joint consultative body composed of Sri Lankan and Indian staff would be established, presumably with broad powers to visit all parts of the country to examine whatever interested it.

Overall, the foreign policy concessions that Sri Lanka extended to India served India's security interests. Sri Lanka was willing to reduce, if not eliminate its security-military connections, in particular with Pakistan and China, to accommodate India's quest for security on its southern flank. It could be argued that Sri Lanka had decided to accept modification of its freedom to choose its friends in exchange for India's guarantee not to invade, not to sponsor anti-Lankan terrorism, and not to permit the use of its territory by forces inimical to Sri Lankan territorial integrity. In effect, this meant that Sri Lanka, in accepting India's terms of friendship, signaled willingness to live under the canopy of Indian foreign policy dominance. The Accord also paved the way for strengthening economic relations between the two countries. The Indo–Sri Lanka joint economic committee was revived after a five-year lapse, and India has promised Sri Lanka US$40 million in loans and grants to finance imports from India. There is even a suggestion that Sri Lanka's electrical power grid be linked to that of Tamil Nadu. Some quarters in Sri Lanka, however, are highly critical of the dependency that such arrangements will create. . . .

Problems of Implementation

The Accord has run into several major problems in its implementation. First and foremost, the Indian troops failed to disarm the LTTE within a reasonable period of time. The latter eventually refused to join the interim administration and decided to continue the war, this time against the Indians. After its defeat in Jaffna in October 1987, the LTTE shifted its operations to the Eastern Province, which is a more sensitive area because it is inhabited in significant numbers by all three communities—Tamil, Muslim, and Sinhalese. Since October, the LTTE has conducted a concerted campaign in the province, using terror tactics to destabilize the region, including the murder of Sinhalese and Muslim civilians. A large number of Sinhalese and Muslim refugees who have fled their homes are refusing to return until the Sri Lankan security forces are redeployed in the area. For propaganda against the Indians, the LTTE has also exploited acts of violence and indiscipline committed by some Indian soldiers on Tamil civilians. The unsatisfactory military situation has prevented the holding of provincial council elections and even the conduct of normal civil administration in the Eastern Province.

The failure to restore peace quickly has put the Accord at risk. The Indians probably overestimated their influence with the LTTE, and underestimated the fighting capability of the Tigers and their commitment to a separate Tamil state of Eelam. Prime Minister Gandhi is running into a host of problems at home on account of the apparently protracted nature of the military engagement in Sri Lanka. The pro–Sri Lankan Tamil lobby in Delhi and especially in Tamil Nadu does not want the Indian army to defeat the LTTE, and Gandhi, anxious to preserve the Congress (I) base in Tamil Nadu following the death last December of Chief Minister M. G. Ramachandran, is now doubly sensitive to Tamil Nadu opinion. The rising casualty figures among Indian troops is also drawing increasing criticism, as are the escalating economic costs of the military engagement. It probably would be premature to describe Sri Lanka as India's Vietnam or Afghanistan, but while Sri Lanka could have been a prestige-enhancing military operation had it been completed quickly, it is turning out to be a rambling, indecisive campaign with no end in sight.

On the Sri Lankan side, many of the government's early optimistic expectations have not been realized. Although the provincial council legislation was passed by Parliament in November 1987, elections for councils in the North-East have been postponed indefinitely. The absence of peace in the Tamil areas and the consequent continued presence of large numbers of Indian troops has become a major electoral liability for the ruling UNP.

There is no doubt that the Indian presence is hugely unpopular among the Sinhalese. It has significantly strengthened the position of President Jayewardene's long-standing rival, Mrs. Bandaranaike and her Sri Lanka Freedom Party, who have also come out against the provincial councils. Even more disturbing for the ruling party and for the survival of the Accord is the anti-Accord and anti-Indian militancy led by the proscribed People's Liberation Front (JVP) in the south. A spate of politically motivated killings generally attributed to the JVP have occurred since August 1987, with most of the victims either members of the ruling party or of left political parties that support the Accord. UNP President Harsha Abeywardene and the charismatic leader of the Sri Lanka People's Party (SLMP), film idol Vijaya Kumaranatunga, are the most prominent among them. This situation forced President Jayewardene to postpone a by-election scheduled for mid-March 1988, as well as elections to some of the provincial councils in the south originally scheduled for late April. Without peace the government is also unable to make use of the US$493 million in rehabilitation aid that it negotiated last December. Thus, the immediate future of the Accord will depend very much on two factors—the success of the Indians in restoring peace in the North and East, and the success with which Colombo is able to implement the devolution package. However, even if peace and local administration become a reality, many other issues in the Sinhala-Tamil ethnic equation are germane to a long-term relationship and these the Accord fails to address.

The Accord and a Long-Term Solution

The Accord can be viewed as a measure that served, at least temporarily, to arrest the hemorrhage of resources and loss of life from the war. The underlying long-term issues that, in the first instance, created the crisis have to be dealt with. Further, it is clear that the society requires positive institutional policies to sustain the coexistence of the different ethnic groups. By developing spheres of intergroup cooperation and expanding areas of amity, the likelihood of conflict may be diminished. In this section, we offer an overview of long-range issues and opportunities toward which the Accord can only be a starting point in institutional conflict resolution.

The underlying practical and symbolic issues that pushed Sri Lanka toward its communal crisis pertain to representation, language, religion, land settlement, and alleged discrimination in the areas of university admission and jobs. Apart from representation, these issues emerged in the post-independence period. As to representation, Tamil spokesmen at the time of the Donomoughmore Commission, fearing the superior numbers of the Sinhalese and wanting to prevent the loss of the comparative advantages in status, jobs, and privileges they had acquired under colonial rule, demanded communal representation instead of the one-man one-vote principle. When this was rejected for a system based on majoritarian democracy, the Tamils sought refuge in a federal arrangement under which they could maximize the value of their concentrated numbers in the Northern and Eastern provinces. This too was rejected. However, Tamil-based political parties have periodically entered into coalition with governing Sinhalese-based parties and obtained important cabinet appointments, thereby giving representation to Tamil interests at the highest decision-making level in the country. But this was a form of representation that was neither predictable nor fully capable of institutionally protecting Tamil rights. In the 1987 Accord, representation stood as the most significant area of Sri Lankan concession: a system of decentralized provincial councils under which the northern and eastern regions would be amalgamated temporarily. However, even this concession was limited in value, as decentralized councils would exist within a unitary system and would lack the level of entrenched protection and jurisdictional prerogative inherent in a federal system. Put starkly, the system of provincial government to be implemented could be dismantled relatively easily by the national legislature. Given the vagaries of party politics in Sri Lanka, especially in the contemporary situation if Bandaranaike's SLFP and its allies were to win the next elections, the provincial councils could be in jeopardy. This sort of vulnerability in an area of vital interest to the Tamil community would have to be eliminated.

While provincial-level representation has been addressed, national-level representation remains problematic. According to population numbers, Tamil representation in the national parliament would be 20% or less. Tamils might or might not be part of the ruling regime and their cabinet representation therefore would be uncertain. This is clearly an important lacuna in the Accord. While Tamil cabinet presence has been left to the vagaries of political alignments in the past, it would appear that some sort of power sharing at the center now is required, both as symbol and as practical assurance to Tamil interests. A proportion of both parliamentary seats and cabinet posts probably would be ideal. A vice-president from a minority community is also a possibility. Thus, the Accord could be conceived as a first step in reconciliation, leading toward negotiation of a wider and more comprehensive agreement covering such issues as cabinet representation.

In the area of language, the Accord stated explicitly that there would be three national languages—Sinhalese, Tamil, and English. In some ways, this was too much and too late. Ideally, the independence constitution of 1947 should have established Sinhalese and Tamil as the national languages, thereby removing this area from party politics. To make English a national language would appear at this time unnecessary and probably costly. Overall, the language provision in the Accord was redundant since the 1956 "Sinhala only" language law had been modified by Article 19 of the constitution of 1978 that recognized Tamil as a national language. In the sphere of religion, the constitution of 1972 proclaimed that Buddhism had a special place in Sri Lanka. This provision had mainly symbolic value, but its place in the constitution of a country could be viewed as unnecessarily provocative. The 1987 Accord called for the "nurturing" of all cultural communities in a multiethnic state, almost requiring the state to offer commensurate amounts of financial support to Hindus, Muslims, and Christians as are offered to the Buddhist sects in Sri Lanka.

Land settlement has been a burning issue in the ethnic conflict. Tamils have accused the government of initiating policies and practices that favored the Sinhalese in settling farmers on state lands and that led to the systematic populating of traditional Tamil areas by Sinhalese settlers. Some facts support this claim. For example, the proportion of Sinhalese in the Trincomalee district increased from 4.5% in 1921 to 33.6% in 1981, and that of the Ampara district from 8.2% to 37.6%. However, other evidence showed that aspects of the claim were unwarranted. The ethnic balance of the north has never changed appreciably through Sinhalese settlement. In the east, the Tamil percentage of the total population dropped from 52% in 1921 to 42% in 1981. However, the Tamil claim of a "traditional homeland" in the Eastern Province is a weak one. All the available historical and demographic evidence points to large Sinhalese settlements in the interior of the province and Tamil settlements along a coastal strip. On the larger canvas, the land settlement problem could be conceived as an "issue" under a government that was intent on diluting Tamil bases of political power. However, under the Accord's "nurturing" outlook, this sort of land policy should terminate.

Discrimination with regard to jobs, scholarships, and university admissions has also been a major grievance of the Tamils. In these matters also, some Tamil claims are closer to the truth than others. For example, Tamils have lost out on jobs in government and state corporations, especially in clerical and lower grades where political patronage is important. Their representation in the security forces is minimal. However, Tamil claims are less convincing in university admissions as President Jayewardene, when he assumed office, removed the system of "standardization" that required Tamils to get higher marks than Sinhalese on university admission examinations. The system of district-based admissions that has prevailed since then has been supported by Tamils outside the Jaffna peninsula who benefit from it. In any event, the present arrangement has generally ensured about 25% of the places in science-based courses for Sri Lankan Tamils who make up 12.5% of the population.

The Accord, by virtue of decentralizing the polity, virtually turned over many employment opportunities to provincial councils, and this was a major reason why the militants wanted not one but two provinces under their control. The combined Northern and Eastern provinces should be controlled in the future by the Tamils, which would provide land, jobs, and other practical opportunities and patronage. At the national level, however, specifically with regard to the public service and national institutions such as the universities, the Accord does not provide for any guaranteed Tamil proportional representation. The civil service of the Northern and Eastern provinces would not be adequate to meet Tamil demands for job opportunities. The Accord does not offer a formula, such as proportionality, for a solution. In the long run, Tamil proportional presence in the national sphere—the public service, the state corporations, the army—is needed to establish a more integrated social and cultural system.

Conclusion

The 1987 Indo–Sri Lankan Accord should be viewed as a first step in a general direction toward a more durable peace. It has attended only to certain significant short-term issues, leaving on the agenda many of the underlying long-term problems for future resolution. The terms of the Accord project both solutions and problems. In this sense, it has to be viewed as a dynamic instrument, clearing away some issues and creating others, a living document always available for amendment and adjustment and not a final static writ unrealistically addressing a fluid situation. It will fall on the shoulders of the joint consultative team not only to monitor the implementation of the Accord, but to recommend changes leading to the larger objective of institutionalizing the peace.

THE ROOTS OF CONFLICT IN SRI LANKA[3]

Despite the peace treaty signed in July by Sri Lanka's Sinhalese-dominated government and Tamil militants, the ethnic conflict on that island country near India's eastern coast is unlikely to end soon. The August 18 grenade attack on the floor of Parliament, apparently planned by Sinhalese extremists to punish President J. R. Jayewardene for his treaty concessions to Tamils, made that ominous point abundantly clear.

One difference between these two ethnic groups is religion. Most of the Tamils, who make up some 18 per cent of the population, are Hindu, while most of the Sinhalese, who constitute about 74 per cent of the island's residents, are Buddhist. But religion is not at the heart of this conflict; more basic are long-standing social and economic inequalities.

The Tamils claim that the Sinhalese majority has discriminated against them socially and politically. One obviously discriminatory policy that is particularly far-reaching concerns language.

---

[3]Reprint of an article by Victoria A. Rebeck, assistant editor of the *Christian Century*. Copyright © 1987 Christian Century Foundation. Reprinted by permission from the September 23, 1987 issue of the *Christian Century*.

Though the government in 1956 recognized both Sinhalese and Tamil as national languages, Sinhalese is the "official" language, which means that Tamils have had to prove proficiency in Sinhalese in order to qualify for jobs, promotions, university acceptance and other means of advancement.

The country's education policy also discriminates against Tamils. In 1971, Prime Minister Sirimavo Bandaranaike altered university entrance requirements to make the minimum grade average higher for Tamil applicants than for Sinhalese. She took this action because the Sinhalese had believed that a disproportionate number of Tamil students were accepted into the nation's four universities, and that Tamil professors graded Tamil students' exams more leniently. Until 1977 the government had favored students on the basis of their speaking Sinhalese, as well as on their place of origin. At that time, the former policy was dropped, but not the latter; students from the nation's areas which are predominantly Sinhalese continue to receive favored treatment.

Perhaps the greatest amount of tension between Tamils and Sinhalese results from employment discrimination. Some reports have placed the 1980 unemployment rate among educated Tamils as high as 41 per cent, compared to 20 per cent among Sinhalese. Tamils complain that there are fewer job opportunities in general for them, partly because many more labor-intensive industries are being developed in Sinhalese-dominated areas.

Some Sri Lankans suggest that much of the Sinhalese animosity toward Tamils is due to their jealousy of Tamils' career successes. Tamils have, in the past, held a disproportionate number of government positions and other white-collar jobs—the result of their willingness to cooperate with the British imperial system. Under British rule the Tamils, who live far away from the commercial developments, saw education as the primary route to advancement and hence were eager for the professional training the British provided. Also, when the British colonized Sri Lanka, the Anglican Church concentrated its mission efforts on the Buddhist majority, allowing American missionaries to work with the minority Hindus. Some Sri Lankans speculate that the Buddhist Sinhalese, who opposed British influence and Anglican proselytizing, resisted the accompanying educational efforts, whereas the Hindu Tamils were inclined to accept the American missionaries, including their schools. This situation gave rise to an educational tradition among Tamils that made them well qualified for university admissions and well-paying jobs—and which in turn stirred the resentment of Sinhalese.

Many Sinhalese actually regard the Tamils as outsiders. Relative newcomers, the Tamils are descendants of the people brought from South India to Sri Lanka by the British in the 19th century to work on tea plantations. However, the Tamils and Sinhalese are in fact closely related ethnically. According to S. J. Tambiah, a Sri Lankan who is now professor of anthropology at Harvard University and curator of South Asian Ethnology at the Peabody Museum, "if it were possible to trace the present-day Sinhalese population's ancestry far enough, all lines would in major part lead back to South India" (*Ethnic Fratricide and the Dismantling of Democracy* [University of Chicago Press, 1986], p. 5). That area of Sri Lanka's huge neighbor is the location of the state of Tamil Nadu, and Sri Lanka's Sinhalese, despite their dominance, have traditionally feared the strength of that state and its support of Sri Lankan Tamils.

Ethnic tensions in Sri Lanka first burst into extensive violence in 1958. Nationalist sentiment among Sinhalese was high—but also frustrated; the government was close to reaching an agreement with Tamil politicians to create a Tamil state that would have some legislative autonomy (which is provided for in the 1987 peace treaty). But protests by a party of Buddhist monks and by the United National Party led by Jayewardene fanned the flames of tension into full-scale rioting against Tamils, and the plan was dropped.

More riots erupted in 1977 shortly after Jayewardene was elected prime minister. Sinhalese zealots drove into Tamil areas (in government vehicles, some observers say) and attacked Tamil people, homes and businesses. Jayewardene did little to curb the violence. He did commission an investigator—who concluded that the Tamils were at fault.

Sinhalese ravaged Tamil areas again in major rioting that occurred in 1981 and 1983. By this time several Tamil militant groups had emerged, most of which have since been subsumed into the Liberation Tigers of Tamil Eelam, who champion the formation of an independent Tamil state in the north to be known as Eelam. Some Tamils claim that the government has had little regard for their physical safety, leaving them no choice but to accept the protection of the militants, even if they do not share the latters' entire ideology. Foreign observers have supported Tamil claims that the government has encouraged attacks on Tamils by the military and by gangs of Sinhalese civilians. (Only recently has Jayewardene acknowledged that "some misguided Sinhalese" were responsible for the 1983 riots.)

This year the conflict developed into a virtual war. The government initiated "Operation Liberation," an offensive against Tamil militants who had taken control of the Jaffna peninsula, a Tamil-dominated area at the nation's northern tip. The government insisted that it was battling only the militants, but hundreds of civilians have been wounded or killed—sometimes in bombings of churches or temples, which the government had claimed it would protect as sanctuaries.

The *New York Times* estimates that about 6,000 Sri Lankans have died in the past four years of fighting. Hundreds of Tamil young men have been detained indefinitely as terrorist suspects, and Amnesty International has published lists of hundreds who have disappeared without a trace, or whom witnesses observed being apprehended by security forces. In many cases, officials have given the detainees' families and friends no information about where the detainees are or how long they will be held. Some former detainees claim they have been tortured, and some female detainees have reported sexual abuse. The security forces' roundup of Tamils has been criticized as random, but under the Prevention of Terrorism Act of 1979, anyone the government deems suspicious can be arrested and held without charge. Fleeing the violence and persecution, several hundred Tamils have sought refuge in Tamil Nadu.

On a recent speaking tour in the U.S. Sri Lanka's minister of national security, Lalith Athulathmudali, denied charges that the military was abusing Tamils' human rights. He questioned the reliability of the reports obtained by Amnesty International because they were based primarily on affidavits, which Athulathmudali claimed are not considered by many court systems to be dependable evidence. When asked how the government is responding to Tamil claims of military harassment, Athulathmudali facilely suggested that citizens with such a complaint could "report it to the police."

In turn, Amnesty International has doubts about the methods of Athulathmudali's government. In its report of disappearances in Sri Lanka, AI states that "in nearly all cases of 'disappearances' in Sri Lanka, no official inquiry has been held to establish the whereabouts or the fate of the 'disappeared.' . . . In the few cases . . . where investigations were reportedly conducted, they were performed by the security forces themselves and not by an independent body. Inquiries either appear to have been stopped or else their findings were never published" (*Sri Lanka Disappearances* [Amnesty International, 1986], p. 4).

This summer's peace treaty came about largely through pressure from India, whose role in the negotiations seemed calculated to appease the demands of Tamil Nadu residents, while minimizing Sri Lanka's criticisms of Indian meddling. As Tamil refugees streamed into Tamil Nadu this summer, local residents called on Prime Minister Rajiv Gandhi to take action. For its part, Sri Lanka does not want to submit to pressure from its powerful neighbor. In early June, when India attempted to deliver by sea supplies of food and medicine to the Jaffna peninsula, resistance from the Sri Lankan government forced it to airdrop the supplies instead. Sri Lanka's main objection was that India had refused to allow the Jayewardene government to distribute the supplies without India's oversight.

The church in Sri Lanka has protested the civil violence only weakly. Christians constitute no more than some 8 per cent of the population, but according to one theology professor at the Theological College of Lanka, they make up nearly half the nation's better-educated citizens. Drawing both Sinhalese and Tamil believers, the church is in a unique position to call for peace, justice and reconciliation, but it has been ineffective. Many Sinhalese Christians trust the government's word, though some Sinhalese church leaders sympathize with the Tamils. Key leaders include Roman Catholic priest Tissa Balasuriya, director of the Center for Society and Religion in Colombo, who has traveled widely in Sri Lanka and abroad to call for peace and cooperation. He has been prevented by the government from holding peace rallies, but his office has helped some people trace missing relatives. While respecting his commitment and vision, some Sri Lankan church leaders are skeptical that his approach can work. Sri Lanka Christians also have the example of the late Anglican Bishop Lakshman Wickramasinghe, who spoke out against the military's participation in attacks on Tamil civilians. He was angry enough to remark that he was ashamed to be a Sinhalese—a comment that earned him no small amount of criticism.

Some church leaders have tried to apply principles of liberation theology to Sri Lanka's struggle, but since that theology has not come from the local grassroots it has not had much impact. Some theologians, such as S. J. Emmanuel, rector of St. Francis Xavier Seminary in Sri Lanka, are trying to call the church to a prophetic stance. In a 1984 pastoral letter, the country's Christian leaders urged Christians to address the conflict's root causes, and to speak out for their resolution. But it took an extended time for the letter to be translated into Sinhalese. Even then, as Father Emmanuel commented in a church newsletter, its statements were too "cautious and safely balanced," and "did not carry a hard-hitting message to those responsible for evil."

An ad hoc interreligious group is attempting to initiate a mass movement under the slogan "Tell the People the Truth." In November 1986, 181 Buddhist and Christian clergy and laypeople (including both Tamils and Sinhalese) signed an appeal, written in verse by church activist Yohan Devananda, decrying oppression and suffering, and pleading for basic rights, compassion and penitence. The document was sent to Parliament and has been passed around to community groups and friends in an effort to mobilize people to demand honesty and repentance from the government.

It remains to be seen whether the peace accord will elicit such repentance. So far it has implemented a tenuous cease-fire (although there have been isolated incidents such as the Parliament shooting). Though the bullets may stop flying for awhile, the government has much to do to convince the people that there is democracy in Sri Lanka and that human rights are heeded. It must locate and release detainees, make restitution for ruined businesses, churches and temples, and repent of the suffering it has afflicted upon its citizens. Sinhalese who have been swept up in a fury of nationalism must acknowledge the injustice of their chauvinism. Militants from both sides must renounce their violent tactics. The government must decide to tell the people the truth, before it can gain their trust, before peace can really begin.

RESOLVING THE SRI LANKAN CONFLICT[4]

I welcome this opportunity to meet with you today to discuss
Sri Lanka and the Administration's policies toward that island nation.

Among today's developing countries, Sri Lanka stands out as
one of the few which have successfully passed more than once the
toughest test facing any democracy—peaceful transition of power from one political party to another. In five general elections
since 1948, voters have turned the party in control out of office.
The country boasts a unicameral legislature elected by universal
adult suffrage, an independent judiciary, and a lively and free
press. Its highly literate citizenry participates enthusiastically in
the political process. This democratic tradition is not new nor is
it fragile. It became a part of Sri Lankan life in 1932 when the
country had its first elections, became especially vigorous since
Sri Lanka became independent in 1948, and remains intact today.

In recent years, Sri Lanka has been noteworthy not only for
its successful practice of democracy but for its economic achievements as well. The quality of life is high for the average Sri Lankan. Even though Sri Lanka's per capita income was only $372
in 1985, the life expectancy of Sri Lankans was 69 years, the highest in South Asia. For the past 10 years, the government has increasingly abandoned an earlier reliance on statist economic
policies and adopted reforms designed to encourage accelerated
economic growth through reliance on liberal and responsible
economic management and expansion of the private sector. Significant numbers of public sector enterprises have returned to
private hands, and this trend is expected to continue as the government adopts new measures.

The Sri Lankan Government's faith in these recent economic
policy reforms has been justified by results. Despite the ethnic
conflict and depressed prices for some of its traditional agricultural commodities, these new policies, combined with the indus-

[4]Reprint of a statement before the Subcommittee on Asian and Pacific Affairs
of the House Foreign Affairs Committee on March 12, 1987 by Robert A. Peck,
Deputy Assistant Secretary for Near Eastern and South Asian Affairs. *Department
of State Bulletin*, May 1987, pp. 68–71.

triousness of the Sri Lankan people, have produced growth rates close to 5%. This is a remarkable achievement and one worthy of our continued support.

U.S. interests in Sri Lanka derive from its strong democratic traditions and its more recent economic success, both of which serve as proof to other developing countries of the efficacy of the political and economic system we advocate. Sri Lanka is, moreover, a good friend of the United States. The Sri Lankan Government recently agreed to upgrade the capabilities of a long-existing Voice of America (VOA) facility, part of a global effort to improve the effectiveness of these broadcasts. We have also been pleased by Sri Lanka's moderate voice in multilateral forums and by its general policy opening its ports to visits by ships of all nations.

Background to the Conflict

Sri Lanka's principal problem, and our principal concern, is the current spasm of ethnic conflict between the majority Sinhalese, who make up 74% of the population, and the Sri Lankan Tamils, who migrated to Sri Lanka from south India centuries ago and who currently comprise approximately 12.5% of the population. There are also smaller groups, most predominantly the so-called Indian Tamils (5.5%), who are more recent immigrants and who work the tea estates in the central part of the country, and Moslems (7%). Each of these groups has unique linguistic, cultural, and religious characteristics, but they have lived side-by-side in relative harmony for most of recent Sri Lankan history. Since independence, however, tensions between the Sri Lankan Tamils and the Sinhalese have grown steadily worse.

Sri Lankan Tamils live throughout the country, including Colombo, but are heavily concentrated in the north and parts of the east. Sri Lankan Tamils have always occupied prominent positions in government, commerce, and the professions. Many are university graduates and significant landowners. At one time, 40% of the university students were Tamils. Tamils believe that since independence, successive governments dominated by Sinhalese have discriminated against them in such areas as access to education and jobs. Sri Lankan Tamils considered government measures after 1956 to promote the use of Sinhala, at the expense of Tamil and English, to be particularly discriminatory.

After assuming power in 1977, the government of President
Jayewardene adopted several measures in an attempt to respond
to Tamil concerns. It scrapped the previous government's university admissions policies, which tended to restrict Tamil
admissions to their percentage of the national population. Approximately 25% of the university students are now Tamils. The
government also increased the number of national universities
from two to eight plus an open university so that there are now
places available for many more students of all ethnic communities. In addition, the government has continued to include Tamils
in high government positions. At present, the chief justice, the
attorney general, three cabinet ministers, and several secretaries
of ministries are Tamils. The just-retired army chief of staff was
a Tamil. Also the government restored Tamil to the status of a
national language in 1978 and began to stress the use and study
of English as a link-language.

Militant Factions

In the mid-1970's, many Tamil leaders and frustrated youths
began to feel that the only way for them to redress their grievances was to separate the Tamil majority areas from Sri Lanka
and form an independent Tamil state, to be known as Tamil
"Eelam." The political leaders, joining together under the banner
of the Tamil United Liberation Front (TULF), contested the
elections of 1977 on a platform of independence and won all 14
seats in the northern province and 2 seats in the east. Tamil
youths, not confident that the political process would provide redress for the grievances or allow the creation of a Tamil state,
formed militant groups and turned to armed struggle as the political process lagged in achieving their goals.

The simmering ethnic conflict came to a head in 1983 after
parliamentary bielections and local government elections. Tamil
militants began to attack banks, government-owned buses and
trains, police stations, and security forces in the north. A backlash
produced communal rioting in the south. In Colombo 387 people, mostly Tamil, were killed.

These events sharply polarized ethnic feelings, eroding the
moderate center on both sides. The number of Tamils entering
lower level government positions after 1983 dropped significantly. Although never high, the Tamil percentage also fell in the se-

curity forces, until now Tamils make up no more than 5% of the police and 2% of the armed forces. The TULF members of Parliament resigned after refusing to take an oath of allegiance to the unity of Sri Lanka required by a new constitutional amendment; many left to take up residence in south India. This left the Tamil struggle in Sri Lanka to the Tamil militant groups, which have grown in strength and power in the years since 1983.

The Tamil militants represent a very heterogeneous group, but all proclaim the goal of a Tamil state which would include the northern and eastern provinces of Sri Lanka. Total militant strength is probably no more than 10,000, with members drawn from young, unemployed Tamil males. Sicne 1983, five militant groups have been the most prominent. These are the Liberation Tigers of Tamil Eelam (LTTE), the Eelam People's Revolutionary Liberation Front (EPRLF), the Tamil Eelam Liberation Organization (TELO), the Eelam Revolutionary Organization of Students (EROS), and the People's Liberation Organization of Tamil Eelam (PLOTE).

Although united by the cause of creating a Tamil state, these different groups do not form a unified fighting force. In fact, the last year has seen repeated attacks by the LTTE against other militant groups. The most hard-line group—the LTTE—has engaged in an apparent campaign to absorb or wipe out the other groups to ensure its dominance of the militant movement. In May 1986, the LTTE attacked members of TELO in northern Sri Lanka, killing between 150 and 170, including TELO's leader. Since December, and after LTTE leader Prabhakaran returned to northern Sri Lanka from India, the LTTE began to attack units of the EPRLF which have been active in the east. At least 100 militants have been killed in these attacks, as well as many Tamil civilians suspected of sympathizing with one militant group or another. As we enter 1987, the LTTE has become the dominant militant group. But intergroup fighting continues.

Since 1983 the militants have expanded areas under their effective control in the northern province, including much of the Jaffna Peninsula. The situation in the multiethnic eastern province is more confused, with some areas largely controlled by the militants and some by the security forces. Increasingly the conflict has shifted to the east, largely because of an apparent attempt by the militants to demonstrate *de facto* control there in support of their claim to the area.

Ideologically all militant groups espouse Tamil nationalism mixed with varying degrees of Marxism. The LTTE and EROS are considered to be the most dogmatic of the groups and are likely to seek to impose single-party rule should they gain power. They have indicated that if they achieve control of the multiethnic eastern province, they may force out its Sinhalese residents. In the areas now controlled by the militants, such as the Jaffna Peninsula, tax collection, licensing, police duties, and judicial functions have been established by the militants without normal democratic procedures. Laws are enforced in a harsh and unpredictable manner, with militants resorting to summary executions of alleged informants or other suspected traitors. Although many Tamil residents of these areas are sympathetic to the goals of the militant groups and see them as their main defense against the government's security forces, many observers believe that a free election would bring the moderate Tamil leaders of the TULF, rather than the militants, back into power.

As is clear from the persistence and severity of the fighting, the militants are well-armed and trained. There have been persistent reports in the Indian press that the Tamil militants acquire arms in and through India and that they have received paramilitary training in special camps which their organizations run there. The Indian Government has categorically denied these charges. The press has also reported that some militant leaders have received support and training from international terrorist organizations, such as the Palestine Liberation Organization (PLO). These reports are difficult to confirm. The Sri Lankan Government believes that the militants have built ammunition and bomb factories within northern Sri Lanka. Much of the funding for militant activities appears to come from money sent by militant sympathizers living abroad and from the proceeds of narcotics smuggling. Many Sri Lankan Tamils have been arrested on narcotics trafficking charges in Europe.

In response to the Tamil insurgency, the Sri Lankan security forces have grown substantially, especially during the past year. Before the insurgency, the army was largely a ceremonial army, with limited training and weaponry. It clearly did not have either the training or experience to wage a protracted guerrilla struggle. Since 1983 the security forces and police have doubled in size, and expenditures on defense have grown accordingly. The armed forces' manpower now exceeds 35,000. The police has grown in size to 20,000, which includes over 1,000 special task force personnel specially charged with counterinsurgency operations. Civilian militia groups have been formed, especially in the east, and their size now approaches 15,000. There has been no need for conscription, since there have been more applicants than can be accommodated.

Escalation of the Conflict

As the security forces and the militants have increased their manpower and obtained better equipment, the conflict has grown, and casualties on both sides have mounted. The number of Sri Lankan civilians killed in the conflict since 1983 probably exceeds 2,000, with 1,500 killed in the last 2 years. During the 4-year period since 1983, at least 515 members of the security forces and police have been killed. As the recent Amnesty International report indicates, many people have disappeared during the conflict. The Amnesty report contends that the security forces are responsible for these disappearances, but the government argues that many of those unaccounted for could have been killed by the militants, changed their names to avoid arrest, joined the militants, or left the country. We estimate that approximately 1,000 persons have disappeared. This figure includes those allegedly abducted by the Tamil militants. Several thousand persons have been reported arrested since the conflict began, although many have since been released.

We estimate that about 4,400 people were killed or wounded in the conflict during 1986, including 800 members of the security forces. As many as 100,000 Sri Lankans have left Sri Lanka since 1983, and over 200,000 were displaced internally in the last 2 years alone. In recent months, there has been a small return flow of Sri Lankan Tamils from southern India back to Sri Lanka. Of those displaced, about one-third are Tamil and two-thirds are Sinhalese, most of them originally living in the northern and eastern provinces. The remaining two-thirds of the country has remained generally calm.

Human Rights Concerns

The fighting has resulted in reports of serious human rights abuses by both sides. In the past year, government security forces

opened fire in civilian areas following hit-and-run insurgent attacks and land mine explosions and launched air strikes or mortar
shellings in densely populated areas, particularly on the Jaffna
Peninsula. Tamil insurgents bombed and mined transportation
facilities and public buildings, attacked Sinhalese villagers living
in areas in the eastern province, and executed approximately 100
suspected government informers or sympathizers. The militants
also mounted a campaign of attacks on Sinhalese targets in the
south which peaked last May when an Air Lanka aircraft was
bombed, killing 17 people. This was followed by the bombing of
the central telegraph office in Colombo in which 12 persons were
killed. Bombs were discovered recently at a Colombo power station, the only such incident sicne last summer.

In a notable development, the government has recently made
an effort to improve the training and discipline of its security
forces. The government has distributed information on human
rights to its troops and formed teams to teach soldiers Tamil and
encourage respect for Tamil culture. Discipline within the army
has improved. In the recent military actions in the north, there
have been virtually no allegations of human rights abuses by the
Sri Lankan Army. This appears to demonstrate the government's
concern with human rights. Unfortunately, this cannot be said
for the police special task force which was accused of summary
executions of a large number of Tamil civilians in an incident last
month in the eastern province. We have encouraged continued
efforts in this area to address the full range of human rights concerns.

Recent Developments

Recent developments affecting the conflict have included the
November seizure by India of the militants' weapons in southern
India and the temporary arrest of some militant leaders. For a
brief period, the communications gear of the Tamil militants,
which enables the leaders to communicate with their forces in Sri
Lanka, was also confiscated. Possibly in reaction to this Indian
pressure, the leader of the LTTE, Prabhakaran, returned to Jaffna. On January 1, the militants in Jaffna announced that they
would begin to expand their takeover of some of the functions
of the local government. This prompted the Sri Lankan Government to institute a limited blockade of the Jaffna Peninsula in an

attempt to cut off fuel and aluminum going to the north. Sri Lankan forces, in a recent offensive, made some advances in the north, captured some weapons, but many militants disappeared into the brush. Fighting continues today in the east, but the north is relatively quiet at the moment. Militant control remains firm in the Jaffna area, and the eastern province remains unsettled.

While the fighting has resulted in great loss of life, its impact on the Sri Lankan economy and the economic well-being of most Sri Lankan citizens has not been as great as might be expected. The Sri Lankan economy continues to grow at about 4.5%, a remarkable figure under the circumstances. This is partly due to the subsistence agricultural nature of the economy and the fact that the fighting has been largely concentrated in the north and east. The fact that only one-third of the north and east are arable and few industries were located there has helped in part to reduce the impact of the conflict on the Sri Lankan economy as a whole. Another factor in the resilience of the economy is the government's increased reliance on the private sector. Still, if the conflict continues, the potential for major economic dislocation is great.

The increase in defense expenditures has already resulted in a widening budget deficit, and inflation is beginning to make itself felt. Concerns about the security situation on the island have resulted in a drop in tourist arrivals, once a major source of foreign currency. Foreign investment has dropped by 50% since 1984. Moreover, the problems associated with the communal conflict have been compounded by lower world prices for Sri Lanka's major export commodities. Tea prices are currently one-half what they were in 1984. Offsetting this have been some gains in coconut and rubber production.

Normal economic activity in the Jaffna area has been disrupted, causing severe hardship. Transport problems and harvesting difficulties have caused localized shortages of rice and other staples. The recent government embargo has raised the price of fuel, although the militants have managed to get limited supplies through. And finally, the continued fighting has made it difficult for aid projects to be implemented in contested areas.

Deadlock in Negotiations

Quite obviously, a negotiated solution to the conflict is urgently needed. The Sri Lankan Government, with the determined assistance of India, is energetically seeking a negotiated settlement to the conflict. I am pleased to report that clear progress has been made in the past year in defining a framework and working out details of arrangements for accommodation of the major demands of the Tamil community. Last summer President Jayewardene proposed the creation of provincial councils which would provide some degree of "home rule" for all parts of the country, including the north and east. Both the United States and India welcomed these proposals as providing an excellent basis for a negotiated settlement. Shortly thereafter the TULF leadership entered into negotiations with the Sri Lankan Government on the specifics of what governmental powers would be devolved and how the proposed councils would govern in practice. TULF delegations traveled to Colombo twice and considerable progress was made, thanks in part to India's useful role in bringing the parties together. By the fall of 1986, there was considerable optimism that a settlement agreeable to the majority of the members of both ethnic communities could be reached.

The militants, however, remained intransigent. They continued to insist on an independent state which would include both the northern and eastern provinces. They refused to participate in negotiations, propose any compromise formulations that might be acceptable to them, and continued the armed struggle. It became increasingly clear to both the Sri Lankan Government and the Indian Government that an effort had to be made to bring the militants into the peace process. Recent negotiating efforts have focused on this objective.

The principal obstacle, both to a settlement and to participation by the Tamil militants in the negotiations, remains the militant demand that the northern and eastern provinces be merged into one Tamil "homeland." The Sri Lankan Government has stated categorically that it cannot accede to this demand. The government points out, correctly, that two-thirds of the population of the eastern province is non-Tamil (about equal numbers of Moslems and Sinhalese) and that their interests and concerns must be taken into account.

In an effort to break the deadlock, the Sri Lankan Government has attempted to shape a compromise that would be acceptable to the militants. One proposal would shift the boundaries of the eastern province to reduce the Sinhalese portion of the population. Another proposal, once under discussion but subsequently dropped, was to cut the province into three parts, thereby creating Tamil, Moslem, and Sinhalese majority states. The militants, however, have not accepted any of these formulations nor have they advanced any alternatives.

U.S. Policy

A negotiated settlement offers the only hope for resolution of the tragic conflict in Sri Lanka. We support the unity and territorial integrity of Sri Lanka, a democratic government with which we maintain very warm and friendly relations. We admire the statesmanship displayed by President Jayewardene and applaud the detailed and far-reaching proposals put forward by his government. We have also urged the Government of India to remain constructively engaged in the search for a negotiated solution and have praised the very positive Indian role during the past year. We have made clear to all concerned that we do not believe that a purely military solution to the conflict is either possible or desirable.

Since the most effective way to end human rights abuses in Sri Lanka is to end the ethnic strife itself, we believe our strong support for a negotiated solution makes an important contribution in the human rights field. We do not, however, believe that efforts to reduce and eliminate human rights problems need await a final settlement; quite the contrary.

Greater attention to the safety and well-being of Tamil civilians innocently caught up in the conflict will help restore the trust and confidence between the communities which will be required to make any settlement viable. To this end, we have maintained an active, though largely private, dialogue with the government both on general human rights issues and individual cases.

Our assistance programs in Sri Lanka focus on fostering private enterprise, improving health and nutrition, agricultural development, and housing. U.S. aid levels, on a per capita basis, remain significant compared to other aid recipients in the Asian region but have declined substantially in recent years. The decline, which we regret, has in part been due to the near completion of major infrastructure projects associated with the Mahaweli River development scheme, though the severe budget constraints of recent years have accelerated the decline. We intend to remain major contributors within the Sri Lanka donors group and are particularly enthusiastic about the economic environment for development being created by the continuing economic reform program of the government.

I have detailed for you the substantial progress made in negotiations to resolve this conflict. For the first time, the outline of a solution is evident. We propose to continue to seek every opportunity to register our support for the negotiating process. My colleagues and I welcome your review of our policies and programs in Sri Lanka.

BIBLIOGRAPHY

An asterisk (*) preceding a reference indicates that the article or part of it has been reprinted in this book.

BOOKS AND PAMPHLETS

Berger, Carl. The Korea knot: a military-political history. Greenwood Press. '86.

Bobilin, Robert. Revolution from below: Buddhist and Christian movements for justice in Asia: four case studies from Thailand and Sri Lanka. University Press of America.'88.

Bonner, Raymond. Waltzing with a dictator: the Marcoses and the making of American policy.

Bresnan, John. Crisis in the Philippines: the Marcos era and beyond. Princeton University Press. '86.

Bunge, Frederica M. and Vreeland, Nena. (American University (Washington, D.C.)/Foreign Area Studies) Malaysia: a country study. The Studies, for sale by the Supt. of Docs., U.S. G.P.O. '85.

Burton, Sandra. Impossible dream: Marcos, Aquino, the unfinished revolution. Warner Books. '88.

Chapman, William. Inside the Philippine revolution. W.W. Norton. '87.

Chua-Eoan, Howard, Corazon Aquino. Chelsea House. '88.

Davis, Leonard. The Philippines: people, poverty, and politics. Macmillan. '87.

Davis, Leonard. Revolutionary struggle in the Philippines. St. Martin's Press. '89.

DeSilva, Kingsley. Ethnic conflict in Buddhist societies: Sri Lanka, Thailand, Burma. Westview Press. '88.

Gombrich, Richard Francis and Obeyesekere, Gananath. Buddhism transformed: religious changes in Sri Lanka. Princeton University Press. '88.

Guzman, Raul P. de and Reforma, Mila A. Government and politics of the Philippines. Oxford University Press. '88.

Howe, Russell Warren. The Koreans: passion and grace. Harcourt Brace Jovanovich. '88.

Johnson, Bryan. The four days of courage: the untold story of the people who brought Marcos down. Free Press. '87.

Kapferer, Bruce. Legends of people, myths of state: violence, intolerance, and political culture in Sri Lanka and Australia. Smithsonian Institution Press. '88.

Karnow, Stanley. In our image. Random House. '89.

Kearney, Robert N. and Miller, Barbara D. Internal migration in Sri Lanka and its social consequences. Westview Press. '87.

Kim, Ilpyong J. and Kihl, Young W. Political change in South Korea. Paragon House. '88.

Komisar, Lucy. Corazon Aquino: the story of a revolution. G. Braziller. '87.

Lee, Yur-Bok and Patterson, Wayne. One hundred years of Korean-American relaitons, 1882–1982. University of Alabama Press. '86.

MacDonald, C. A. Korea, the war before Vietnam. Free Press. '87.

Manogaran, Chelvadurai. Ethnic conflict and reconciliation in Sri Lanka. University of Hawaii Press. '87.

Myers, Robert John. Korea: the year 2000. University Press of America, Carnegie Council on Ethics & International Affairs. '87.

Nadel, Laurie. (CBS Television Network) Corazon Aquino: journey to power. J. Messner. '87.

Nam, Joo-Hong. America's commitment to South Korea: the first decade of the Nixon doctrine. Cambridge University Press. '86.

O'Brien, Niall. Revolution from the heart. Oxford University Press. '87.

Romulo, Beth Day. Inside the palace: the rise and fall of Ferdinand and Imelda Marcos. Putnam. '87.

Rosca, Ninotchka. Endgame: the fall of Marcos. F. Watts. '87.

Rubin, Barnett R. (Asia Watch Committee, U.S.) Cycles of violence: human rights in Sri Lanka since the Indo–Sri Lanka agreement. Asia Watch. '87.

Samarasekara, Dhanapala. Take a trip to Sri Lanka. F. Watts. '87.

Samaraweera, Vijaya. Sri Lanka. Clio Press. '87.

Seagrave, Sterling. The Marcos dynasty. Harper & Row. '88.

Siegel, Beatrice. Cory: Corazon Aquino and the Philippines. Dutton. '88.

Starrels, John M. United States/ Congress/ Joint Economic Committee. The Korean economy in congressional perspective: a study. U.S. G.P.O. '86.

Tambiah, Stanley Jeyaraja. Sri Lanka: ethnic fratricide and the dismantling of democracy. University of Chicago Press. '86.

United States/Congress/House/Committee on Foreign Affairs/ Subcommittees on Human Rights and International Organizations and on Asian and Pacific Affairs. Political developments and human rights in the Republic of Korea: hearing and markup before the Subcommittee on Human Rights and International Organizations and the Subcommittee on Asian and Pacific Affairs of the Committee on Foreign Affairs, House of Representatives, Ninety-ninth Congress, second session, on H. Con. Res. 345 and H. Con. Res. 347, April 16, May 21, and June 5, 1986. U.S. G.P.O. '86.

United States/Congress/House/Committee on Foreign Affairs/ Subcommittee on Asian and Pacific Affairs. Developments in Korea, September 1987: hearing before the Subcommittee on Asian and Pacific Affairs of the Committee on Foreign Affairs, House of Representatives, One Hundredth Congress, first session, September 17, 1987. U.S. G.P.O. '87.

United States/Congress/House/Committee on Foreign Affairs/ Subcommittee on Asian and Pacific Affairs. Implications of recent developments in the Philippines: hearing before the Subcommittee on Asian and Pacific Affairs of the Committee on Foreign Affairs, House of Representatives, Ninety-ninth Congress, second session, December 1, 1986. U.S. G.P.O. '87.

United States/Congress/House/Committee on Foreign Affairs/ Subcommittee on Asian and Pacific Affairs. Investigations of Philippine investments in the United States: hearings before the Subcommittee on Asian and Pacific Affairs of the Committee on Foreign Affairs, House of Representatives, Ninety-ninth Congress, first and second sessions, December 3, 11, 12, 13, 17, and 19, 1985; January 21, 23, and 29; March 18 and 19; April 9 and 17, 1986. U.S. G.P.O. '87.

United States/Congress/House/Committee on Foreign Affairs/ Subcommittee on Asian and Pacific Affairs. Philippine elections, May 1987: hearing before the Subcommittee on Asian and Pacific Affairs of the Committee on Foreign Affairs, House of Representatives, One Hundredth Congress, first session, May 19, 1987. U.S. G.P.O. '87.

Wee, Jessie. Philippines. Chelsea House Publishers. '88.

Wilson, A. Jeyaratnam. The break-up of Sri Lanka: the Sinhalese-Tamil conflict. University of Hawaii Press. '88.

Wurfel, David. Filipino politics: development and decay. Cornell University Press. '88.

ADDITIONAL PERIODICAL ARTICLES WITH ABSTRACTS

For those who wish to read more widely on the subject of the political changes in Southeast Asia, this section contains abstracts of additional articles that bear on the topic. Readers who require a comprehensive list of materials are advised to consult the *Readers' Guide to Periodical Literature* and other Wilson indexes.

OVERVIEW OF POLITICAL TRENDS IN ASIA

Southeast Asia (special issue). *Current History* 86:145–86 Ap '87

An issue devoted to Southeast Asia examines U.S. policy in the region and the political situation in Vietnam, Laos, Cambodia, the Philippines, Thailand, Malaysia, and Indonesia.

No room at the inn (Vietnamese refugees). William McGurn
National Review 41:26 Je 30 '89

With thousands of Indochinese refugees languishing in camps throughout Southeast Asia, the United Nations High Commissioner for Refugees (UNHCR) has agreed to support a screening program that would distinguish between genuine refugees and those leaving for socio-economic reasons or reasons of personal convenience. This program, which would force the majority of refugees back to Vietnam, merely supports those countries that want to keep refugees off their shores at any cost. If the United States is serious about helping people flee totalitarian regimes, it should consider redirecting the proposed $82.9 million grant to UNHCR toward other refugee organizations.

Journey among tyrants (East Asian dictators). A. M. Rosenthal
The New York Times Magazine 20-5+ Mr 23 '86

Americans often support dictatorships in other countries rather than seek to further political freedom. It is incredible that people in the United States, who have benefited so richly from their freedom and prize it so highly, can argue in favor of tyranny for others. Liberals and conservatives nonetheless defend authoritarians on the Left or Right with almost identical arguments: that poor nations are not culturally or economically prepared for freedom and that temporary protective dictatorships will eventually be replaced by free societies. Such arguments are preposterous. There are signs that learning to recognize and oppose both Communist and anti-Communist dictatorships, but the double standard still prevails. The United States must consistently stand up for political freedom. Political and economic conditions in Korea, the Philippines, and Indonesia are described.

Moslem militants take aim at Southeast Asia. Robert Kaylor
U.S. News & World Report 98:35-6 Mr 11 '85

Islamic fundamentalism is destabilizing several Southeast Asian countries and, in some instances, has led to violence. This Muslim radicalism, inspired by the success of Ayatollah Khomeini in Iran, could cause problems for Washington if anti-American governments are established in countries that are strategic to U.S. interests. In Indonesia, which is 90 percent Muslim, bloodshed has resulted from the Islamic movement's growing opposition to President Suharto's military-backed regime and his state ideology of Pancasila. In Malaysia the Parti-Islam SeMalaysia is calling for a separate Islamic state. Prime Minister Datuk Seri Mahathir is concerned about the danger of Iranian support for his country's radical extremists. Young Muslims in the Philippines are joining Communists in opposing the Marcos government. So far, no Southeast Asian government is in serious jeopardy.

Boat people sail into closed harbors. James M. Fallows *U.S. News & World Report* 105:36 Ag 1 '88

The number of refugees from Vietnam is increasing dramatically, but many countries that once accepted the boat people are refusing to do so. The collapse of the Vietnamese economy and continuing repression are playing a role in the flight. Since the exodus began ten years ago, Hong Kong, Thailand, Malaysia, and Indonesia have offered first asylum but no permanent homes, placing refugees in camps until they are taken away by the United States, Australia, Canada, and other resettlement countries. Last January, however, Thailand announced that it would no longer offer first asylum. Indonesia is turning most refugees away; Malaysia will close its main camp next year; and Hong Kong is considering imposing limitations. An international conference that might take place next year could set new guidelines, but one U.S. refugee official says that repatriation is the key.

America's East Asia policy (address, July 26, 1986). John Franklin Cooper *Vital Speeches of the Day* 52:738-41 O 1 '86

The Stanley J. Buckman Distinguished Professor of International Studies at Rhodes College addresses the Annual Conference of the Asian-Pacific Interparliamentary Union in Taipei, Taiwan. He traces the history of American foreign policy toward Asia, especially U.S. attitudes toward China, under presidents Nixon, Carter, and Reagan. He describes several major policy problems in Asia, including Asian reluctance to accept a rearmed Japan as a counter to Soviet power, the U.S. trade deficit with Japan, the unresolved issue of Korea, and the Vietnamese occupation of Kampuchea. He argues that the United States must continue to play a leadership role in East Asia—an area he considers vital to America's interests—and not retreat into protectionism.

SOUTH KOREA

The Pyongyang puzzle: trick or trade? Laxmi Nakarmi *Business Week* 47-8 F 20 '89

Expanding business ties between North and South Korea are sure to create sensitive issues for President Bush, who plans to visit Seoul on February 27. Reunification is an explosive political issue in the South. Because Washington cannot afford to be perceived as an obstacle to progress, the U.S. military presence may need to be scaled back. The North already appears to be using the prospect of economic ties as a ploy to get South Korea to cancel an upcoming joint military exercise with the United States. Another possibility is that the North may be trying to create problems for South Korean president Roe Tao Woo, who would suffer if the North suddenly stepped back. On the other hand, the North Korean leadership may be sincere. Selling to the South would provide hard currency, and Moscow and Beijing, North Korea's traditional benefactors, have an interest in expanded ties.

President's trip to Japan, China, and South Korea (special section). George Bush *Department of State Bulletin* 89:1–22 My '89

A special section examines President Bush's trip to Japan, China, and South Korea on February 22–27, 1989. The section includes a news briefing with Secretary of State James Baker; excerpts from a news conference with Bush; responses by Bush to questions from the Kyodo News Service of Japan, Chinese television, Xinhua of China, and South Korea's Yonhap News Agency; excerpts from an interview with Baker on *Face the Nation*; Bush's remarks following a meeting with President Roh of South Korea; Bush's address before the National Assembly of South Korea; and Bush's remarks on arriving back in the United States.

An act of contrition (Chun Doo Hwan). Ric Dolphin *Maclean's* 101:34 D 5 '88

As an estimated 30 million of his countrymen watched him on television, former South Korean president Chun Doo Hwan apologized for the corruption and brutality of his regime. Chun, a general who became president in a 1979 coup, is widely credited with creating South Korea's strong economy and with bringing the Olympics to Seoul. He has been condemned, however, for an unofficial death toll of 2,000 during the suppression of an uprising against martial law in the city of Kwangju in 1980, for at least 54 deaths in military reeducation camps, and for the extortion of more than $95 million from industrialists. Chun's successor and former protégé, President Roh Tae Woo, has begun trying to rid the government of corruption. His political survival will greatly depend on whether the public accepts Chun's act of repentance. Meanwhile, Marxist students have intensified their protests calling for Chun's execution and Roh's ouster.

Ending a battle but not the war: labor unrest at Hyundai. Adam Platt *Newsweek* 113:37 Ap 10 '89

When some 2,000 striking workers at the Ulsan shipyard of Hyundai Heavy Industries in South Korea began assembling pipe bombs and other weapons, President Roh Tae Woo responded with his strongest antilabor demonstration to date, sending thousands of riot police to storm the strikers. Most of the workers responded by slipping away without a fight. Striking and protests continued elsewhere around the country, however. In the first three months of 1989, there have been more than 300 strikes, many of them violent. Workers want a greater share of Korea's prosperity, more benefits, and better working conditions.

The South Korea behind the Olympic glitz. William K. Tabb
The Progressive 52:26-9 N '88

Behind the smooth, sanitized facade presented by South Korea during the 1988 Olympics is a system of exploited workers. Korea has indeed made substantial economic progress, achieving 12.2 percent growth in 1987 while reducing its foreign debt by 18 percent. These accomplishments, however, have been made at workers' expense. Koreans work the longest hours and suffer accidents at the highest rate of any workers in the industrialized world. According to a government study, 86 percent of workers earn less than the government-set minimum subsistence level. Life in Korea is marked by control of workers through company unions, police repression, and tough management supervision. The 1987 election of Roh Tae Woo was hailed in the United States as a fundamental shift toward democracy, but this may be a misconception. Roh has disdained corruption and wholesale repression but has shown no interest in basic democratic reforms that would empower ordinary Koreans.

Labor stirrings in Korea. Jim West *The Progressive* 53:12 Mr '89

South Korea's fledgling labor movement is growing and consolidating in the face of heavy opposition and intimidation. The new Korean unions have their origins in the massive wave of strikes that occurred in 1987. They have, however, just begun to improve the miserable conditions under which most Koreans work. The unions have formed regional federations in a number of areas, and most union leaders would like to form a national federation as an alternative to the government-controlled Federation of Korean Trade Unions. Because the unions threaten to end the cheap labor that supports Korea's export-based economy, labor activists must deal with blacklisting, thuggery, and other repressive measures.

Asia's next giant. Alice H. Amsden *Technology Review* 92:46-53 My/Je '89

Korea seems ready to become Asia's next technological giant. Fueled by cheap but relatively well-educated workers and an ability to improve on borrowed technology, the country's gross national product has grown at 8.8 percent annually over the last 25 years. The Korean government's ability to get businesses to follow a national industrial policy has also been crucial to economic growth. Through a nationalized banking system, the government influences businesses and entire industries by offering loans to preferred borrowers. Foreign investment in Korea is difficult, however, unless the companies make products for export, and an illegal overseas transfer of $1 million or more is punishable by a minimum sentence of ten years in prison or a maximum sentence of death. Now that Korea is investing large amounts of money in research and development, it could become an industrialized nation in a class with the United States and Japan.

Can South Korea bat in the big leagues? Mike Tharp *U.S. News & World Report* 106:35-8 F 27 '89

As South Korea moves closer to becoming an advanced industrialized nation, it is torn by tensions between modernity and tradition. South Korea's success or failure in making the transition from an isolated, Confucian society to a cosmopolitan, world-class trading nation will depend partly on factors beyond its control, such as a possible rise of protectionism abroad, and partly on internal factors. Koreans are extremely hard workers, the result of a cultural dedication to the work ethic and a national belief that the country's destiny will be shaped by the character of its people. Moreover, Korean society has proved remarkably resilient for thousands of years despite repeated invasions. The country is just beginning to move toward accepting political pluralism and implementing political liberalization, however, and it has yet to overcome its traditional insularity.

THE PHILIPPINES

Aquino's biggest problem: the United States? Denis Murphy *America* 158:30-3 Ja 16 '88

Despite the many problems plaguing the Philippines, the country has the potential to achieve great progress under the leadership of Corazon Aquino. Aquino's biggest problem at this point may be the unrelenting pressure from the United States to combat the Communist revolution with force and to pay off national debts. Military campaigns against the Communist New People's Army have been ineffective in the past. The insurgency now shows signs of falling apart over internal disagreements. Further reliance on force would only increase the rebels' solidarity. Devoting 40 percent of the national budget to repaying foreign debts, as the United States demands, would starve the population and make growth impossible. Instead of pressuring the government, the United States should support President Aquino and native institutions like the church in their efforts to enhance the attractions of peace and democracy through measures such as land reform.

Plenty of nice people. Denis Murphy *America* 160:150-2 F 18 '89

In the Philippines, the poor must help themselves by using the tenuous democratic institutions provided by President Corazon Aquino. Aquino remains committed to democratic reform, but her efforts to provide democratic solutions to the problems of land reform, human rights abuses, workers' rights, the insurgent Communist rebels, and corruption in high places are not supported by the bloated military or the irresponsible Filipino elite. Meanwhile, the grossly inefficient Aquino government has done little to improve garbage removal, the delivery of basic services, housing for the poor, and other, similar matters that a more efficient government could handle. The years since the people's revolution that ousted Ferdinand Marcos have shown poor Filipinos that their one hope lies in organizing nonviolently to gain some measure of power that can be used for constructive change.

A damaged culture. James M. Fallows *The Atlantic* 260:49–54+ N '87

The current social and economic problems of the Philippines are not the result of Ferdinand Marcos's misrule but the manifestations of a damaged culture. While there have been some positive developments since Corazon Aquino's ascension to power, the economy is still plagued by extremes of wealth and poverty, a lack of manufacturing opportunities, an agricultural system skewed to plantation crops and huge haciendas, and monopolistic and corrupt industries. Capitalism has worked for other economies in the region and can therefore not be blamed for the Philippines' economic woes. Philippine immigrants to the United States have shown themselves to be industrious, so it seems unlikely that a character deficiency is to blame. Philippine society is enfeebled by a lack of nationalistic feeling and a contempt for the public good. For each Filipino, the boundaries of decent treatment are limited to family or tribe and do not extend to the nation.

Human rights problems persist in the Philippines. Dorothy Friesen *The Christian Century* 104:348 Ap 15 '87

According to the Philippine Alliance of Human Rights Associations, Corazon Aquino's government has been unable to eliminate human rights abuses. The government has a weak grip on the military and has not been able to prosecute abusive military personnel, some of whom hold key positions. Government troops target civilians and engage in the forcible relocation of families, searches of remote population centers, and food blockades. Most human rights abuses are committed against farmers and workers who are demanding reform and economic justice. Between February and September 1986, there were reportedly 88 cases of extrajudicial executions, 36 massacres, and 238 cases of torture.

A peaceful transition (Marcos's last days). Sharon Mumper *Christianity Today* 30:28–30 Ap 18 '86

The events surrounding the leave-taking of former president Ferdinand Marcos of the Philippines may have been made easier as a result of the unified effort of the country's Roman Catholics. Catholics prayed for a nonviolent transition to the presidency for Marcos's successor, Corazon Aquino, who is herself a devout Catholic. Protestants make up only 3.5 percent of the country's population, and they were not very active during the election period. Aquino's government has vowed not to restrict freedom of religion, but some Protestants express anxiety over the genuineness of her commitment.

In the grotto of the Pink Sisters. Anne Nelson *Mother Jones* 13:18-24+ Ja '88

Corazon Aquino has inherited the disenfranchised, the vigilantes, and the guerrillas left over from Ferdinand Marcos's troubled reign. When she first came to power, Aquino seemed interested in instituting social reforms, but the emphasis soon shifted to controlling the insurgency. She has come to support the various vigilante groups, which commit atrocities against nonviolent organizers for peace as well as against Communist guerrillas. Widespread vote buying ensured that most of Aquino's slate of candidates won the recent congressional elections, and as a result the new congress is composed primarily of landowners who are opposed to land reform. As the country's poor come to recognize that Aquino is unable to address their needs owing to her privileged background, their frustration may lead to another revolution.

The bartered bride. Ian Buruma *The New York Review of Books* 36:7-11 Je 1 '89

Submission and betrayal loom large in the history of the Philippines. There is, perhaps, a masochistic streak in Filipino submission to superior might. In the 19th century, the mestizo elite submitted to foreign powers so that it could, in turn, rule over its darker-skinned compatriots. The last of these foreign powers, the Americans, were racist and brutal but also benign, generous, and idealistic. American institutions were partly the basis of the first Philippine democratic republic's constitution, promulgated in 1899. The Filipinos, however, did not have a chance to prove themselves as a nation because they were preempted by the Americans, who through their largess kept the Filipinos from becoming their own masters. The writer comments on *In Our Image: America's Empire in the Philippines*, by Stanley Karnow; *The US and the Philippines: In Our Image*, a television series; and *Ermita: A Filipino Novel*, by F. Sionil Jose.

The embattled Mrs. Aquino. Seth Mydans *The New York Times Magazine* 42-3+ N 15 '87

Philippine president Corazon C. Aquino is still defining herself as a leader after more than a year and a half in power. Aquino has forcefully met direct challenges to her authority, such as a nearly successful coup attempt last August, but in general she is somewhat passive and hesitant. She has been slow to address the issue of land redistribution and corruption, has failed to firmly lead local governments or to head off the growing Communist insurgency, and has tolerated an escalation of lawlessness and violence. Her worst failure is that she has not come to terms with the Philippine military, the most immediate threat to her presidency. The image of Aquino as incompetent, however, is as unrealistic as the outside world's image of her as a savior. She maintains that she is increasingly comfortable with the exercise of power but emphasizes that she is determined to remain the complete opposite of Ferdinand Marcos.

From Marcos to Aquino (I). Robert Shaplen *The New Yorker* 62:33-8+ Ag 25 '86

Part of a two-part article examining the transition of power in the Philippines. The extraordinary popular rebellion that unseated Philippine president Ferdinand Marcos will not easily be translated into social and political stability. Violence and volatile civil discord remain a very real prospect. The principal figures in the struggle for influence and leadership in the post-Marcos era fall into three basic groups: the ranks of local, regional, and national politicians; the military; and an amorphous aggregation of scholars, clerics, and businessmen who banded together in opposition to Marcos. President Corazon Aquino faces a monumental task in steering the Philippines back to a clear democratic course and engineering enduring economic recovery. Two decades of corruption and misrule by Marcos have so crippled the country that it will take years to restore any sort of workable representative government.

From Marcos to Aquino (II). Robert Shaplen *The New Yorker* 62:36-40+ S 1 '86

Part of a report on the deposition of Philippine president Ferdinand Marcos by Corazon Aquino. While election returns remained controversial, nonviolent demonstrations by Aquino supporters began to flourish. As Marcos hesitated to crush them with military force, the demonstrations intensified. Finally, military leaders, the Catholic hierarchy, and many other moderate forces joined in the resistance, and Marcos could only concede defeat. Corazon Aquino faces a difficult political and economic task, but her character, beliefs, and positive qualities show promise.

Cheap thrills in Manila. P. J. O'Rourke *Rolling Stone* 72-4+ Mr 10 '88

The writer describes a visit to the Philippines, which included an encounter with the New People's Army, the Communist insurgents who have been waging a civil war for the past ten years. Although Corazon Aquino is an upright and honorable person, she hasn't been able to contend with the country's many problems, which include crime, disease, lack of investment capital, shortage of energy resources, endemic corruption, and exploding population growth.

Please speak into the microphone (F. Marcos' plans for insurrection). Susan Tifft *Time* 130:50 Jl 20 '87

Deposed dictator Ferdinand Marcos planned to stage an armed invasion of the Philippines in hopes of regaining control of the invasion of the Philippines in hopes of regaining control of the nation. The insurrection, which had been scheduled for last week, would have taken Marcos from Hawaii to his home province of Ilocos Norte. The invasion plans also included a scheme to kidnap Philippine president Corazon Aquino. Marcos's plot was uncovered by Robert Chastain, an American businessman posing as an arms dealer, and lawyer Richard Hirschfeld, whom the former Philippine president had contacted about arranging a loan. Marcos had wanted to buy $18 million worth of weapons and ammunition to equip 10,000 soldiers for three months.

A sense of foreboding in the Philippines (assassination of U.S. Army colonel N. Rowe). Brian Duffy *U.S. News & World Report* 106:35–6 My 15 '89

The recent assassination of American military adviser Col. James N. Rowe by the New People's Army in the Philippines should not have come as a shock to American and Philippine officials. Despite the vast amount of aid that the United States is providing to the Philippines, American interests have been under mounting pressure. U.S. installations have been bombed, and military personnel have been threatened by the Communist guerrillas. No agreement on the future of two U.S. military bases in the Philippines has yet been reached. Meanwhile, the guerrillas continue to make gains in the countryside against the poorly equipped and often languid Philippine military. While Corazon Aquino's government continues to try to consolidate its authority, the Filipino people, with a per capita income of just $2 per day, appear to be more restive than ever.

CAMBODIA

Update on Cambodia (statement, March 1, 1989). David F. Lambertson *Department of State Bulletin* 89:37–40 My '89

In a statement before the subcommittee on Asian and Pacific affairs of the House Foreign Affairs Committee, the deputy assistant secretary of state for East Asian and Pacific affairs discusses the current situation in Cambodia. He calls for a complete withdrawal of Vietnamese troops from Cambodia and urges Hanoi to issue a timetable for withdrawal. He says that an acceptable settlement in Cambodia should also include a restoration of self determination for the Cambodian people and safeguards against the return to power of the Khmer Rouge. He notes that the United States is prepared to normalize relations with Vietnam if an acceptable settlement is reached. He also discusses the role of ASEAN in resolving the Cambodian situation and proposals by ASEAN, Prince Sihanouk, China, and others for controlling the Khmer Rouge.

Killing time (Cambodian refugee camp). Margaret Drabble *Harper's* 278:69–72 Ap '89

At Site 2, the largest of Thailand's refugee camps, 174,000 Cambodians live in small thatched huts on intersecting grid rows. Technically, they are displaced people from Cambodia, not refugees. At least in theory, they are awaiting resettlement, but some have waited ten years. Disease and famine aren't the major problems in the camp, which the United Nations supplies with free rice and water. As one might expect in a city with no real employment and no prospects, however, there is violence, rape, robbery, extortion, banditry, depression, psychosis, drug abuse, and suicide. Governmental and nongovernmental agencies supply services and training, but some of the projects seem rather pointless. Like animals in the zoo, the people are cared for, but their efforts to comprehend their lot are doomed to frustration.

Zbig deal in Cambodia (U.S. responsibility for continued strength of Khmer Rouge). *The Nation* 248:109 Ja 30 '89

The United States loves to pretend otherwise, but it is largely responsible for the resurgence of the Khmer Rouge in Cambodia. It was Zbigniew Brzezinski who, in 1979, bragged that he had rallied Chinese support for Pol Pot. Consequently, the Khmer Rouge today is powerful enough to overpower the non-Communist resistance.

Looking to the private sector. Susan Blaustein *The Nation* 248:226-8 F 20 '89

Prime Minister Hun Sen's People's Republic of Kampuchea (PRK) government faces grave difficulties. Years of virtual isolation have hurt the Cambodian economy. While the Vietnamese withdrawal—scheduled for 1990—should help restore Western aid and investment, Phnom Penh may be hard pressed to maintain peace without calling the troops back. Meanwhile, it will have to keep its promises to ensure free elections, rebuild an adequate food supply, and continue rehabilitating the economy. The PRK initially patterned its central planning of agriculture and industrial production after Vietnam's socialist economy, but it has since begun to support private enterprise. Its encouragement of foreign investment, decision to float the Cambodian currency on the international money market, and incentives for growers of high-yield rice crops are all steps in the right direction, but recovery still seems remote.

The specter of the Khmer Rouge. Mary Kay Magistad *The Nation* 248:228+ F 20 '89

The Khmer Rouge purports to accept the idea of a multiparty democracy in Cambodia after the Vietnamese withdraw, but evidence suggests that, as in the early 1970s, this is a ruse to obscure its intention to begin a new war. The non-Communist resistance factions and the Phnom Penh government believe that the figures who are now touting a new Khmer Rouge are merely front men and that Pol Pot and the original senior leadership are still very much in power. It is reported that refugees in the Khmer Rouge-controlled camps on the Thai-Cambodian border are expected to help carry arms into Cambodia and to eventually relocate to Cambodia to be the vanguard of the new revolution. Indeed, the Khmer Rouge has become a highly organized and well-armed force. Few believe

that the Khmer Rouge can seize power immediately, but Prime Minister
Hun Sen worries about giving it a chance to win votes when Cambodia
finally holds a free and fair election.

Killing fields II. Elizabeth Becker *The New Republic* 200:10+ Ja
2 '89

The Bush administration could aid in averting a new holocaust and facilitate Vietnam's withdrawal from Cambodia if it were to take a stronger
position against Pol Pot and the Khmer Rouge, which now has the strongest single Cambodian army. The Khmer Rouge clearly plans to return to
power when Vietnam pulls out. Supplied by China, it has assassinated
scores of local officials and launched guerrilla attacks, particularly in
provinces where the Vietnamese presence is diminished. It now controls
about 75,000 Cambodian refugees, some of whom have been forced to
return to Cambodia to prepare for the new war. It appears that Washington has yet to realize that it is in a good position to help ensure that the
Vietnamese leave, that the Khmer Rouge never returns to power, and
that Cambodia becomes a democracy.

Stop Pol Pot. *The New Republic* 200:7-9 Ap 3 '89

The United States should work to ensure that Pol Pot's Khmer Rouge
does not return to rule Cambodia when the Vietnamese withdraw. After
Pol Pot came to power in 1975, his Khmer Rouge army massacred a million people, a third of the Cambodian population. He is thought to be still
in command of the Khmer Rouge force of around 30,000 fighters, which
is the largest of the three anti-Vietnamese resistance groups. The United
States could conceivably decide to support Hun Sen, prime minister of
the Vietnamese-installed People's Republic of Kampuchea, if he proves
to be the only alternative to the Khmer Rouge. However, the United
States should not consign Cambodia to a foreign-dominated Communist
dictatorship until everything possible has been done to bring about a freely elected democracy backed by international guarantees and peacekeeping forces.

The unmaking of a quagmire. Nancy Cooper *Newsweek*
113:38-40 Ja 30 '89

Ten years after forcing Pol Pot's Khmer Rouge regime from power in
Cambodia, Vietnam is beginning to withdraw its forces, raising concerns
about who will control the country in their absence. Vietnamese troops
have helped the People's Republic of Kampuchea (PRK) regime gain control of all cities and towns and more than 90 percent of the countryside.
Hanoi has paid a high economic and diplomatic cost for its occupation,
however. It has reportedly agreed to an international supervision mechanism for managing Cambodia after its withdrawal, and it has also implicitly conceded that the Khmer Rouge must be included in any peace talks.
So far, the PRK's 40,000 troops and more than 100,000 local militiamen

have kept the Khmer Rouge and other rebels in check, but the Khmer Rouge maintains a force of up to 30,000 guerrillas. PRK prime minister Hun Sen is attempting to solidify his base of popular support in preparation for the pullout of his Vietnamese backers.

Sihanouk on the high wire. Adam Platt *Newsweek* 113:45 My 15 '89

In a remarkable display of political versatility, Prince Norodom Sihanouk, the former monarch of Cambodia, recently expressed his willingness to join forces with the head of the regime he has formerly denounced. Sihanouk met with Hun Sen, prime minister of the Vietnamese-backed People's Republic of Kampuchea regime, in Jakarta, where Hun agreed to adopt a new national flag and to change the nation's name to the State of Cambodia. Hun also agreed to consider Sihanouk's demand for the establishment of a multiparty government and political system prior to elections. Sihanouk indicated that he would return to Phnom Penh as head of state of a non-Communist Cambodia. He noted, however, that he does not expect the Khmer Rouge, which joined him and another group in forming the Coalition Government of Democratic Kampuchea in 1982, to approve any political accommodation with Hun. Sihanouk cannot afford to risk a split with the Khmer Rouge until Vietnam has fully withdrawn from Cambodia.

Cambodia's line of death. C. S. Manegold *Newsweek* 113:30 Je 26 '89

The Khmer Rouge, Prince Norodom Sihanouk's National Army, and Son Sann's Khmer People's National Liberation Front, which have fought among themselves for years, recently formed a loose alliance, the Coalition Government for Democratic Kampuchea, to win power from the Vietnamese-backed government of Cambodian prime minister Hun Sen. Attacks along Cambodia's western border have already increased. Officials in Phnom Penh claim to be in control of the situation, and troops are being added to replace the 70,000 Vietnamese soldiers scheduled to pull out of Cambodia on September 30. The Bush administration said that it would ship rifles and light arms to Sihanouk's army, but Congress blocked the move, fearing possible involvement in a war in Indochina.

Better times for a ravaged land. William Stewart *Time* 133:42 My 15 '89

Cambodia has a renewed sense of vitality after years of hardship, thanks to the government of Prime Minister Hun Sen. Installed by the Vietnamese after they drove the Khmer Rouge from power, Hun Sen has begun pursuing liberal economic policies that could win him popular support. He may be able to retain power after the last Vietnamese troops leave his country on September 30 if he can obtain the cooperation of the country's former head of state, Prince Norodom Sihanouk. Sihanouk has indicated that if demands for a more liberal, multiparty government are met, he will return as head of state in October or November without his partner in opposition, the Khmer Rouge forces. Hun Sen appears ready to meet these demands, but he must also design a political settlement that will please the foreign sponsors of Cambodia's warring factions: the Soviet Union and Vietnam on one hand, and the United States and China on the other.

United Nations pursues Kampuchean settlement. *UN Chronicle* 26:64 Mr '89

As part of its efforts to secure a peaceful resolution to the situation in Cambodia, the United Nations General Assembly recently adopted Resolution 43/19. The resolution includes calls for the withdrawal of foreign forces from the country; the creation of an interim administrative authority; the restoration and preservation of Cambodia's independence, sovereignty, territorial integrity, and nonaligned and neutral status; the right of the Cambodian people to determine their own destiny; promotion of national reconciliation under the leadership of Prince Norodom Sihanouk; and the commitment by all states to noninterference and nonintervention in Cambodia's internal affairs. Extensive debate was raised by the assembly's call for the forswearing of recent practices and policies. Some countries welcomed it as an acknowledgment of the need to prevent the return to power of Pol Pot, while others felt that it either went too far or did not go far enough.

As China agonizes, the U.S. wavers and Cambodia waits. Louise Lief *U.S. News & World Report* 107:34 Jl 3 '89

With Vietnamese troops scheduled to leave Cambodia by September 30, four factions are vying for control of the country. The Bush administration wants to supply weapons to the non-Communist resistance (NCR) factions led by Prince Norodom Sihanouk and Son Sann in order to strengthen them in negotiations with the Chinese-backed Khmer Rouge and the Vietnamese-backed Hun Sen government. Sihanouk, who once ruled Cambodia, is generally considered the only person capable of achieving a national reconciliation. Critics charge that the administration's policy could lead to deeper American involvement, and they argue that because Sihanouk has an alliance of convenience with the Khmer Rouge, arming him would legitimize Khmer leader Pol Pot's role in the future government.

MALAYSIA

Asian journal (shift of power from America to Japan). James M. Fallows. *The Atlantic* 261:20+ Mr '88

The writer discusses the implications of a debate between Singapore prime minister Lee Kuan Yew and New York Times columnist William Safire on the shift of power from the United States to Japan and probes the racial problems currently afflicting Malaysia: Although Japan has a limitless supply of capital and a lead in commercial technology, the country is not more powerful than the United States. Rather, the two countries may now have a balance of power. In Malaysia, a racial struggle between Chinese and Malay citizens has recently threatened to deteriorate into civil war. As a result, Malaysian prime minister Dr. Mahathir bin Mohamad has passed a disturbing new law that cripples the country's free press. Although some experts believe that this clampdown is only temporary, it could lead to a full-fledged tyranny.

A straw that broke the economy's back (Pan-Electric Industries affair damages stock trading and embarrasses government). Cheryl Debes *Business Week* 41+ D 16 '85

The collapse of Pan-Electric Industires triggered a crisis that may have irreparably damaged the economic reputations of Singapore and Malaysia. Slumps in the shipping, commodities, oil, and electronics industries had already taken their toll on the Singaporan and Malaysian economies, once among the world's fastest growing. The failure of Pan-Electric, a marine salvage, property, and hotel company, raises concerns about Singapore prime minister Lee Kuan Yew's ability to bring the nation through an economic downturn and about whether other companies in the region have engaged in widespread pyramid training. Both nations' stock exchanges were forced to close temporarily, and the drain in confidence may affect the future of regional investment as well as the financial markets. The crisis could also threaten Malaysian prime minister Mahathir Mohamad's bid for another term. If the region cannot stabilize itself, however, this crisis may seem minor compared to what follows.

Minority report. Christopher Hitchens *The Nation* 246:6 Ja 9 '88

Anti-Chinese racism contributed to the Malaysian government's recent decision to suspend almost all political and civil liberties. Western observers were surprised by the government's apparently irrational behavior. However, in the mind of Malaysia's leader, Mahathir bin Mohamad, repression is an appropriate response to a racial competition that he believes the native Malays are losing.

Dreaming of the forty-hour week. Denis MacShane *The Nation* 248:658–60 My 15 '89

The Malaysian government continues to block the formation of free trade unions as pressure builds for better treatment of workers. For example, the government has thwarted numerous attempts to organize workers in Malaysia's electronics industry. Late last year, Labor Minister Lee Kim Sai appeared to end that stand when he announced that an elec-

tronics workers' union would be permitted. Lee reversed himself within
weeks, however, declaring that the government would allow only in-
house unions, which workers reject as extensions of company control.
The turnaround may have come in response to pressure from the elec-
tronic companies, including U.S. firms, that benefit from imposing long
hours and low pay on their employees. Nonetheless, Malaysia is just one
example of how trade unionism is on the rise in the newly industrializing
countries of Asia.

Malaysia's improbable triumph. William Maxwell McCord *The
New Leader* 68:9-13 S 23 '85

The fourth in a series of articles on the records of Third World governments: Despite ethnic conflict, religious extremism, and a forbidding environment, Malaysia has preserved its democracy and developed one of
the most successful economies in Asia. Malays, a Sunni Muslim group,
make up 52 percent of the population and dominate the government.
Preferential treatment for Muslims in education, business, and the government's New Economic Policy have created tensions with the Chinese,
Indians, and other minorities. Under Prime Minister Mahathir Mohan-
ned, Malaysia has moved away from the cyclical commodities business and
into industry. A tradition of tolerance and democracy, as well as capitalist
development policies, an industrious population, and Japanese investment have enabled Malaysia to maintain its pluralistic and prosperous society. Despite economic threats and a disruptive Islamic fundamentalist
movement, Malaysia seems likely to weather any storm.

Deadly traffic. Michael Schwarz *The New York Times Magazine*
54+ Mr 22 '87

Malaysia has instituted drastic measures to deal with its overwhelming
drug problem but recognizes that, without international cooperation,
stopping the flow of drugs will be difficult. Convicted drug dealers receive
the death penalty in Malaysia, and drug users must undergo two years of
rehabilitation in prison. Although everyone knows the law, there are as
many as 500,000 heroin addicts in Malaysia. Critics say that the draconian
punishment has no effect on the drug problem and violates constitutional
protections. Supporters admit that some democratic procedures had to
be sacrificed for the strict laws to succeed but say that the number of drug
addicts is declining. As long as international drug trafficking exists, however, Malaysia, which is situated in the midst of the poppy-growing triangle, will continue to fight the drug problem.

Malaysia: natural wealth, few industries. Lorraine Hopping
Scholastic Update (Teachers' edition) 119:12 Ap 6 '87

Part of an issue on Japan and the Pacific Rim. For two decades after Malaysia gained independence from Britain in 1963, the country's natural
resources helped the economy expand at a rapid rate. In the mid-1980s,

however, prices for resources such as rubber and tin began to drop, cutting Malaysia's growth rate and increasing unemployment. Prime Minister Datuk Seri Mahathir bin Mohamad wants to industrialize his country, but Malaysia may not be able to afford the other raw materials needed to manufacture goods. Malays are poorly educated, and many laborers would have to be retrained and moved to cities. Mahathir faces political headaches as well, the worst being racial tension between the majority Malays and the minority Chinese. He is also under pressure from Muslim extremists who want to turn Malaysia into a strict Islamic state. The country's economic woes have helped the extremists gain ground in recent years.

Malaysia's changing market. James Clad *World Press Review* 32:60-1 Je '85

An excerpt from the February 28 issue of Hong Kong's Far Eastern Economic Review. Malaysia has one of the most varied of media audiences. There are forty-two daily and weekly newspapers in English, Malay, Chinese, and Tamil, with a total circulation of approximately 1.4 million. Readership of Malaysian and English newspapers has increased. Video viewing of foreign films has become extremely popular, while movie house patronage has dropped; few changes have been seen in radio listening. The government directly or indirectly maintains tight censorship control over television, but the new private channel TV3 was given permission to show some racy American soap operas and entertainment shows.

Sri Lanka

The siege of Jaffna. Kevin Scanlon *Maclean's* 100:33 O 26 '87

Indian troops stationed in Sri Lanka to stop Tamil extremists' attacks on the majority Sinhalese population launched a five-pronged attack on the Jaffna peninsula, the Tamil rebels' stronghold, but stopped their advance on the outskirts of Jaffna city. The Indians wanted to limit civilian casualties within Jaffna, according to foreign military analysts, but were also worried by the extent of their own casualties: 79 Indian soldiers were killed and 260 were wounded in the weeklong fighting. The Indians rejected a cease-fire offered by the rebels last week because it did not provide for rebel disarmament. At the Commonwealth conference in Vancouver, Indian prime minister Rajiv Gandhi stressed that he and Sri Lankan president Junius Jayewardene remain committed to their July 29 agreement to end the civil war. Many Indian citizens, however, are deeply opposed to the Indian army's action, and moderate Tamils in Sri Lanka criticize the scale of the Indian attack.

Voting for peace. Mary Nemeth Maclean's 102:44-5 Ja 2 '89

Despite death threats from Marxist radicals, about 55 percent of Sri Lanka's eligible voters went to the polls in the country's recent presidential elections. The island has been racked by violence since 1983, with the mainly Hindu Tamil minority waging a struggle for independence from the Buddhist Sinhalese majority. Marxist and nationalist terrorists in the south have been retaliating against President Junius Jayewardene's concessions to the Tamils and his 1987 Indo–Sri Lankan accord, which invited Indian peacekeeping forces to the northern part of the island. The winner of the election was Prime Minister Ranasinghe Premadasa, a Sinhalese, who will be Sri Lanka's first leader from outside the high-caste elite.

The gods and the stars. Mary Anne Weaver *The New Yorker* 64:39–42+ Mr 21 '88

The writer chronicles the political unrest and violence in Sri Lanka. Age-old tensions between the majority Sinhalese Buddhists, led by Junius Richard Jayewardene, the nation's president, and the minority Tamil Hindus have erupted. The most prominent Tamil leader is Velupillai Prabakaran, who organized the militant Liberation Tigers of Tamil Eelam in 1972. In 1983, Prabakaran and other Liberation Tigers ambushed an army group and killed 13 soldiers. This incident led to escalating violence, which has claimed thousands of lives. Last May, following two brutal terrorist acts the month before, Jayewardene launched a military offensive against Tamil strongholds in the northern Jaffna Peninsula. India's assistance to the Tamils brought the campaign to a standstill, and since then Jayewardene and Indian prime minister Rajiv Gandhi have signed a settlement. Many Sinhalese, however, are offended by the deal with India.

India's quagmire in Sri Lanka. William McGowan *The Nation* 246:896–9 Je 25 '88

India's intervention into Sri Lanka's bitter ethnic conflicts has created a militarily and politically disastrous quagmire. India, which entered the Sri Lankan conflict on the side of the Tamil minority in May 1987, hoped that it could tame the separatist rebels under the terms of the July Indo-Lankan Peace Accord, an attempt to end the long-standing antagonism between the Tamils and the Sinhalese Buddhist majority. The Indians overestimated their own leverage, however, as well as underestimating the determination of the Tamils and the unrepentant bloody-mindedness of the Sinhalese. The intervention has turned into a brutal occupation that threatens to destabilize the government of Indian prime minister Rajiv Gandhi even as it fails to alleviate the situation in Sri Lanka.

Sri Lanka: a nation disintegrates (cover story). Steven R. Weisman *The New York Times Magazine* 34–8+ D 13 '87

Sri Lanka continues to suffer the effects of a bloody civil war, but the four years of fighting between the Sinhalese majority and Tamil minority is only the latest episode in a long history of conflict marked by clashes between Sinhalese and Tamil kingdoms and a series of invasions by India. When the British colonized the island in 1815, unity was imposed for the first time in a thousand years. Following the island's independence from Britain in 1948, the Sinhalese and Tamils managed to avoid conflict for a time, but tensions reemerged in the mid-1950s and deepened during the 1970s. The historical pattern remains evident: Tamil separatists seek establishment of an independent state in the northern and eastern sections of Sri Lanka, often through guerrilla tactics, and India maintains both a military and a diplomatic role in the conflict. Whatever hope there is for Sri Lankan unity may spring from a common desire to be free from Indian domination.

If this is peace . . . (agreement signed by India and Sri Lanka).
Edward W. Desmond *Time* 130:18-20 Ag 10 '87

Indian prime minister Rajiv Gandhi and Sri Lankan president Junius R. Jayewardene have reached a tenuous agreement that would end Sri Lanka's four-year-old civil war. The conflict between the Sinhalese majority and the Tamil minority has threatened the stability of Jayewardene's government and has raised the possibility of increasing New Delhi's reluctant involvement in the war. At the heart of the agreement is Jayewardene's concession to allow local rule in a Tamil province that will be created in northern and eastern Sri Lanka. In return, Gandhi has pledged to disarm the Tamil rebels. The agreement, which is a major gamble for Jayewardene, faces strong opposition from the Sri Lankan military, the ruling United National Party, and members of his Parliament. In addition, Indian troops sent to Sri Lanka to disarm the Tamils may have a tougher job ahead of them than they expect.

The battle for Jaffna (Indian troops mount assault on Tamil stronghold). Thomas A. Sancton *Time* 130:52 O 26 '87

Bloody fighting between 6,000 Indian troops and about 2,000 guerrillas from the Liberation Tigers of Tamil Eelam in Jaffna, Sri Lanka, has claimed scores of lives. The assault came just 2 months after the signing of a peace pact by Indian prime minister Rajiv Ghandi and Sri Lankan president Junius R. Jayewardene. The treaty, which aimed to end the strife between Sri Lanka's Sinhalese majority and Tamil minority, called for an Indian peacekeeping force to disarm the Tamils. Tiger leader Velupillai Prabakaran has continued to push for political concessions from the Sri Lankan government, however, using his group's cache of weapons as a deadly bargaining chip. Tens of thousands of civilians have been caught in the midst of the subsequent fighting between the Tamils and the peacekeeping force, and it is impossible to determine how many noncombatant deaths occurred. Gandhi has sent some 1,000 additional troops to help with a final assault.

Blood on the ballot box. Michael S. Serrill *Time* 132:55 O 24 '88

Sri Lanka's Tamil and Sinhalese militants are moving to reject an agreement designed to give the nation's Tamil minority a greater measure of autonomy. The accord would merge Sri Lanka's northern and eastern provinces, where Tamils form a majority, but Tamil militants argue that the pact is worthless. Indian soldiers, who were sent to Sri Lanka to help enforce the agreement, are the main target of the Tamil insurgency. Meanwhile, Sinhalese extremists, claiming that the accord gives too much power to the Tamils, recently organized a strike to protest elections that would form a provincial council in the new Tamil province. The ability of Sinhalese radicals to paralyze the country reinforces the impression that Sri Lanka is on the verge of anarchy.

Sri Lanka: no taming the Tigers. Walter A. Taylor *U.S. News & World Report* 103:28-9 Jl 27 '87

Sri Lanka's civil war is dragging into its fifth year with no end in sight. Tensions between the Tamil minority, who are mostly Hindu, and the Buddhist Sinhalese majority had been high since Sri Lanka (then Ceylon) gained independence from Britain in 1948. Violence between Tamils and Sinhalese erupted in 1983; since then, some 6,000 people have been killed. Tamil Tiger terrorists have killed nearly 400 people since early April. The army is currently sealing off 1,000 Tamil Tigers in Jaffna Peninsula in the north. The military could probably take Jaffna, but that would scatter the terrorists into other areas and likely end all prospects of a settlement. The Tamils demand a separate state as a condition for peace, and the government refuses to compromise. Meanwhile, the fighting has destroyed an economic revival, leaving high unemployment, double-digit inflation, and debt.

Wrong side, wrong war, for India (fighting between Indian troops and Tamil rebels). Walter A. Taylor *U.S. News & World Report* 103:38 O 26 '87

In an ironic twist of history, Indian prime minister Rajiv Gandhi's effort to establish peace in neighboring Sri Lanka has resulted in the greatest bloodshed outside India since the 1971 invasion of East Pakistan. Although India sympathizes with the Tamil separatist rebels, it has been politically compelled to side with the Sinhalese majority. Gandhi's peace accord with Sri Lankan president Junius Jayewardene—Gandhi promised to disarm the rebels in exchange for political autonomy for Tamils in two areas—has unraveled mainly because Indian troops have been unable to completely disarm the Tamils. Sri Lanka's civil war seems unlikely to end soon, and its continuation is a major blow to Gandhi's diplomatic credibility.

M